AQA History

A2
Unit 3

British State and People, 1865–1915

Ailsa Fortune

OXFORD
UNIVERSITY PRESS

Great Clarendon Street, Oxford, OX2 6DP, United Kingdom

Oxford University Press is a department of the University of Oxford.
It furthers the University's objective of excellence in research, scholarship,
and education by publishing worldwide. Oxford is a registered trade mark of
Oxford University Press in the UK and in certain other countries

First published by Nelson Thornes Ltd in 2009

British Library Cataloguing in Publication Data
Data available

978-1-4085-0319-5

10 9 8 7 6 5 4 3

Printed in China

Acknowledgements

Cover: Photograph/illustration by Getty Images

Illustrations: Thomson Digital, Bob Moulder (c/o Graham Cameron
Illustration), David Russell Illustration

Page make-up: Thomson Digital

Although we have made every effort to trace and contact all
copyright holders before publication this has not been possible in all
cases. If notified, the publisher will rectify any errors or omissions at
the earliest opportunity.

Links to third party websites are provided by Oxford in good faith
and for information only. Oxford disclaims any responsibility for
the materials contained in any third party website referenced in
this work.

Contents

Introduction

The publisher has worked hard to ensure that this book offers you excellent support for your A2 course and helps you to prepare for your exams. You can be confident that the range of learning, teaching and assessment practice materials has been checked and is closely matched to the requirements of your specification.

How to use this book

The features in this book include:

Timeline

Key events are outlined at the beginning of the book. The events are colour-coded so you can clearly see the categories of change.

Learning objectives

At the beginning of each section you will find a list of learning objectives that contain targets linked to the requirements of the specification.

Key chronology

A short list of dates usually with a focus on a specific event or legislation.

Key profile

The profile of a key person you should be aware of to fully understand the period in question.

Key terms

A term that you will need to be able to define and understand.

Did you know?

Interesting information to bring the subject under discussion to life.

Exploring the detail

Information to put further context around the subject under discussion.

A closer look

An in-depth look at a theme, person or event to deepen your understanding. Activities around the extra information may be included.

Sources

Sources to reinforce topics or themes and may provide fact or opinion. They may be quotations from historical works, contemporaries of the period or photographs.

Cross-reference

Links to related content within the book which may offer more detail on the subject in question.

Activity

Various activity types to provide you with different challenges and opportunities to demonstrate both the content and skills you are learning. Some can be worked on individually, some as part of group work and some are designed to specifically 'stretch and challenge'.

Question

Questions to prompt further discussion on the topic under consideration and are an aid to revision.

Summary questions

Summary questions at the end of each chapter to test your knowledge and allow you to demonstrate your understanding.

Study tip

Hints to help you with your study and to prepare for your exam.

Practice questions

Questions at the end of each section in the style that you may encounter in your exam.

Learning outcomes

Learning outcomes at the end of each section remind you what you should know having completed the chapters in that section.

Web links in the book

Because the publisher is not responsible for third party content online, there may be some changes to this material that are beyond our control. In order for us to ensure that the links referred to in the book are as up-to-date and stable as possible, the websites provided are usually homepages with supporting instructions on how to reach the relevant pages if necessary.

Please let us know at **schools.enquiries.uk@oup.com** if you find a link that doesn't work and we will do our best to correct this at reprint, or to list an alternative site.

Introduction to the History series

When Bruce Bogtrotter in Roald Dahl's Matilda was challenged to eat a huge chocolate cake, he just opened his mouth and ploughed in, taking bite after bite and lump after lump until the cake was gone and he was feeling decidedly sick. The picture is not dissimilar to that of some A level history students. They are attracted to history because of its inherent appeal but, when faced with a bulging file and a forthcoming examination, their enjoyment evaporates. They try desperately to cram their brains with an assortment of random facts and subsequently prove unable to control the outpouring of their ill-digested material in the examination.

The books in this series are designed to help students and teachers avoid this feeling of overload and examination panic by breaking down the AQA history specification in such a way that it is easily absorbed. Above all, they are designed to retain and promote students' enthusiasm for history by avoiding a dreary rehash of dates and events. Each book is divided into sections, closely matched to those given in the specification, and the content is further broken down into chapters that present the historical material in a lively and attractive form, offering guidance on the key terms, events and issues, and blending thought-provoking activities and questions in a way designed to advance students' understanding. By encouraging students to think for themselves and to share their ideas with others, as well as helping them to develop the knowledge and skills they will need to pass their examination, this book should ensure that students' learning remains a pleasure rather than an endurance test.

To make the most of what this book provides, students will need to develop efficient study skills from the start and it is worth spending some time considering what these involve:

▓ Good organisation of material in a subject-specific file. Organised notes help develop an organised brain and sensible filing ensures time is not wasted hunting for misplaced material. This book uses cross-references to indicate where material in one chapter has relevance to material in another. Students are advised to adopt the same technique.

▓ A sensible approach to note-making. Students are often too ready to copy large chunks of material from printed books or to download sheaves of printouts from the internet. This series is designed to encourage students to think about the notes they collect and to undertake research with a particular purpose in mind. The activities encourage students to pick out information that is relevant to the issue being addressed and to avoid making notes on material that is not properly understood.

▓ Taking time to think, which is by far the most important component of study. By encouraging students to think before they write or speak, be it for a written answer, presentation or class debate, students should learn to form opinions and make judgements based on the accumulation of evidence. These are the skills that the examiner will be looking for in the final examination. The beauty of history is that there is rarely a right or wrong answer so, with sufficient evidence, one student's view will count for as much as the next.

▓ Unit 3

The topics chosen for study in Unit 3 are all concerned with the changing relationship between state and people over a period of around 50 years. These topics enable students to build on the skills acquired at AS level, combining breadth, by looking at change and continuity over a period of time, with depth, in analysing specific events and developments. The chosen topics offer plentiful opportunities for an understanding of historical processes enabling students to realise that history moves forward through the interaction of many different factors, some of which may change in importance over a period of time. Significant individuals, societies, events, developments and issues are explored in a historical context and developments affecting different groups within the societies studied from a range of historical perspectives. Study at Unit 3 will therefore develop full synoptic awareness and enable students to understand the way a professional historian goes about the task of developing a full historical understanding.

Unit 3 is assessed by a 1 hour 30 minute paper containing three essay questions from which students need to select two. Details relating to the style of questions, with additional hints, are given in the accompanying table and helpful tips to enable students to meet the examination demands are given throughout this book. Students should familiarise themselves with both the question demands and the marking criteria which follow before attempting any of the practice examination questions at the end of each section of this book.

Answers will be marked according to a scheme based on 'levels of response'. This means that an essay will be assessed according to which level best matches the

Unit 3 (Three essay questions in total)	Question Types	Marks	Question stems	Hints for students
Two essay questions	Standard essay questions addressing a part of the Specification content and seeking a judgement based on debate and evaluation	45	These are not prescriptive but likely stems include: To what extent… How far… A quotation followed by, 'How valid is this assessment/view?'	All answers should convey an argument. Plan before beginning to write and make the argument clear at the outset. The essay should show an awareness of how factors interlink and students should make some judgement between them (synoptic links). All comments should be supported by secure and precise evidence.
One essay question	Standard essay question covering the whole period of the unit or a large part of that period and seeking a judgement based on debate and evaluation	45	As above	Evidence will need to be carefully selected from across the full period to support the argument. It might prove useful to emphasise the situation at the beginning and end of the period, identify key turning points and assess factors promoting change and continuity.

historical skills it displays, taking both knowledge and understanding into account. All students should keep a copy of the marking criteria in their files and need to use them wisely.

Marking criteria

Level 1 Answers will display a limited understanding of the demands of the question. They may either contain some descriptive material which is only loosely linked to the focus of the question or they may address only a part of the question. Alternatively, they may contain some explicit comment but will make few, if any, synoptic links and will have limited accurate and relevant historical support. There will be little, if any, awareness of differing historical interpretations. The response will be limited in development and skills of written communication will be weak. *(0–6 marks)*

Level 2 Answers will show some understanding of the demands of the question. They will either be primarily descriptive with few explicit links to the question or they may contain explicit comment but show limited relevant factual support. They will display limited understanding of differing historical interpretations. Historical debate may be described rather than used to illustrate an argument and any synoptic links will be undeveloped. Answers will be coherent but weakly expressed and/or poorly structured. *(7–15 marks)*

Level 3 Answers will show a good understanding of the demands of the question. They will provide some

assessment, backed by relevant and appropriately selected evidence, which may, however, lack depth. There will be some synoptic links made between the ideas, arguments and information included although these may not be highly developed. There will be some understanding of varying historical interpretations. Answers will be clearly expressed and show reasonable organisation in the presentation of material. *(16–25 marks)*

Level 4 Answers will show a very good understanding of the demands of the question. There will be synoptic links made between the ideas, arguments and information included showing an overall historical understanding. There will be good understanding and use of differing historical interpretations and debate and the answer will show judgement through sustained argument backed by a carefully selected range of precise evidence. Answers will be well-organised and display good skills of written communication. *(26–37 marks)*

Level 5 Answers will show a full understanding of the demands of the question. The ideas, arguments and information included will be wide-ranging, carefully chosen and closely interwoven to produce a sustained and convincing answer with a high level of synopticity. Conceptual depth, independent judgement and a mature historical understanding, informed by a well-developed understanding of historical interpretations and debate, will be displayed. Answers will be well-structured and fluently written. *(38–45 marks)*

Introduction to this book

Fig. 1 *Workers in a textile factory about 1865. What does this picture tell you about working conditions in the textile industry at this time?*

British State and people in 1865

By 1865, the nature and character of the British State was changing in response to changes in British society. Political power was no longer the preserve of the landed classes. Industrial power had become more important than ownership of land, and this was reflected in the increasing concentration of political power in the hands of the middle classes. The continuing development of manufacturing industry had created more opportunities for the working classes, particularly the skilled 'artisan'. Healthy profits from industry, trade and overseas investments had increased the overall standard of living. However, this was not the case for everyone. The rapid growth in industrial power and prosperity disguised the ugly realities of harsh working conditions, slum housing and desperate poverty, which it had helped to create. There was an increasing expectation and pressure from middle- and working-class groups that the **government** would accept responsibility to improve the worst social problems. The beginnings of a national system of education gave the working classes a greater knowledge and understanding of how the State was run, and gave them the confidence to demand the same share in government as that enjoyed by their middle-class contempories.

In 1865, Britain could not claim to be a democracy, although its constitutional monarchy was regarded as liberal and admired abroad.

There had been no further parliamentary reform since the 1832 Reform Act had extended the **franchise** to middle-class men. No working-class men had the vote, not because they belonged to the working class, but because they did not own or rent property of a high enough value to qualify. As a result, only one in six men could vote. It was almost taken for granted that women were excluded from political power. There was no secret ballot and so there were opportunities to bribe and intimidate voters. This made elections expensive and, as there was no salary for MPs, only wealthy candidates could put themselves up for election. Some limited redistribution of seats had taken place, but the industrial areas, situated largely in the north and the Midlands, were seriously under-represented, while the rural areas and small towns were over-represented. A Register of Electors was introduced, but was incomplete as many men would not pay the registration fee of 1 shilling and so were unable to vote.

The disappointment of the working man that he had been completely excluded from the franchise reform and had no political voice led to the setting up of the Chartist Movement after 1838. It petitioned for universal male **suffrage**, but it lacked strong leadership and as a working-class organisation it lacked the ability to raise sufficient funds.

In the 19th century, as now, Britain was recognised as a constitutional monarchy. The institutions of government comprised the monarchy, the House of Lords (unelected hereditary peers) and the House of Commons (elected representatives). A great deal of political influence was held by the Lords, who had the power to block measures passed by the Commons. The monarch was head of State, but left the making and passing of laws to the elected parliament and could not impose his or her will directly. The monarch acted on the advice of the ministers of State and was required to provide approval for legislation. The monarch had the power to make certain appointments, for example, officially appointing the Prime Minister, and could bestow honours on people he or she wished to reward. The monarch was also head of the established Church of England and titular head of the armed forces.

The balance of power between the monarch and parliament had changed over past centuries. The Bill of Rights of 1689 had established the principle of the supremacy of parliament over the monarch and prevented the monarch from interfering with the law. By 1865, Britain's monarch, Queen Victoria, was about half way through her long reign, which stretched from 1837 to 1901. She took a great interest in government, including foreign policy and wielded considerable influence over the appointment of ministers, bishops and army chiefs. According to H. C. G. Matthew in *Gladstone 1875–1898* (1995): 'Victoria saw herself as an integral part of the making of policy, with the right to instruct, to abuse and to hector.' Walter Bagehot, a political philosopher, in his study of the parliamentary system, *The English Constitution* (1867), defined the monarch's rights as 'the right to be consulted, the right to encourage and the right to warn.' He was in effect giving an opinion on what he believed to be the appropriate political boundaries within which Queen Victoria should operate. Throughout her reign, Queen Victoria interfered in affairs of State. She was most often humoured by her ministers, but did not always get her own way. She was obliged to accept Gladstone as Liberal prime minister on four occasions during her reign, although she detested him. She was opposed to the extension of the franchise and too much social reform, and she always sought closer ties with Prussia (later Germany) than her ministers chose to pursue.

The extension of the franchise was high on the political agenda in 1865. The First Reform Act of 1832 had proved a great landmark in parliamentary reform, as it pinpointed the start of Britain's move towards

Key terms

Franchise: in historical and political terms, the franchise is a voting qualification – 'the right to vote' or simply 'the vote'. During the 19th century, only 'male persons' had the franchise and that was based on a property qualification.

Suffrage: a very similar meaning to franchise, but is more of a concept of having the power or right to exercise the vote. For example, we talk about the campaigns for female suffrage when referring to attempts to persuade government to give women the vote.

Cross-reference

The British political system is covered in more detail on in chapter 1.

Cross-reference

Walter Bagehot is profiled on page 12.

Exploring the detail

Whigs, Tories and Liberals

In the early 19th century, there were two main political parties in Britain – the Whigs and the Tories. They lacked the unity and organisation of modern political parties. There were factions within the parties who often opposed each other in parliament. Both parties derived from the landed classes. The Whigs believed that the monarch should not interfere with the will of parliament, nor have power to appoint ministers and officials. However, the Tories were great supporters of the monarch. Whigs became associated with liberal ideas and reform, while the Tories were regarded as reactionary and anti-reform or change. By 1865, another group was emerging: many of the new urban middle-class and skilled workers, often Nonconformists (see Chapter 1), were becoming known by a newer term – the Liberals.

Key terms

Free trade: the economic policy that involves a free exchange of commodities (goods) between nations without imposing duties or tariffs. Adam Smith's book *The Wealth of Nations* (1776) inspired the free trade movement, which was taken up by Gladstone and the Liberals.

Cabinet: the committee at the centre of the British political system that is responsible for making decisions in government. Its members are chosen by the Prime Minister from among their ministers. Both Disraeli and Gladstone had small Cabinets by today's standards (of approximately 15 members). Cabinet meetings have been held in the same room, the Council Chamber at 10 Downing Street in London, since 1856.

becoming a democratic society. This was not the intention of the Whig government that passed the act. It had argued for a reform that made the House of Commons more representative of the industrial society that Britain had become. However, the Whigs wished to maintain the principle that owning land or property was an essential qualification for political power, and they continued to believe that the landed aristocracy played a part in maintaining stability and social order. Although the Whigs were the reforming party, many of them sat in the Lords and did not wish to threaten their own position.

The reform meant that the landed aristocracy lost their monopoly of political power and were forced to share it with the recently enfranchised middle-class merchants, manufacturers and professional classes, in the rapidly expanding and previously unrepresented industrial towns. A steadily increasing number of them became MPs in the ensuing parliaments. They represented the new industrial wealth of Britain. The majority of this new entry voted with the Whigs and this enabled the Whigs to form majority governments for most of the following three decades.

The other main political party of the day was the Tory Party, which had been absolutely opposed to the reform as it feared it would bring revolution. The party achieved brief political success under the leadership of Sir Robert Peel, who formed a government from 1841 to 1846. Peel had rebranded the Tories; he had given them a softer, more moderate, image and renamed them as the Conservative Party. During the 1840s, Britain faced an economic crisis. One of Peel's remedies to get the economy moving again was to remove duties on imports. His policies were a success; the economy revived and there followed an extraordinary period of prosperity for Britain, which continued into the 1870s. Peel was in effect moving away from the old concept of protected trade, where duties were levied on imported goods to protect the home markets, and towards a system of **free trade**, where few duties would be imposed. Many people associated free trade with Britain's prosperity.

Peel had been sufficiently impressed with a young ambitious Tory MP, William Ewart Gladstone, to give him the **Cabinet** post of president of the Board of Trade in 1843. Gladstone retained a deep admiration for Sir Robert Peel, and later acknowledged him as his political guiding light when he came to formulate his own policies.

Irish affairs dominated much of the political landscape in the 19th century and contributed to Peel's downfall in 1846. In 1800, an Act of Union with Ireland had been pushed through parliament at Westminster and brought to an end the Irish parliament in Dublin. One hundred Irish MPs took seats in the House of Commons and 32 peers took seats in the House of Lords at Westminster. Yet Catholics, who made up 90 per cent of the Irish population, were barred from sitting in parliament. In 1829, Peel had been forced to give way to the Irish over Catholic emancipation to avoid civil war and, as a result, had weakened the Tory Party.

Emancipation did not settle Irish grievances. In 1843, civil unrest and calls for the repeal of the Act of Union were surpressed by Peel's firm action. The majority of the Irish population made a poor living by renting small parcels of land from the absentee Protestant landlords. The failure of the Irish potato crop in 1845, the staple diet of the Irish peasant, led to widespread suffering, starvation and death among an already impoverished population. The political solution was to repeal the Corn Laws, in place since 1815, which kept the price of British corn artificially high by stopping the import of cheap foreign corn. In theory, this would bring down the price of bread, which in the short term could replace the blighted potato and provide food for the starving population. The repeal of the Corn Laws in 1846 in effect did little to ease Irish suffering. The potato blight continued the following year. There was a general shortage of corn because of poor harvests, and no readily available surplus stocks from Europe because of the previous imposition of the Corn Laws but, worse still, Irish corn was exported to England to ease the situation there. Almost a million Irish peasants either starved to death or succumbed to disease. Many hundreds of thousands, who could scrape together the fare, emigrated to England and Scotland or America and Canada.

The Irish Famine increased feelings of bitterness against the British. The repeal of the Corn Laws destroyed Peel and split the Conservative Party. Peel died in 1850, but his supporters including Gladstone continued to call themselves Peelites and eventually became part of the new Liberal Party. The remainder, the Protectionists, formed the Conservative Party under Lord Derby; they were ineffective and out of office for most of the next two decades, except for two brief governments in 1852 and 1858.

Both Whig and Conservative governments were responsible for some measures of social reform, which had begun to scratch the surface of the problems of the industrial society. The method was to set up a Royal Commission of Enquiry into the problem, investigate, call witnesses and produce a detailed report with recommendations for government action. The recommended reforms affected factories, coal mines, railways, local government, public health, education and the poor law. All these laws required an army of administrators to oversee them. This led to the development of the Civil Service, an important component in a modern State, although it was not until 1870 that Gladstone made it possible for a young man, born into a working-class family, to enter the Civil Service by passing a competitive exam. The machinery of the British State was beginning to accept the necessity of working harder for the benefit of its people.

The Liberal Party was formed in 1859 by combining several political groups in parliament – Whigs, Liberals, Radicals and Peelites. Although personal differences and political backgrounds divided the party members, by 1859 they increasingly had pursued similar aims, the most pressing of which at the time was to remove the minority Conservative administration led by Lord Derby. It made sense to unite into one political party and mount a stronger challenge against the Conservatives. A meeting was held by the key members of the four groups in Willis's Rooms near St James Palace in London, and a motion was passed to come together under the banner of the Liberal Party to achieve this aim. A few days later on 10 June 1859, after a vote of no confidence in the Conservatives in the House of Commons, the first true Liberal government took office, with Lord Palmerston as prime minister and W. E. Gladstone as chancellor of the exchequer.

By 1865, Gladstone had become leader of the Liberals and Benjamin Disraeli leader of the Conservatives in the House of Commons. Both men represented the powerful prosperous middle class of Victorian Britain. Over the following months, both vied with each other to introduce political and social reforms and to uphold British and Imperial interests abroad.

As you read the following pages, you will gain an appreciation of how the British State evolved over the next 50 years, and of how the relationship between State and people was influenced by a variety of forces, such as Liberalism, Socialism, Nationalism and economic change. By 1915, there were many aspects of British politics and society that remained the same, but look out for the key elements that changed Great Britain and reflect on the extent to which young Britons of 1915 lived in a world that was very different from that of their parents.

Fig. 2 *Woman on the shore of Ireland holding up a sign asking for help to passing ships bound for America. This illustration from* Harper's Weekly *dated February 1880 demonstrates that famine continued to be a problem in Ireland after the 1840s*

Exploring the detail

The Corn Laws

The Corn Laws were passed in 1815 at the end of Britain's lengthy wars with France against Napoleon. They stopped the import of cheap foreign corn into Britain, until the price of British corn reached 80 shillings a quarter ton. This measure was to protect the farmers and landed classes, but it made the price of bread very high. Bread was the staple diet of working people and so the measure caused them great hardship.

Table 1 *Population for Ireland from 1841 to 1881*

Date	Population
Census return 1841	8,175,124
Census return 1851	6,552,385
Census return 1861	5,798,967
Census return 1871	5,412,377
Census return 1881	5,174,836

Timeline

The colours represent different types of event as follows: Social, Political, Economic.

1865	1866	1867	1867	1868	1868	1869	1870
Death of Lord Palmerston clears way for reform	Most of London is connected to an efficient sewage network, through the skills of Joseph Bazalgette	Second Reform Act, passed by a Conservative government, which gives the right to vote to some working-class men for the first time	Fenian disturbances occur in England and Ireland, including the bombing of Clerkenwell prison	Disraeli's first term as prime minister, but ministry only lasts from February to December	Gladstone's first term as prime minister, during which he carries out a series of far-reaching administrative reforms and establishes an interest in settling the problems of Ireland reforms	Opening of the Suez Canal in Egypt creates a shorter route to India and the Far East	Gladstone's Irish Land Act to protect tenants from unfair eviction

1876	1876	1877	1878	1879	1880	1881
Bulgarian uprising savagely repressed by the Turks in what is known as the Bulgarian atrocities	By the Royal Titles Act, Queen Victoria is made Empress of India. This is a masterstroke by Disraeli, because as a result Victoria is indebted to him	Russia declares war on Turkey	Treaty of San Stefano is followed by secret agreements between Britain and Turkey before the Congress of Berlin in July, a personal triumph for Disraeli and from which Disraeli returns home claiming to have achieved 'peace with honour'	Formation of the Irish Land League by Michael Davitt and others to secure land reform for Irish tenants. This marks the start of the Irish Land Wars	Gladstone starts his second term of office	Death of Disraeli

1886	1889	1892	1892	1893	1895	1898
Lord Salisbury's Second Ministry as leader of Conservative government begins. Conservatives dominate the political scene for most of the next 20 years	The Dockers' strike ends in success when the employers give in to their demands. It gives confidence to other unskilled workers to form unions	Gladstone becomes prime minister for the fourth time and fails in his second attempt to introduce Home Rule for Ireland	Keir Hardie and John Burns become first independent labour MPs	Independent Labour Party formed through efforts of Keir Hardie	Opening of the Kiel Canal in Germany	British conquest of the Sudan

1903	1904	1906	1906	1906	1907	1908	1908
Emmeline Pankhurst founds the Women's Social and Political Union and leads the campaign for women's suffrage	Entente Cordiale with France marks the beginning of improved relations between France and Britain in the face of increasing German aggression	General election in January sweeps the Liberal Party to victory. With the influence of New Liberalism, they introduce a large number of measures of innovative social reform	Trade Disputes Act is passed	Provision of Meals Act gives free meals to needy school children	Medical inspections introduced in schools to improve the health of the nation's children	Campbell-Bannerman dies and H. H. Asquith becomes prime minister	Old-age pensions introduced

1870	1870	1871	1872	1873	1874	1874	1875
Forster Education Act marks the beginning of State education	Civil Service reforms make entry on the basis of a competitive examination	Trade Union Act legalises trade unions, but a Criminal Law Amendment Act makes striking illegal	The Secret Ballot Act enables newly enfranchised working-class men to vote without fear of reprisals from employers	Cardwell's army reforms end system of purchasing commissions	Trade unionists, Thomas Burt and Alexander McDonald, are the first working-class men elected to parliament	Disraeli starts his second term of office and defines 'Tory democracy'	Artisans' Dwellings Act is an early attempt at slum clearance

1880	1882	1882	1884	1884	1885	1886
Charles Parnell becomes leader of Irish Nationalist Party	Kilmainham Treaty agreed between Gladstone and Parnell	The Phoenix Park murders	Third Reform Act gives the vote to labouring men in the countryside and ends the distinction between county and borough franchises	Fabian Society set up by Sidney and Beatrice Webb. They are very influential and seek to influence the government to carry out social reform through their political writings	November general election gives balance of power to Irish Home Rule Party in Commons	Gladstone's Home Rule Bill defeated and a damaging split occurs in the Liberal Party. The breakaway group is led by Joseph Chamberlain and forms the Liberal Unionists, who ally themselves with the Conservatives

1898	1899	1900	1901	1901	1902	1902
Kaiser approves German Navy Laws to build up German navy	Start of the Boer War	Setting up of the Labour Representation Committee	Publication of Seebohm Rowntree's Poverty: A Study of Town Life	The death of Queen Victoria after a reign of 63 years. Her reign marked a period of great social, economic and technological development and coincided with the expansion of the British Empire. She is succeeded by her son, the 59-year-old Edward VII	The Anglo–Japanese Alliance ends Britain's period of 'splendid isolation'	Balfour's Education Act establishes State responsibility for secondary education

1909	1910	1910	1911	1911	1911	1914
The 'People's Budget' is rejected by the House of Lords and sparks a constitutional crisis	Death of Edward VII; George V becomes king	Asquith calls a general election in order to seek popular approval to curb the power of the House of Lords, the results of which give the Liberals a tiny majority, and Irish Nationalists balance of power	Parliament Bill becomes law when it is finally passed in the House of Lords by 131 votes to 114 and reduces the power of the House of Lords by abolishing their power of veto over finance bills	National Insurance Act for health and unemployment	Payment of MPs is introduced, which enables them to draw a salary of £400 a year	Britain declares war on Germany on 4 August, in response to Germany's invasion of neutral Belgium. It is the start of hostilities that continue for four years

1 Reforms for a modern state

In this chapter you will learn about:

▦ the nature and composition of the Liberal Party

▦ the problems that faced the Conservative Party

▦ the issues surrounding parliamentary reform

▦ the importance of the Second Reform Act of 1867 and the Ballot Act of 1872

▦ the impact of the reforms of Gladstone's First Ministry from 1868 to 1874.

Fig. 1 *A formal portrait of Queen Victoria at the time of her Golden Jubilee in 1887. What does this portrait tell you about Queen Victoria's character?*

From God downwards through the Queen and the established order, there were those whose place it was to give orders and those whose duty it was to obey. Obedience was one of the first of many duties exacted of a child by parents, and it was a virtue highly prized throughout society by those who considered they had a right to demand it. The political system, though it permitted a degree of personal liberty, was at the same time deeply permeated with the **authoritarian idea**, especially the principle that social standing carried **authority** with it. This was in the main long accepted by the working classes themselves, even after the Second Reform Bill had given the working class the vote.

1

Adapted from Reader, W. J. (1967)
Life in Victorian England

Key terms

Authoritarian idea: belief that stresses the importance of authority.

Authority: power that comes from holding an influential or official position, e.g. a headteacher in school.

The Liberals, 1865–73

In 1865, Britain was on the threshold of social and political change. The Great Reform Act of 1832 had shaped the British political system for over 30 years. It had increased the franchise and brought about a redistribution of seats. However, in reality, the landed classes still held political power, although they had been forced to share it with the new, prosperous middle classes. Out of a total population in Britain of 30 million, approximately 1.2 million had the right to vote and these were men. There was no system of voting in private and this meant that the voters were open to bullying, bribery and corruption by the political elite. After the Second Reform Act in 1867, the franchise was extended to include the respectable working-class men in the towns – the artisan class. In the general election that followed, these new voters ensured a victory for the Liberal Party, which was led by William Ewart Gladstone. During his period of office, Gladstone introduced a number of wide-ranging innovative reforms. These reforms could be said to have been responsible for helping to establish the basis of our modern democratic State, in which meritocracy (government by people selected for merit) is preferred to advancement by privilege.

The nature of the Liberal Party

Emergence of the Liberal Party

The Liberal prime minister, Lord Palmerston, died in office in 1865. By this time, Liberalism was becoming firmly established as a political creed in Britain, and people began to talk about a Liberal Party. The Liberal Party dominated the political scene for the next 20 years under the forceful and inspiring leadership of Gladstone.

Key profile

William Gladstone

Gladstone (1809–98) was born into a privileged background as the son of a wealthy Liverpool merchant, who had made his money in shipping and the West Indian slave and sugar trade. Gladstone went to Eton and Christ Church, Oxford, where he enjoyed the advantages of a son of Britain's upper classes. He began to take an interest in politics at the time of the debate on the 1832 Reform Act, and became Tory MP for Newark in 1832. At this stage, Gladstone was opposed to reform and was described by Macaulay as 'the rising hope of the stern unbending Tories'; in other words, incredibly clever and fiercely reactionary. It was said of Gladstone that 'he could do in four hours what it took any other man 16 to do and that he worked 16 hours a day'. Gladstone was a follower of Sir Robert Peel, and split with the rest of the Conservative Party in 1846, following the repeal of the Corn Laws. As chancellor of the exchequer under three prime ministers during the 1850s and 1860s, he extended free trade and cut government expenditure. He was renowned for his strong moral principles and religious convictions. Gladstone believed in individual liberty and equality of opportunity. He joined one new Liberal party, with the other Peelites, in 1859 and became party leader in 1867, and such was his force of character and influence that Liberalism became synonymous with Gladstone and was referred to as 'Gladstonian Liberalism'. He held office as prime minister four times in 1868–74, 1880–5, 1886 and 1892–4.

Fig. 2 *William Ewart Gladstone (1809–98). How has the artist chosen to represent Gladstone in this portrait?*

Cross-reference

To recap on Whigs, Tories and Liberals, look back to page 4.

Key terms

Nonconformists: Protestants who do not accept the practices of the Anglican Church. They were sometimes known as 'dissenters', but this word has an unpleasnt edge to it, and the blander term 'Nonconformist' became more common. Nonconformists include Presbyterians, Quakers and Methodists. Their numbers grew in the 19th century as religious, civil and political restrictions against them had been withdrawn. Their political allegiance lay mainly with the Liberal Party.

Protectionists: protection or protected trade is when the government imposes a tax on imported goods to support home production.

Cross-reference

The repeal of the Corn Laws in 1846 is outlined on pages 4–5.

Fig. 3 *John Bright (1811–89), an English Radical statesman, campaigned for the passing of the Second Reform Act*

Composition of the Liberal Party

The **Whigs** belonged to powerful aristocratic landowning families. They differed from their traditional political opponents, the Tories, in that they believed in a constitutional monarchy, in which the monarch's powers of patronage were limited. They had been instrumental in passing the First Parliamentary Reform Act in 1832 and were in favour of a further extension of the franchise, as long as it was controlled. The Whigs were generally supportive of the **Nonconformists**, yet also included in their number the Roman Catholic Lords. Titled Whigs sat in the House of Lords, while the junior branches of their families sat in the House of Commons.

Some of the junior Whigs began to disassociate themselves from their more aristocratic and politically cautious kinsmen and call themselves **Liberals**. But most Liberals were from middle-class business and commercial backgrounds, or were lawyers and professional men and had come into parliament after 1832. They believed in individual liberty, free trade, freedom of the press and religious freedom. Many of them were 'dissenters' or Nonconformists, who believed that the Church should be separate and free from State patronage and control.

The **Peelites** had followed Sir Robert Peel over his repeal of the Corn Laws in 1846. This split the Conservative Party into **Protectionists** and Peelite free traders, and ensured that the Conservatives did not have a majority in the Commons for a long time to come. Intially, the Peelites held a balance of power in parliament, but they increasingly voted with the Whigs. Gradually their numbers fell away and they were content to fuse with the Liberals by 1859. The Peelites came from wealthy industrial and commercial backgrounds. Gladstone was regarded as one of the leading Peelites.

The **Radicals** in parliament were free thinking middle-class individuals who adopted the doctrine of Utilitarianism. This was a belief in taking actions that would be of greatest pleasure to the greatest number of people. Generally speaking, the Radicals wanted change in the social order. They opposed the political and economic dominance of the landowning classes and the privileged position of the Church of England as the established Church. They wanted an extension of the franchise, the removal of government restrictions and free trade. Perhaps the most influential Radical in the Liberal Party was John Bright.

Key profile

John Bright

Bright (1811–89) was a leading Radical and perhaps the greatest of the mid-19th century moralists. Born the son of a Rochdale (Lancashire) textile manufacturer, into a Quaker Nonconformist household, Bright entered parliament as a Radical in 1843. He made his reputation as leader of the Anti-Corn Law League, which set Britain on the road to free trade. He was a leading light in Nonconformist politics. He campaigned tirelessly for the extension of the franchise and was a driving force behind the Reform League. Bright was an outstanding orator and toured the country drawing huge crowds to listen to his crusading speeches. He was the first Quaker to hold Cabinet office in Gladstone's First Ministry. He and Gladstone had a deep regard for each other. Bright's political creed was in line with Liberal principles of peace, retrenchment and reform. It would be a fair assessment to say that he was instrumental in defining 'Gladstonian Liberalism'.

Table 1 *Occupations of the 456 Liberal MPs sitting between 1859 and 1874 for English constituencies*

Occupation	Number of MPs
Large landowners (aristocrats)	198
Gentlemen of leisure	49
Lawyers	84
Radicals	20
Big businessmen	74
Local businessmen	43
Radical businessmen	34

(Note: Total adds up to 502 as some landowners were also practising lawyers, etc.)
*Vincent, J. (1967) **The Formation of the British Liberal Party***

Half of the parliamentary Liberal Party drew their wealth from the land. The other half (including Gladstone) had no aristocratic or landed connections, but had gained recent wealth through industry and commerce, and associated themselves with the aristocracy through public school education and social habits. Historian John Vincent characterises the middle-class Liberal MPs as 'middle-class intruders [who] blended into the aristocratic landscape, or wished to'. It was the small group of Radicals in the party who consistently supported change and reform and who acted 'spasmodically, in conjunction with the people, public opinion and the front bench, to achieve … progress'. It is not surprising, given both the social and political mix, that division and disagreement dogged the Liberal Party during this period.

'Gladstonian Liberalism'

The emergence of the Liberal Party coincided with the emergence of Gladstone to national prominence. Gladstone's personal and firmly held principles gave weight to the wider Liberal beliefs of peace, retrenchment and reform. They centred on his religious devotion and his admiration for Sir Robert Peel, in whose Cabinet he had served as a Conservative in the 1840s. However, sometimes Liberals found Gladstone's deeper motivating forces difficult to understand.

E. J. Feuchtwanger identifies the importance of Gladstone's belief in God on his political life (Source 2).

> The young Gladstone was strongly drawn to a career in the Church, but was persuaded that with his gifts he might serve God's will better if he went into politics. This view of politics, that it was subject to a divine purpose, remained characteristic of him.

2 *Feuchtwanger, E. J. (1996) **Gladstone, New Perspective**, Vol.2, September*

'Peace, retrenchment and reform' was the catchphrase of Gladstone and the Liberal Party. They both believed that if peace could be maintained with other nations, this would enable trade and industry to develop unhindered by the disruptions of war. It would also mean that taxation could be more easily kept under control. Gladstone wanted to 'live to see the day when income tax would be abolished' and so a policy of cutting back in government spending or retrenchment (as it was called in 19th century Britain) would also

Activity

Talking point

1. What were the common threads, if any, that united the different voices in the Liberal Party?

2. There was no working-class representation in parliament. Which group, if any, would be likely to support the working-class cause? Based on the evidence in Table 1, what was their chance of success?

Laissez-faire: doctrine that the State should not interfere in the workings of the market economy. It was a basic principle of 19th century Liberal governments and came from the teachings of the great political economists Adam Smith (1723–90) and David Ricardo (1772–1823). It was closely associated with Gladstone's activities as chancellor of the exchequer (1852–5 and 1859–66) when he followed a policy of free trade by abolishing duties on goods.

Self-help: this could be seen as a by-product of *laissez-faire*. It was made popular by Samuel Smiles in his book *Self Help* (1859), in which he praised the hard-work ethic of inventors and engineers who succeeded through their own efforts. A good standard of living and prosperity was the reward of the middle class for thrift and hard work. Self-help became the virtue of the skilled workers in their campaign to promote themselves as respectable and hard working.

■ Cross-reference

Laissez-faire, free trade and self-help are discussed further on pages 57–59.

■ Activity

Thinking point

1. What were the uniting factors for Gladstone's Liberal Party?

2. What were the areas of potential conflict?

3. On the basis of your findings, what problems were the Liberal Party likely to face after 1865?

reduce the necessity of raising taxes. Taxation was seen by the Liberals as depriving people of the freedom to spend their money as they wished. By reform, they were concerned with bringing about changes in laws and institutions that prevented people from acting freely.

These three Liberal principles tied in with **laissez-faire** principles and the doctrine of **self-help**. The Liberals were influenced by the great political philosophers of the day, Jeremy Bentham, John Stuart Mill and Walter Bagehot. They believed in the liberty and freedom of the individual and religious toleration. They supported free trade and saw it as a means of creating prosperity for all. They upheld the principle of parliamentary government, within a limited democracy. However, they accepted that an overhaul of the parliamentary system was necessary to reflect the changes in the distribution and wealth of the population that had occurred after the Industrial Revolution. The development of Britain into an urban Nonconformist and perhaps more secular society was reflected politically in the growth of Liberalism and the Liberal Party.

■ Key profiles

Jeremy Bentham (1748–1832)

The writings of Bentham (1748–1832) influenced Victorian political ideology and especially Liberalism. Bentham called for an extension of franchise for all men, but conditional on property ownership or fixed residency and so not really universal. His most important and radical contribution was the idea of Utilitarianism – organisation of society to benefit the greatest number. Ideally, he sought a balance between individual freedom and what was in society's best interests. He was influential, radical and progressive, yet not extreme in his views.

John Stuart Mill

The son of political writer James Mill, John Mill (1806–73) was married to Harriet Taylor who spoke out for women's rights. Mill was influenced by Bentham's political and social theories. He was a great supporter of Liberalism and believed in the political domination of the middle class. He supported extension of the franchise to all who contributed to the country's economy, even to women, but feared the majority uneducated masses gaining political power, in his words 'the tyranny of the majority'. Mill's views were expressed in his acclaimed work *Representative Government* (1861).

Walter Bagehot

A Liberal, from a middle-class banking family, Bagehot (1826–77) displayed a great talent for political journalism. He was a friend and contemporary of Mill, but possibly jealous of Mill's acknowledged intellectual success as a political thinker and writer. Bagehot was best known for his study on the British parliamentary system *The English Constitution* (1867), written just before the 1867 Reform Act changed the system. He believed in the superiority of the upper and middle classes and that the labouring classes were too ignorant to have the responsibility to vote or make good decisions. Bagehot, too, was against universal male suffrage.

Liberal support in the country

If the election results in this period are examined, it is clear that most support for the Liberals came from the towns and **boroughs**. The urban centres of population were still expanding and were full of prosperous middle-class men of commerce and industry, who saw the Liberal Party as reflecting their aspirations and values. They enjoyed a comfortable lifestyle, were well educated and were regular church goers. They had a sense of justice and respected authority, and they desired an ordered society in which they could at least maintain and possibly increase their status and wealth. The skilled craftsmen, who made up a significant proportion of the population of the industrial towns, had similar ambitions to the middle classes, but on a reduced scale. After the 1867 Reform Act gave them the vote, they helped to keep the Liberals in power for almost 20 years. In his book *The Formation of the British Liberal Party, 1857–1865*, John Vincent looks at what kind of people supported the Liberal Party and helped to create its national identity. Vincent argues that support grew from the impact of three key developments:

- the rise of the provincial press
- the growth of the new model unions
- the appearance of a political dimension to Nonconformist movement.

The rise of the provincial press

Until the 1860s, the London press had dominated the newspaper industry. With the coming of the railways, the invention of the telegraph and the removal of stamp duties, the provincial press saw a dramatic increase both in titles and circulation. Most of this new press was Liberal in terms of ownership, employees and readership. Newspapers, such as the *Newcastle Chronicle*, were able to influence large numbers of voters across the industrial towns of north-east England and were of considerable benefit to the Liberal Party.

The growth of the new model unions

The **new model unions**, which had developed during the 1850s, gave their support to the Liberal Party. They represented the interests of skilled workers such as engineers and boilermakers. It was these workers who benefited from the extension of the franchise in 1867. They regarded themselves as the elite of the working classes and sought to improve their conditions by self-help and self-education. The unions, functioning as **friendly societies**, set up schemes to give benefits to members in times of hardship. The legal position of the **trade unions** was not clearly defined, and their funds could not be protected by law. By supporting the Liberal Party, the unions hoped that once the party was in government, it would strengthen the unions' legal position.

The political activities of the Nonconformists

The most pressing wish of the Nonconformists was to achieve equal treatment with the Church of England (the Anglican Church) and to end its privilege as the established Church. This campaign was led by the Liberation Society, which became a kind of political wing of the Nonconformists and whose steady backing of the Liberal Party over the years helped to ensure the Nonconformist vote 'was bound hard by habit to the Liberal Party' (John Vincent). The support of Nonconformists was crucial to the Liberal Party. Nearly 50 per cent of the church-going population was Nonconformist. They were geographically spread, but the

Key terms

Borough: a town granted special privileges often by royal charter became known as a borough and had the right to send two representatives to parliament. Its origin dates from medieval times.

New model unions: after 1850 skilled workers formed unions for their own craft/skill. Their subscriptions were high and they paid out generous benefits to members for illness or unemployment. These unions were generally against taking strike action.

Friendly societies: (or mutual societies) were formed among workers to enable them to make savings as an insurance against an event such as accident or sudden death. Every subscriber became a member of the society.

Trade union: an association of workers, often belonging to a single trade, who act together to protect their economic interests and welfare in the workplace. Trade unions began to form with the growth of industry.

Cross-reference

The 1867 Reform Act is described on pages 17–21.

wealthiest and most influential lived in the industrial areas where the Liberals were strongest. Nonconformists were also numerous in Wales, Scotland and the West Country.

Problems of the Conservatives

Finding a suitable leader

While the Liberals were establishing their new political party, the Conservatives were absorbed with the problem of regaining the political power that they had lost years before over the repeal of the Corn Laws in 1846. Between 1846 and 1865, the Conservatives held office for two very short periods in 1852 and 1858–9. On both occasions they were **minority governments** and, therefore, it was always difficult to pass any legislation. Lord Derby was the Conservative Party leader, but because he held a peerage he sat in the House of Lords, and was not entitled to sit in the House of Commons. The power of the Lords over the Commons had weakened after the formation of new constituencies in industrial towns, where peers like Derby had little control over elections. This made it difficult for the Lords to influence procedings in the Commons, although they could still use their veto to block measures they disliked in the Lords.

■ **Key profile**

Benjamin Disraeli

Disraeli (1804–81) was born into an Italian Jewish immigrant family. To distance himself from his Jewish roots, his father changed the family name from D'Israeli to Disraeli and Benjamin was baptised into the Anglican Church. Disraeli had a privileged upbringing, though he was educated at a small obscure private school rather than one of the well-known English public schools. He entered parliament in 1837 as a Tory after unsuccessful attempts at standing as a Radical. He gained a reputation as a gifted and persuasive speaker, but was scorned and distrusted by traditional Conservative MPs. He helped to bring down Peel in 1846, siding with the Protectionists against the Free Traders. During Lord Derby's three minority Conservative ministries, Disraeli served as chancellor and leader of the Commons. He and Gladstone became political arch rivals. He out-manoeuvred Gladstone over parliamentary reform and passed the Second Reform Act under his nose. He served as prime minister briefly in 1868 and then from 1874–80, when he adopted a programme of social legislation. In 1876, Disraeli was created Earl of Beaconsfield by his great admirer Queen Victoria.

There were few Conservative politicians of real quality to lead the party in the House of Commons – apart from Benjamin Disraeli, who acknowledged that he did not come from a traditional Tory aristocratic background and whose family was Jewish. Disraeli had been baptised into the Church of England, but there was still a great deal of prejudice against him. He fought hard to be accepted, proved himself an excellent debater in the House, and made himself as indispensible as possible to the Tory elite. But even as Conservative leader in the House of Commons, Disraeli was still despised and distrusted by many in his party.

■ Key terms

Minority government: the government in office has fewer seats in the House of Commons than the opposition. This can occur when a prime minister resigns and a new government is formed from the opposition party without holding a general election. It can reduce the government's ability to carry out its legislative programme.

■ Cross-reference

To revise the repeal of the Corn Laws in 1846, look back to pages 4–5.

■ Did you know?

The last prime minister to sit in the House of Lords was Lord Salisbury, who held the post for his third and last time from 1895 to 1902. It became part of 20th century democratic convention that a prime minister must be an elected member of parliament and not a hereditary Lord.

Fig. 4 Benjamin Disraeli, 1st Earl of Beaconsfield (1804–81), portrait by Millais, 1881

It is certainly true that Disraeli was only tolerated by the Conservatives in the House of Commons because he was clearly subordinate to Derby, the acknowledged overall party 'chief'. Derby's patrician presence was reassuring to the country gentlemen on the backbenches making it easier to accept the unavoidable necessity of Disraeli's leadership in the absence of any viable alternative candidate.

3   *Jenkins, T. A. (1996)* **Disraeli and Victorian Conservatism***, Palgrave MacMillan*

Disraeli's leadership was an unavoidable necessity as he appeared to be the person with clear ideas about developing party policy. He realised that to win the support of the electorate it was vital to present them with new policies. In an era when many ordinary people could not read or write, it was important to get the party message across by holding public meetings and finding good speakers to inspire the crowd. There was considerable competition from a number of outstanding orators (public speakers) in the Liberal Party – particularly Gladstone and John Bright – who could successfully work a crowd.

On policy matters, Disraeli persuaded the Conservatives that it was no good following a policy of trade protection when it was clear that the Whigs' free trade policy had resulted in a rise in living standards. He brought the party around to accepting the principle of parliamentary reform, in order to update the party's image with the electorate. He developed ideas on the need for social reform, which he spoke about at great length, without committing himself to any detailed proposal. After the Conservative defeat in the 1868 general election, he set about managing the reorganisation of the party machinery, which helped to bring about a Conservative victory in the election of 1874.

Fig. 5 *'Climbing the greasy pole' at the Gifford annual fair in Scotland in the late-19th century*

Issues of parliamentary reform

As most of our readers know, the Reform Bill of 1852 did not become law, and the cause of Parliamentary Reform was shelved for a time. For several years afterwards the country was too busily engaged with the affairs of Eastern Europe to pay much attention to other political questions affecting the interests of the people of Great Britain.

4   *Dent, R. K. (1880)* **Old and New Birmingham**

Did you know?

Before Disraeli entered politics he was renowned as a romantic novelist, though he is not in the same class as the Victorian greats such as Charles Dickens and George Eliot. One of his best-known novels is *Sybil*, published in 1845, the object of which was to bring to public notice the concept of a Britain divided between the rich and poor, a Britain of two nations. It hints at Disraeli's earlier Radicalism.

Did you know?

Disraeli is credited with coining the phrase 'climbing the greasy pole' to refer to the difficulties encountered by an ambitious person when trying to get to the top in an organisation. Its origins are much earlier. It was a popular event at village fairs among the men. They would climb a wooden pole smeared in animal fat as a test of strength. A piece of mutton at the top ot the pole was the prize for the winner.

Activity

Talking point

1 Why would Disraeli's background count against him in the 19th century Conservative Party?

2 Why did the Conservatives accept him as leader of party in the Commons?

Source 4 gives a good indication of the general attitude to parliamentary reform in Britain in the 1850s. The series of reform bills introduced between 1851 and 1866 appear to have failed because there was little public pressure and the middle-class voters who were enjoying a period of prosperity were generally satisfied with the parliamentary system in 1865. However, several factors brought about a change in attitude towards the question of reform.

Changing attitudes towards reform

There was a change in attitude within the political parties and also changes in the make-up of those parties, which helped to bring parliamentary reform to the forefront. The old Whig Party, dominated by landed aristocrats, was transforming into the Liberal Party, in which the commercial and industrial members had growing influence. These successful businessmen, who lived in the large under-represented towns and cities, sought to extend their political status and power, even if it was only through redistribution of seats. The Liberal leader in the House of Commons, William Gladstone, was converted to a belief in reform and began to lead the party in this direction. The Radicals in parliament, who often spoke for the working man, were becoming more effective within the Liberal Party. The leading Radical John Bright increased his influence on Gladstone. The Conservative Party also accepted the need for change, though for Disraeli and the progressive Tories there was a degree of opportunism to win the wider support of a larger electorate.

The conversion of Gladstone to belief in reform

In a speech in parliament in 1864 Gladstone underlined his position on reform: 'Every man who is not incapacitated by some consideration of personal unfitness … is morally entitled to come within the pale of the constitution'. In other words, Gladstone was defending the moral right of decent working men to have the vote. He believed that there was enough evidence to be confident they would vote responsibly as they possessed 'self-control, respect for order, patience under suffering, confidence in law and respect for superiors'. Gladstone's statement offered encouragement to Radical reform groups. Gladstone had become convinced of the necessity of reform.

The growth in interest in the democratic ideal

Both the American Civil War (1861–5) and the movement for Italian unification (1859–61) were seen by many British people as struggles for freedom and democracy, and were therefore instrumental in creating a popular surge of interest in reform. The visit of Garibaldi, the hero of the Italian unification movement, to London in 1864 excited the crowds and 'quickened the demand' from leading Radicals for a revival of interest in British politics and reform. Thousands of people flocked to hear Garibaldi speak and when the authorities clamped down on his public meetings, there were angry protests from his supporters. This repressive response led directly to the setting up of a new political organisation in February 1865 – the Reform League. The writings of political philosophers such as John Stuart Mill, elected MP for Westminster in 1865, were influential in raising interest in the political debates surrounding the extension of the franchise.

The Reform League (1865), the Reform Union (1864) and trade union pressure

The Reform League was a mainly working-class alliance with strong trade union support and a few wealthy middle-class backers. The League's aim was to work towards democracy through universal male

Cross-reference

John Bright is profiled on page 10.

Exploring the detail

Gladstone's 'conversion' to supporting reform was linked to the American Civil War. Raw cotton supplies to the Lancashire mills from the southern states were cut off by a blockade of the northern states. The 'cotton famine' that followed dealt a major economic blow to north-west England. The Lancashire cotton workers endured great hardship, which they bore without complaint. Gladstone was deeply impressed with their restrained conduct and came to the conclusion that it was 'a scandal that bodies of men such as these should be excluded from the parliamentary franchise'.

suffrage and a programme of radical reform. Local branches sprang up in the manufacturing towns and, although the central organisation was sometimes chaotic, it was able to mobilise its considerable force of trade union members and make its presence felt. Additional pressure came from leading trade union men in the London Trades Council, who met in 1866 and started to organise a campaign for reform.

The Reform League was more active and more successful than its counterpart the Reform Union, which was created a few months earlier in April 1864. This, by contrast, was a largely middle-class organisation that called for a secret ballot, and focused on seeking the redistribution of seats to correct the imbalance caused by the changes and movement in the population. Radical John Bright encouraged the two organisations to work together towards an extension of the franchise for working men, but the class divide created tensions between them.

Radical pressure

The Radicals kept up the pressure for reform both inside and outside parliament. John Bright, who was MP for Birmingham, toured the country encouraging ordinary men to demand their democratic rights. He was frustrated that the thousands who turned out to listen to him were his 'countrymen, who have no political power, who are at work from the dawn of the day until evening, and who have, therefore, limited means of informing themselves on great questions' (R. K. Dent, *Old and New Birmingham*, 1880). Bright put forward convincing arguments on behalf of the skilled workers in favour of extending the franchise.

The impact of rise in living standards and population changes

Economic prosperity after 1850 had led to an overall rise in the standard of living, especially of skilled artisans. The improvement in the standard of living among the skilled working class, coupled with their improved level of education, made the Liberals more prone to accepting the idea of extending the franchise to include this group. They saved wages in friendly societies and the Post Office Savings Bank set up by Gladstone in 1861. They formed responsible trade unions through which they provided self-help and some form of social security. In the opinion of leading Liberals like Gladstone, they had proved themselves to be responsible. One good example of this was the Lancashire cotton workers.

The responsible attitude of the skilled workers had not brought them any political advantage. Few of them had the right to vote, and many of them lived in the huge, sprawling industrial cities that still had only one or two MPs – therefore they were largely under-represented. The size of **constituencies** had become very uneven as a result of continuing population growth and movement from the countryside to urban areas. No new constituencies had been formed even though the industrial revolution of the early 19th century had helped to create new towns and cities. The Liberal middle-class manufacturing MPs also had a vested interest in securing an increase in the number of seats in these areas to extend their political influence. In reality, the demographic changes were forcing the issue of reform on to the political agenda and they would have to be tackled by whichever party was in power.

The Second Reform Act, 1867

The death in October 1865 of the elderly prime minister, Lord Palmerston, who had remained persistently hostile to any idea of electoral reform, cleared the way for the Liberal government to address the question of reform.

Cross-reference

For more on the Lancashire cotton workers, refer back to page 16.

The rise in prosperity is covered in more detail on pages 54–57.

Key terms

Constituency: a district that is represented by a member of parliament. Britain is now divided into constituencies of equal size in terms of population, for the purpose of electing representatives to parliament at each general election. A large city such as Manchester is divided into several parliamentary constituencies. In the 19th century, rapid industrial growth made constituencies very uneven and many districts had no MP to represent their interests.

Activity

Revision activity

Why was there an increased demand for parliamentary reform by 1865? Summarise the key points in note form.

Gladstone's 1866 Reform Bill

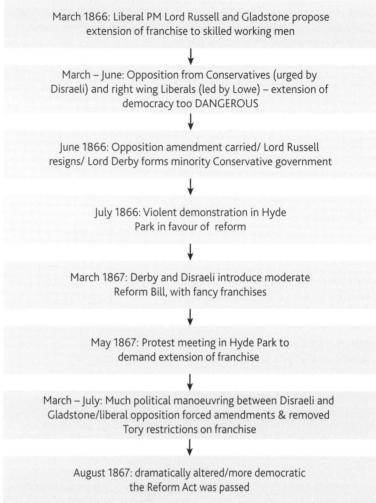

March 1866: Liberal PM Lord Russell and Gladstone propose extension of franchise to skilled working men

↓

March – June: Opposition from Conservatives (urged by Disraeli) and right wing Liberals (led by Lowe) – extension of democracy too DANGEROUS

↓

June 1866: Opposition amendment carried/ Lord Russell resigns/ Lord Derby forms minority Conservative government

↓

July 1866: Violent demonstration in Hyde Park in favour of reform

↓

March 1867: Derby and Disraeli introduce moderate Reform Bill, with fancy franchises

↓

May 1867: Protest meeting in Hyde Park to demand extension of franchise

↓

March – July: Much political manoeuvring between Disraeli and Gladstone/liberal opposition forced amendments & removed Tory restrictions on franchise

↓

August 1867: dramatically altered/more democratic the Reform Act was passed

Fig. 6 *The passage of the 1866 Reform Bill*

In response to the renewed interest and pressure for parliamentary reform, Gladstone and Lord John Russell, the new Liberal prime minister, drew up a Reform Bill. It was well reasoned and moderate and had the backing of Radical John Bright. It proposed an extension of the vote to those in the towns (boroughs) who owned or rented a property with a rateable value of £7 a year, instead of the existing £10 qualification. In the counties, the vote would be given to those who rented property valued at £14 a year. This would give the vote to skilled workers who lived mainly in the industrial towns and, in the country, would include smallholders. It would extend the electorate by about 400,000 men.

When the Reform League heard that Lord Russell and Gladstone were putting together a Reform Bill, they called a meeting in the Town Hall on 23 November 1865 to demonstrate their approval (Source 5).

> Having regard to the time-honoured name of Russell and the great services and high reputation of Mr Gladstone, this meeting expresses its confident hope that a large instalment of political rights will be now conceded to the working manhood of this country, and that the principle of manhood suffrage will be recognised as the basis of our representation.

5

Dent, R. K. (1880) Old and New Birmingham

However, the Reform League was to be disappointed. The Bill was thrown out. Gladstone and Russell expected opposition from the Conservatives who claimed it went too far, but more damaging was the fierce opposition of a group of about 40 Liberals, led by Robert Lowe, who claimed the reform would give political power to the 'ignorant'. Lowe rejected Gladstone's argument that the skilled workers had proved themselves worthy of getting the vote. He rejected the idea of improving working-class status by lowering the franchise qualification 'to the level of those persons who have no decency or morality'. He saw the vote as 'a privilege of citizenship', to be awarded to working men who improved themselves to the extent that they could meet the existing qualification.

When an amendment, which would have had the effect of cutting the number of new skilled voters in the boroughs, was put forward in June 1866 by one of Lowe's supporters and carried, Russell resigned. The Conservatives formed a minority government under Lord Derby. It was a sad end to Lord Russell's long political career. As a Whig minister in 1832, he had helped bring in the first Great Reform Act that began the process of making parliament accountable to the people, under Prime Minister Earl Grey, setting Britain on the road to democracy.

The Reform League responded by organising demonstrations across the country. The message to the new Conservative government was clear. The protesters were not going to give up until they had obtained 'registered, residential manhood suffrage, as the only just basis of representation and the (secret) ballot to protect them from undue influence and intimidation in elections' (R. K. Dent, *Old and New Birmingham*, 1880).

Disraeli tackles parliamentary reform

> ### ◼ Did you know?
>
> Robert Lowe's supporters were nicknamed 'Adullamites' by John Bright the leading Radical reformer. It was a reference that would have been clearly understood at the time. It comes from the Old Testament story where David and his friends take shelter in the Cave of Adullam to escape from King Saul, whom David has apparently betrayed.

Fig. 7 *Meeting of supporters of the Reform Bill in Hyde Park, London, from the* Illustrated London News, *May 1867. What strikes you about the composition of the crowd?*

Lord Derby led a minority Conservative government into office, with Disraeli as leader in the Commons and chancellor of the exchequer. It is not entirely clear whether Derby and Disraeli had already decided to go ahead with another attempt to introduce parliamentary reform, before the deteriorating condition in the economy and the growing working-class frustration at the lack of progress over reform persuaded them to act quickly and introduce another reform bill. The main argument had become how low the franchise could be set and still avoid giving the vote to the uneducated 'masses', who were seen as unreliable and a bad risk, rather than whether or not to go ahead with a reform bill.

The historian Asa Briggs in *The Age of Improvement* (1967) maintains that the 'break in economic prosperity' in 1866 and 1867 was the main catalyst for the reform to be successfully passed through parliament. Apart from frustration at the lack of progress on the franchise, the working classes were feeling the effects of the bad harvest of the previous year. There had been another outbreak of cholera, which caused panic in London and other large towns. At the same time, there had been a spectacular collapse of one of London's most successful finance houses, Overend and Gurney, followed by a stock market tumble. The domino effect brought about the collapse of many other businesses, threatened high unemployment and helped to spark off the huge demonstrations. There was considerable alarm at the outbreak of violence near Hyde Park on 23 July 1866, after a Reform League meeting, which had attracted a huge crowd, was prevented from taking place. A similar demonstration by the League took place in Hyde Park in May 1867. Asa Briggs' argument is that the resulting pressure from outside parliament persuaded Disraeli to seize the moment and take the credit for what had generally been regarded as a Liberal reform.

When the Conservative Reform Bill was first introduced, it contained checks to restrict the number of working-class voters, and balances with 'fancy franchises' and dual votes for many members of the middle classes. Disraeli dropped these when there was fierce opposition from Gladstone and a chance the Bill would be lost. Disraeli also accepted the radical proposals in the amendment of George Hodgkinson, simply in order to get the Bill through the Commons and get the better of Gladstone. Derby secured its smooth passage through the Lords by convincing them it would ensure a Conservative victory in the next election.

Historians have highlighted the paradox of the political events of 1866 and 1867. The final legislation turned out to be much more democratic than either Derby or Disraeli had imagined. Hodgkinson's amendment enfranchised the skilled worker in the towns. The result was a further shifting of the centre of political power away from the landed classes. This was surprising as the Conservatives were traditionally anti-reform and would not naturally support a measure that further eroded the political power of the upper classes. Disraeli, however, was an opportunist. He reckoned it was possible that, by pushing through a measure of parliamentary reform, the Conservatives might win over those skilled workers who were about to be enfranchised. In this way, the Conservatives could perhaps break the long record of poor election results that stretched back to the days of the party split in 1847. To win the loyalty of the potential new voters on a longer-term basis, Disraeli could see it was essential to change the public perception of the Conservatives as an anti-reform party. Disraeli knew that if the Conservatives did not seize this chance to bring in the reform themselves, then Gladstone would do it as soon as he got back into power. Thus, a Conservative

Cross-reference

The Reform League is outlined earlier on pages 16–17.

Activity

Talking point

Historian Robert Blake suggests that both the Liberal and Tory leaders were subject to the pressure of mass working-class agitation expressed through the activities of the Reform League. How important was the Reform League in bringing about the Second Reform Act?

Exploring the detail

Hodgkinson's Amendment concerned the central debate over whether compounders should get the vote; this would determine how low the franchise would be set.

- Compounders were tenants who paid their rates as part of the rent collected by the landlord.

- Householders (i.e. those who owned the property) paid their rates direct to the local authority.

- Hodgkinson proposed to abolish compounding. This would enfranchise *all* ratepayers, whether they owned or rented property.

minority government introduced parliamentary reform legislation that was more far-reaching than the Liberal Bill of the previous year, which the same group of Conservatives had helped to defeat.

In the event, the Conservatives lost the 1868 general election that followed, as the new largely urban electorate rewarded Gladstone for his consistent support of the Reform Act. In opposition, Gladstone had united the Liberals and pleased the Nonconformists by putting Irish Church reform on the political agenda. An unfavourable economic climate and the raising of income tax had reduced Conservative popularity at the polls. Disraeli's Reform Act had failed to break the Conservatives' long record of poor election results and the pattern of Liberal domination continued.

The franchise was extended:

In the boroughs (towns) to

- All male householders over 21, who had lived at the same address for 12 months.
- Lodgers who paid £10 a year in rent and had lived at the same address for 12 months.

In the counties to

- The forty-shilling **freeholders** (as in the 1832 Act).
- The £5 **copyholders** and £12 **tenants.**

These terms only applied to men. No women could vote.

Redistribution of seats:

- 53 seats were taken from boroughs with a population of under 10,000
- 25 seats were given to English counties
- 20 seats were given to larger English boroughs and towns
- 8 seats to Scottish burghs and counties

Fig. 8 *Terms of the 1867 Second Reform Act*

 Key terms

Freeholder: owned his land and, if it was worth 40 shillings in annual rateable value, he could vote.

Copyholder: possessed a written copy of his lease over his land and qualified for a vote if the land had an annual rateable value of £5 or more.

Tenant: rented land on a less secure basis than copyholders, but qualified for a vote if the land had an annual rateable value of £12 or more.

Activity

Challenge your thinking

Can you explain why the issue of parliamentary reform no longer seemed to divide the Liberals and Conservatives in 1866–7?

Effects of the 1867 Reform Act

The number of voters had increased from 1.2 million to approximately 2.5 million, which was roughly one-third of the male adult population. No women could vote. The greatest increase of voters occurred in the boroughs, where skilled workers had the vote for the first time.

However, the impact of this landmark victory for the artisan class was reduced because of the limited nature of the redistribution of seats. For example, Birmingham, Liverpool and Manchester, with their huge populations, were given only one extra seat in addition to the two they already had. Overall, the distribution of seats did not correspond to the size of population. Rural areas remained over-represented whilst the industrial Midlands, the North and Scotland remained under-represented. There was a smaller increase in the electorate in the counties, where most voters were relatively prosperous smallholders or middle class. Boroughs with a population of just over 10,000 had the same representation (i.e. two MPs) as boroughs with a population of almost 400,000.

The increase in the electorate led to both parties improving their party organisations in order to capture the new voters at elections. The Reform Act led indirectly to the 1870 Education Act, as many politicians thought it expedient to educate the new voters.

The Ballot Act, 1872

Although the Second Reform Act was effective in moving the British people closer to a democratic State, bribery, corruption and intimidation remained a common feature of elections. Voting was still carried out in public by a show of hands and allowed landlords and employers to put pressure on tenants and employees to vote for a particular candidate

 Activity

Talking point

1. How could the Conservative Party justify passing the Reform Act in 1867 when it had so recently thrown out the Liberals' Reform Bill?

2. What impact did the Second Reform Act have on: (a) the electorate; and (b) the distribution of seats in both the short and long term?

3. Which section of the electorate gained most from the changes? Explain your answer.

or party. At worst, a man could lose his job for not voting as he was told. Money was often laid out by candidates for free transport and free beer on polling days and there were very few eyebrows raised. To many politicians, irrespective of party, the right to vote was a privilege and a responsibility that should be carried out in public.

However, in 1867, a parliamentary enquiry revealed the extent of corrupt practices in many boroughs. As a result of that enquiry, the constituency of Lancaster was disenfranchised for spending £14,000 to bribe its 1,400 voters in the 1865 general election. Gladstone's response to the results of the enquiry was to introduce the Secret Ballot Act (1872), whereby voters were free to choose their preferred candidate by using the ballot box. It was a further step towards democracy and, although it reduced intimidation of voters at the polls, it failed to stamp out corruption.

The reforms of Gladstone's First Ministry, 1868–74

Key chronology

A catalogue of reforms

1869	Vote in local elections for women ratepayers.
1870	Forster Education Act marks the beginning of State education. Entry to the Civil Service on the basis of a competitive examination. Married Women's Property Act.
1871–3	Cardwell's Army Reforms ends system of purchasing commissions.
1871	Universities Tests Act ends the Anglican monopoly of teaching posts in Oxford and Cambridge. Trade Union Act legalises trade unions. The Criminal Law Amendment Act makes almost any action they take illegal! Local Government Board set up to supervise poor law and public health.
1872	Public Health Act. Compulsory appointment of medical officers of health. Licensing Act restricts opening hours.
1873	Judicature Act produces a major reform of courts.

'The best can be the enemy of the good'

As a result of the 1868 general election, Gladstone became prime minister for the first time in a high-profile political career that had already stretched almost 40 years. The Liberal majority was 106 over the Conservatives and it gave them a clear mandate to implement policies based on the principles of Gladstonian Liberalism. Many of the reforms passed during this government reflected these principles of administrative efficiency, cutting back on government spending, pursuing free trade and promoting the freedom of the individual.

The make-up of Gladstone's Cabinet (his committee of ministers) revealed the different political groupings that made up the Liberal Party: Peelites (including Gladstone); Liberals; Radicals; and Whigs. All were Anglican except for John Bright who was a Quaker and a Nonconformist, the first to hold a Cabinet post.

At the centre of the Liberal administration was the highly principled and deeply religious Gladstone. Gladstone was a committed Christian and his religious beliefs shaped his understanding of the function of politics and the role of political change. For him, politics and religion seemed to go

Cross-reference

Details of Gladstone's Corrupt and Illegal Practices Act (1883) can be found on page 79.

Cross-reference

The principles of Gladstonian Liberalism are described on pages 11–12.

For the composition of the Liberal Party, refer back to page 10.

Exploring the detail

Gladstone: politics and religion

There are differing views on the extent to which Gladstone was guided by his religious and moral convictions. Martin Pugh in his book *The Making of Modern British Politics* (2002) appears to subscribe to the view that politics and religion were interlinked for Gladstone, when he comments: 'no-one could rival his capacity to articulate a sense of morality in politics and lift men's sights above vulgar materialism'. John Vincent, in *The Formation of the British Liberal Party* (1967), however, contends that expediency guided Gladstone in his political decisions, rather than his belief in God.

hand in hand, and his policies were often guided by what he believed to be morally right.

The reforms were vast in number and addressed important social and political issues of the period. The extent to which they satisfied the various interests within the party and the **pressure groups** outside, is a matter for debate. In some ways, the Liberal Party was an awkward coalition, in which the over-riding desire of each group was to follow its own agenda and please its own lobby. At the outset, Gladstone insisted on unity within the party and held it together at least on the surface for five years.

Pressure groups

Several key pressure groups operated outside the parliamentary party. They were single issue groups, but shared some of the same membership and the thread of Nonconformism ran through most of them.

- The Liberation Society aimed at the **disestablishment** of the Church of England. In 1871, pressure was put on Nonconformist MPs to accept a disestablishment motion, but it was firmly defeated with a clear lead from Gladstone.

- The National Education League led the campaign for free, compulsory and non-religious education in State schools. Its leadership was Nonconformist and included Joseph Chamberlain. Its dissatisfaction with the 1870 Education Act caused potential division in the party.

- The United Kingdom Alliance founded in 1852 was a temperance movement. It was based in Manchester, a strong Nonconformist area, and sought to outlaw the sale of alcohol. It lobbied its supporters in parliament to pass a Permissive Bill, to make the banning of alcohol an issue for local ratepayers. It regarded the 1872 Licensing Act as a partial success.

Position of Labour and trade union leaders

At this time, there was little concept of a separate Labour Party and the few working-class men to enter parliament did so as Gladstonian Liberals. Regional trades councils, whose importance lay in the opportunities they provided for the different unions to exchange ideas, encouraged the setting up of a national organisation for the unions. As a result, a Trades Union Congress (TUC) met for the first time in 1868 in Manchester to bring pressure to bear on the government to give trade unions legal recognition. Union leaders were keen to cooperate with the Liberal government and promote their members as hard working, respectable and god fearing.

The TUC became an annual event after its London meeting in 1871. From this time, it represented the trade union movement as a whole.

Key terms

Pressure group: a number of like-minded people who by their actions and words try to influence public opinion or government policy on an issue that is important to them.

Disestablishment: separation of the Church from the State so that the State no longer takes any official part in supporting the Church or upholding its decisions.

Activity

Talking point

Michael Winstanley in *Gladstone and the Liberal Party* (1991) suggests that while 'Faddists' (pressure groups) gave the party its 'reforming reputation', they 'threatened to undermine its unity'.

1. To what extent do you agree with this assessment of the leaders of the pressure groups?

2. How important do you think pressure groups are in persuading governments to pass difficult legislation? Use some present-day examples.

The main reforms

The Forster Education Act, 1870

Fig. 9 *The junior class writing on their slates at the London Board School in Islington. The setting up of board schools was a provision of the Forster Education Act*

Reform of the mishmash of **voluntary schools** that existed in England was overdue. The schools had been run mainly by Church groups on an inadequate government grant since the 1830s. There were not enough schools for the growing population and the expanding towns. After the extension of the franchise in 1867, it was in the government's interest to have an educated electorate. There were obvious benefits to society as a whole, but, in Gladstonian terms, a national system would be efficient and contribute to the development of a meritocracy. It would bring economic advantage in the longer term by creating workers with technical and vocational skills and, therefore, assist Britain in international competitiveness.

The main provisions of the Forster Education Act were as follows:

▓ The country was divided into school districts.

▓ **Board schools**, providing elementary education for pupils aged 5–12, were to be built where provision was inadequate and maintained out of the local rates.

▓ **School boards** were to be set up, elected by ratepayers in each district, to run the new schools. They had autonomy over attendance and fees, but had to pay fees for poor children.

▓ Attendance at religious lessons was voluntary.

However, problems arose over the place of religion in education and the continuing existence of the denominational schools, most of which were run by the Church of England. The National Education League called for the exclusion of churches in the running of schools and no religious teaching in the new board schools. The Anglican National Education Union retaliated with demands for the continuation of religious education. The Cowper-Temple amendment excluded **denominational** religious teaching in the new board schools and the final act was a compromise. Nevertheless, the Nonconformists continued to see it as a threat to religious equality.

There were bitter disputes over the election to school boards and Nonconformist support was withdrawn from any Liberal by-election candidate who failed to pledge to amend the Education Act further. The resulting Liberal by-election losses helped to destroy the Liberal government.

The Education Act was important in that it indicated a move away from *laissez-faire* in government social legislation, and acknowledged the role of the State in educating its children.

 Activity

Talking point

Robert Lowe commented on the passing of the 1867 Reform Act: 'I believe it will be absolutely necessary to compel our new masters to learn their letters.'

Why do you think it was in the government's interest to have an educated electorate?

Administrative reforms

Civil Service and Army Reform created ill feeling towards the government from the traditional Whigs. Entry to both was based on family connections and wealth, not on the ability to perform the job.

In the reform of the Civil Service, the principle of entry by competitive examination was established. This innovation brought in candidates with intellect and ability and improved professionalism and efficiency at a minimal cost to the government. The reform allowed bright young men from ordinary backgrounds the chance of a steady career with good prospects and a comfortable standard of living. It won the approval of many middle-class Liberals.

Edward Cardwell, Secretary for War, was charged with rooting out incompetence and inefficiency in the army. The existing system was based almost entirely on privilege and was seen as the preserve of the aristocracy. The Commander-in-Chief was appointed through royal patronage and was often a junior royal lacking in military skill and intelligence. Wealthy families bought their sons commissions as officers. These commissions could be sold on to the highest bidder, and were regarded as an officer's property. The disasters of the Crimean War had underlined the need to improve the competency and professionalism of the army. More recently, British newspapers had carried reports of the astonishing victories of the Prussian army over Austria (1866) and France (1870). Bismarck's reform of the Prussian army had produced a highly disciplined, well-equipped, professional fighting force that could be seen as a potential future threat to Britain.

Cardwell established political control of the army by making the Commander-in-Chief answerable to the Secretary for War. The Army Enlistment Act 1870 changed the 12-year service to six years active service and six in the reserve, following the Prussian model, and peacetime flogging was abolished. A new breech-loading Martini-Henry rifle was introduced to replace the muzzle-loading Enfield rifle for the infantry. Britain was divided into military districts, usually counties, and the regiments took the name of the county, e.g. The Northumberland Fusiliers. These changes were in the interests of creating a modern force, but almost coincidentally raised morale among the ranks, which was beneficial to army discipline. To increase efficiency, The War Office was divided into three main departments, but all were housed in one building at Whitehall.

Exploring the detail

Will Thorne, the Gas Workers' leader, was one of several union leaders who grew up illiterate. Although the Education Act of 1870 had provided school places for all children, it was not necessarily free. Many labouring families could not afford to send children to school. There were still high levels of illiteracy among the working class. A good indication of literacy levels is the percentage of men and women who were able to sign the marriage register. In England in 1880 it was 86% and by 1900 it had risen to 97%. However, for most of those who could write their name, their level of literacy was very basic.

Key terms

Civil Service: the body that is responsible for the public administration of the State.

The abolition of the system of purchase of commissions presented a different challenge to Cardwell. By its abolition, he was attacking a fundamental belief of society – the right by birth and wealth to privilege. It was bound to be controversial. The furious opposition in the House of Lords, which was encouraged by Queen Victoria, was overcome by Cardwell's threat to abolish existing commissions without compensation. The act ending the purchase of commissions was passed in 1871, whereby in future the selection and promotion of officers was to be based on merit.

Further administrative changes were made in the least contentious Liberal reform, the Judicature Act of 1873. This aimed to simplify the British legal system by uniting the existing seven major courts, which had developed independently of each other over centuries, into the Supreme Court of Judicature. The act tidied up the organisation and roles of the courts and simplified the cumbersome and lengthy appeals.

Labour laws

Until 1871, the working-class electorate were still firm supporters of the Liberals. In that year the government passed two pieces of trade union legislation, which changed that support to frustration and anger. The leaders of the new model unions, confident that the Second Reform Act had given them bargaining power, pressed the government for a Royal Commission of Inquiry into Trade Unionism, to clarify the ill-defined legal position of the unions. During the 1860s, the unions had been weakened by dishonest officials and the violent behaviour of some of their striking members.

The Trade Union Act of 1871 established the legal right of the unions to hold property and funds and have them protected by law. They also had the right to strike. The Criminal Law Amendment Act, passed immediately after, made any form of **picketing** illegal. Therefore, the trade unions were legalised, but almost any action they took to achieve their objectives was illegal. Historians have identified this act as Gladstone's most serious misjudgement as it cost him working-class support at the general election in 1874. Historians believe that the passing of two such contrasting pieces of legislation can be explained by Gladstone's strong religious faith that abhorred violence or threat of violence. The skilled artisans who had helped to ensure the government's success in 1868 were left bitterly disappointed with the lack of any real support for trade union reform.

Licensing laws

Gladstone's missionary zeal to improve the moral fibre of the ordinary man probably contributed to his enthusiasm to support the Licensing Act (1872). It was a mild enough measure, giving magistrates the power to issue licences to publicans, to fix opening and closing hours, and to prohibit the adulteration of beer. It satisfied neither side who took part in the debate that had preceded it. The United Kingdom Alliance and other temperance groups did not think it went far enough and the 'Beerage' felt it attacked their industry. The Licensing Bill had repercussions beyond the term of Gladstone's First Ministry, as it alienated the brewers and distillers who in future voted Conservative and gave generously to Conservative Party funds. Public houses became centres of Conservative propaganda.

Legislation affecting women

MILL'S LOGIC; OR, FRANCHISE FOR FEMALES.

"PRAY CLEAR THE WAY, THERE, FOR THESE—A—PERSONS."

Fig. 10 *This* Punch *cartoon of March 1867 is a satirical comment on John Stuart Mill's campaign to extend the franchise to include women. What does this cartoon tell you about attitudes towards the idea of women having the vote at this time?*

Perhaps almost unnoticed among this flurry of reforms were a number of measures that involved the first stirrings of a women's rights movement and female emancipation. John Stuart Mill had introduced an amendment to the Reform Bill to allow women a parliamentary vote. Although it was defeated, 73 MPs voted in favour of it. In 1869, it was Gladstone who agreed to the principle of female emancipation by giving women ratepayers the vote in local elections. A year later, one of the most important pieces of legislation regarding women's rights was passed. The Married Women's Property Act gave married women legal status and allowed a woman to keep £200 of her own earnings. The Education Act was enlightened as it made provision for girls to attend school. It would possibly be the daughters of that generation who benefited from the introduction of women's suffrage in 1918 and 1928.

Cross-reference

John Stuart Mill is profiled on page 12.

Activity

Group activity

1 In groups, study the brief outline of the Liberal government's key reforms. Group them under the following headings:

- Electoral reform.
- Labour laws.
- Education, social reform.
- Equality laws.
- Administrative reforms.

2 Identify who would benefit from these reforms. Does a pattern emerge? Can you explain Gladstonian Liberalism (see page 11) in terms of these reforms? Which groups, if any, would be dissatisfied with the reforms and why? Present your findings to the class. Have you all reached similar conclusions?

Assessment of Gladstone's First Ministry

The Liberals passed a range of reforms, constitutional, legal, religious (and administrative), which reflected their desire to restrict excessive privilege, to open up opportunities and to improve civil liberties for the individual.

6

*Pugh, M. (2002) **The Making of Modern British Politics**, Blackwell*

Martin Pugh's assessment suggests that the Gladstonian Liberals set out on their reform programme with good intentions. Yet, in spite of passing laws to overcome injustice and abuses in the army, the Civil Service and the universities, by 1874 they had succeeded in antagonising almost every group of former supporters, leaving the way open for a Conservative victory by Disraeli in the 1874 election.

There was disappointment over the compromise policy of the Education Act from Radicals and Nonconformists. Cardwell's abolition of the purchase of commissions caused outrage among the elite classes and obscured the far-sightedness of the other army reforms. The Licensing Law had adverse political repercussions for the Liberal Party for decades. The Liberals' concentration on winning support from the lower-middle and artisan classes, who were mainly Nonconformist, caused the established Church to ally itself with the Conservatives. More costly was the irritation of the businessmen and industrialists at the Liberals' wooing of the working classes, for they too turned to the Tories. The Liberals even mismanaged the working class and lost the support of the trade unions. The loss of a series of by-elections should have given Gladstone the message, but it was not until the defeat over the Irish Universities Bill in February 1873, that Gladstone resigned, although he returned to office for a short time once his First Ministry was at an end.

Nevertheless, the reforms were innovative and far reaching. They improved the efficiency of the nation's key institutions, the army, the Civil Service, education and the judiciary. The Trade Union Act gave legal status to the unions and allowed them to develop into bastions of support for the whole labour movement. The Ballot Act signified a key step towards Britain achieving democracy and gave voters freedom of choice at elections. Gladstone's reforms challenged the notion of privilege, encouraged the promotion of meritocracy and, taken as a whole, underlined the principles of equality in a just society. In his own words, Gladstone concluded that his First Ministry was 'one of the finest instruments of government that ever were constructed'!

Cross-reference

The situation in Ireland at the end of Gladstone's first ministry is covered on pages 40–42.

Study tip

Remember that to assess 'success' you will need to define terms – successful for Gladstone, his party, the country, the people? Be careful you don't simply judge by present-day standards and expectations. Placing your answer within historical context is essential.

Summary questions

1 What were the main strengths and weaknesses of the Liberals and the Conservatives in 1865?

2 Why was there a need for parliamentary reform in 1867?

3 How successful were the reforms of Gladstone's First Ministry? Write down the strengths and weaknesses of each of the reforms and draw up an overall conclusion.

Gladstone, Ireland and abroad

Fig. 1 *An emblem of Irish Nationalism showing a portrait of Robert Emmet, executed after leading an abortive rebellion against the British government in 1803*

In this chapter you will learn about:

- Fenianism, the activities of the Fenians and the development of Irish Nationalism

- the emergence of the Home Rule for Ireland movement

- Gladstone's mission to pacify Ireland and how he sought to achieve this. This includes the passing of the 1869 Irish Church Act and the 1870 Land Act

- Gladstone's foreign policy.

Release the Fenians? Yes, how could we think of doing less.

They only made a slight mistake, which still they say they didn't make:

Mistook themselves and did suppose they were our fair and open foes,

Forgot they were but private 'gents' and claimed to be 'belligerents'

And gallows-free to shoot police on duty while they kept the peace;

To blow, as in some hostile town, a prison up and houses down,

Reckless of death and mutilation, dealt round to neighbouring population.

Release those Fenians? If they please to go down humbly on their knees

The pardon of the Queen implore, promise they will offend no more.

| 1 | *Pity the poor Fenians (adapted)* |

Pity the Poor Fenians first appeared in *Punch* magazine during Fenian unrest in Britain, and was reprinted in *The Scotsman* newspaper in September 1869 when their release from prison was being considered. It indicates a patronising attitude to the Fenians from the British press. It condemns their criminal acts, but shows a willingness to forgive.

After the Act of Union in 1800 between England and Ireland, the British nation was styled 'The United Kingdom of Great Britain and Ireland'. The detailed attention Gladstone gave to domestic affairs once he became prime minister in 1868 can also be seen in his zealous attempts to deal fairly and justly with Ireland as part of the United Kingdom. Legend has it that his first words on hearing that he was to become prime minister were 'my mission is to pacify Ireland'. Whatever truth there is in this story, Gladstone put Ireland at the top of his list of priorities, and almost his first piece of legislation was the Irish Church Act in 1869. This act sought to address pressing religious grievances. Gladstone's motives for his concentration on Ireland have been questioned by historians, particularly when compared with his handling of Britain's foreign policy. His attitude to foreign affairs was entirely different. Indifference and incompetence have been suggested as explanations for Gladstone's lacklustre foreign policy. In spite of this, Britain's status as the most powerful and wealthiest country in the world, with a vast empire and a strong navy to guard and support the country's overseas interests, was not diminished. In Gladstone's defence, it could be said that in his foreign policy he was simply applying the main **tenets** of Gladstonian Liberalism – to seek justice and maintain peace.

Key terms

Tenets: the opinions or principles that a person or a group believes in and believes to be true. It comes from the Latin word *tenet* meaning 'he holds'.

Key chronology

Fenian activity – government response

1858	Beginnings of Fenianism in Ireland and USA.
1866	Fenian incursions into Canada.
1867 February/March	Fenian disturbances in England and Ireland.
1867 September	Fenian attack on police prison van in Manchester.
1867 23 November	Execution of Fenian 'Manchester Martyrs'.
1867 13 December	Fenian bombing of Clerkenwell Gaol.
1868	Foundation of amnesty association by Isaac Butt.
1869	Irish Church Act disestablishes Anglican Church of Ireland.
1870 May	Isaac Butt founds Home Government Association.
1870 August	Gladstone's Land Act to protect tenants.
1870	Coercion Act to deal with agrarian unrest.
1873 January	Foundation of Home Rule Confederation of Great Britain.
1873 March	Defeat of Gladstone's Irish University Bill.
1873 May	Religious tests abandoned for Trinity College.
1873 November	Home Rule League founded.
1874 February	General election returns 59 Home Rulers.
1874 July	Butt's Home Rule motion defeated in Commons.

Fenianism and the emergence of Home Rule

Background to the 'troubles'

One of the most important areas of policy for Gladstone during his First Ministry was dealing with Ireland. At the outset, Gladstone made it clear that he wished to take up the challenge, where other British politicians had failed, to find a solution to Ireland's problems. The dissatisfaction among the Irish centred on the Church, the land (the economy was land based) and their **national identity**. Any attempt by British politicans to deal with Irish issues made matters worse, as they lacked a basic understanding of the problems and lacked sympathy for the Irish people when they suffered as a result of the British government's indifference.

During the 1840s, and before Irish politics became interwoven with the cataclysmic effects of the Irish Famine, a new group 'Young Ireland' was formed with the aim of repealing the union with England. There were sporadic outbreaks of violence, culminating in an abortive rising in 1848 that was easily put down by the police and the deployment to Ireland of extra troops from mainland Britain. Yet this rising, although inept and idealistic, was nationalist in character and, to some extent, marks the start of a long period of troubles for the British government in Ireland and increasing demands from several sections of Irish society for political independence and Home Rule for Ireland.

Fig. 2 *Ireland, 1867*

The growth of Fenianism

Fenianism evolved gradually. A Fenian Society as such was never formally set up. The Fenian movement arose from the remnants of the Young Ireland group and can also be seen as the political legacy of the famine, and in this sense it was a response to the increasing suffering of the Irish people. The Fenians were militant but romantic nationalists, whose aim was to achieve an independent Ireland by forcing the government to repeal the Act of Union. In spite of the idealism of some of the leaders, they were prepared to use violence to achieve their aim. The Fenians are sometimes described as separatist republicans, because they wanted an Irish government completely separate from the British government, with their own president, rather than to be subjects of the British monarchy.

The original inspiration for the Fenian movement came from two Young Ireland rebels, James Stephens and John O'Mahony – both fugitives in Paris after the failed rising in 1848. When Stephens felt it was safe for him to return to Ireland, he set up a secret society in 1858, 'to make Ireland an independent democratic republic'. It eventually became known as the Irish Republican Brotherhood or the IRB. At much the same time,

Key terms

Nationalism/national identity: akin to patriotism, especially in the 19th century, in having a love of one's country. Nationalism includes the belief that one's country is a sovereign State, which means it accepts no other country's authority over it. Nationalism is the attitude that people conscious of a common language, culture and tradition, and sometimes religion, should join together into an independent nation State. National identity addresses a basic need in people to belong to a country they can call their own.

Fenianism: an Irish republican movement that grew up in the aftermath of the Irish famine in the 1840s. Its members swore a secret oath and vowed to work towards Irish independence.

Cross-reference

Details of the Irish Famine of the 1840s can be found on page 5.

Did you know?

The name 'Fenian' is derived from the old Irish Gaelic 'Fianna', and was the name given to the warrior class, a legendary heroic group in the early history of Ireland. The name was inspired by John O'Mahony, who studied Gaelic and wanted to connect the movement to Ireland's heroic past. The Fenians operated as a secret society partly because of the revolutionary nature of their organisation, but they also wanted to follow a tradition of secret societies in Ireland, especially in the countryside.

Key terms

Ribbonmen: Ribbon Societies were a network of secret societies across Ireland based mainly in the towns, with political aims and a tradition of violence and direct action. The Ribbonmen included clerical workers, school masters and artisans. Its members wanted freedom from British rule and civil and religious liberties for all. The Ribbonmen formed a direct link with the Fenian movement after 1858.

John O'Mahony set up a parallel organisation in North America that became known as the Fenian Brotherhood, which also had the aim of achieving independence for Ireland.

Key profiles

James Stephens

Few facts are known about Stephens (1825–1901), except that he was born in Kilkenny. He was an engineer and probably from a comfortable background. He was adventurous, self-confident and dedicated to the Irish cause through the Young Ireland movement. In 1856, he toured Ireland for 3,000 miles on foot, to 'suss out' the strength of feeling for revolution among the grass roots. Stephens founded the Irish Republican Brotherhood in 1858. He was dictatorial and arrogant. He never lost belief in his own genius and qualities of leadership, although in 1865, he failed to start the Fenian rising in Ireland. He fled to the USA.

John O'Mahony

O'Mahony (1816–77) was from a prosperous landed Co. Cork family. Most leaders and supporters were lower-middle class. A founder member of the Fenian Brotherhood, he started up the movement in the USA. He was a romantic nationalist, emphasised the importance of Irish national traditions and encouraged a pride in Irish history. Mahony regarded Ireland as a nation in cultural terms as it had its own Gaelic language. He had an idealistic vision of an Ireland rooted in its Celtic past, but organised as a socialist democratic republic. He lost his political influence in the movement in 1866, when a new wing tired of his dictatorial style.

Support for Fenianism

In *Modern Ireland 1600–1972* (1988), R. F. Foster quotes Lord Strathnairn's remark in 1869 that in Ireland the Fenian supporters tended to be 'the class above the masses', or lower-middle class. This referred to the fact that about 50 per cent of the Fenians' followers came from the artisan class. The movement also attracted support from school teachers and *petit bourgeois* in the towns, and small farmers and labourers in the countryside. A number of **Ribbonmen** became integrated into the movement. Irish soldiers serving in the British army were always targeted for recruitment to Fenianism. The Fenian leadership came from a mixture of backgrounds, a few from the landed or clerical families, but most from the commercial and shopkeeping class.

Fig. 3 *The Knave, with horns and tail, represents an Irish American trying to persuade his naïve brother back in Ireland to join the Fenian rising, by promising him freedom, but, in reality, the hangman's noose*

In spite of the secret nature of the brotherhood, many thousands of supporters in Ireland and America were drawn into it. In America, they came largely from among the Irish immigrant population who had been driven out of Ireland as a result of the famine. Many were still poor and embittered. They filled the downtown areas of big cities like New York and Boston and welcomed the opportunity to belong to a group that nurtured their Irish identity and allowed them to give expression to their anti-English feelings. There was also significant Fenian support in England and Scotland among the Irish immigrant populations of Liverpool, Manchester and Glasgow. The word 'Fenian' became the generally accepted term to describe all the groups associated with seeking independence for Ireland.

The movement rapidly gathered momentum in the 1860s. Stephens claimed a membership of 80,000 supporters in Great Britain and Ireland, although this figure has been questioned as Stephens was prone to exaggerate, and when the rising occurred the numbers of insurgents were thin on the ground and largely ineffective. *The Times* on 12 March 1867 described them as: 'the wretched herd of shop-boys, clerks and draper's assistants who are now fleeing like sheep, even when no-one pursues them'.

There was outright hostility towards the Fenians from the Roman Catholic Church, which disliked the cult of secret societies that already existed in Ireland as it threatened the Catholic Church's influence over the peasant population. The Catholic Church argued that the Fenians were 'secret, anti-government, anti-clerical and dangerous to society' and they believed it was wicked to 'lead out ignorant and ardent young men to a struggle that might well end in their extermination'. The Catholic Church therefore denounced Fenianism as wicked. This reduced vital support among the Irish peasantry who were in awe of the Catholic Church and feared **excommunication** if they disobeyed a Church ruling.

The failure of the Fenian rising

Despite the strength of feeling for Irish Nationalism and the popularity of the concept of an independent Ireland, the Fenians met with little obvious success. They wanted an end to English rule in Ireland, but the dilemma was how and when to make an attempt to achieve it. There were problems at the outset. There was the geographical divide between the Fenians in America and those in Britain and Ireland. This created difficulty in mobilising and arming their forces and accessing the necessary funds, most of which came from successful immigrant Irish in America. There were personality clashes between the leaders – Stephens and O'Mahony. There were constant misunderstandings, which led to bitter disputes between them, as to what strategies to adopt to achieve their aims. Stephens wanted to publicise the movement by setting up a newspaper, the *Irish People*, believing it would increase their support. O'Mahony believed it would antagonise the authorities and lead to trouble, and the whole idea of using public propaganda was inconsistent with a secret society.

In September 1865, the offices of the *Irish People* in Dublin were raided and the leaders arrested on charges of conspiracy to overthrow the British government in Ireland. Stephens escaped, and it was expected he would take overall command and give the word for a rising to start. He hesitated and the moment was lost. According to F. L. S. Lyons in *Ireland Since the Famine* (1973), '1865 marked the high point of the movement and, the chance of a rising once missed, circumstances were never again to be so favourable.'

Stephens fled to America and, after the usual disagreements among the leadership, a decision was taken to invade Canada from America. The object was to play on the tense relationship between Britain and America

Key terms

Excommunication: expulsion from membership of a Church. If a Roman Catholic was excommunicated from the Church, he/she feared eternal damnation and hell when they died.

caused by the American Civil War, in the hope of provoking a dispute between the two countries. After 1865, there were hundreds of Irish soldiers discharged from fighting at the end of the Civil War and trained in arms, and only too ready to join the Fenians to fight for the cause of Irish Nationalism. However, informers had been at work and the rebel force was quickly rounded up over the Canadian border.

Afer 1865, the centre of activity moved back to Britain. The idea was to attempt a further rising in Ireland. It was a forlorn plot from the outset. Britain was enjoying a period of peace and prosperity. The tensions between Britain and America were never serious enough to end in conflict between the two countries. Most of the Fenian leadership were in prison, the authorities were firmly in control with government spies infiltrating groups of Fenian sympathisers, and plenty of informers ready to betray their comrades. A young Fenian, Thomas Kelly, who had taken over the leadership from Stephens, organised a simultaneous rising in England and Ireland in February 1867, using Irish–American Civil War veterans. The original orders to launch an attack were called off when Kelly realised that their plans had been leaked to the government forces. A new date was fixed for the night of 5 March. The weather was atrocious, with heavy snowfalls across Dublin and the south of Ireland. The small disorganised groups of poorly armed men were soon apprehended by police and troops.

> The Fenian war has ended almost as soon as it has commenced. The Fenians themselves have been taught a lesson by bitter experience. They counted no doubt on being able to seduce, intimidate or beat the constabulary in their isolated stations; they thought they had corrupted some of the military and that the peasantry would rise as soon as they raised the green flag. They thought that above all the men that had drilled so long would fight bravely for the Irish Republic. They now know too well, how grievously they miscalculated on all these points.

2   *The Times, 16 March 1867*

The Fenian plot appeared to have failed. However, the effect of the arrests turned out to be more damaging for the British establishment than the rising itself. Long prison sentences rather than death sentences were imposed on those brought to trial and convicted of treason. But the harsh conditions suffered by the prisoners elicited sympathy from many who had previously opposed the Fenians and there were calls for an **amnesty**. Isaac Butt, a Dublin lawyer, once a convinced Unionist, set up an Amnesty association, which kept the fate of the political prisoners in the public eye.

Key terms

Amnesty: a general pardon usually granted by a government to political prisoners who are then released without further penalty.

Key profile

Isaac Butt

Butt (1813–79), son of a Protestant clergyman from Co. Donegal, was a brilliant lawyer, political economist and union supporter. He saw the poor relationship between landlord and tenant as one of the root causes of Ireland's hopelessly inefficient economy. He believed the solution to Ireland's problems lay in constitutional Nationalism and established the Irish Home Rule Party. Butt's chaotic personal life and financial problems interfered with his ability to keep a firm hold over his party. When he refused to join in obstructionist tactics in parliament, in 1878, there was an attempt to oust him as party leader. He died shortly after.

Fig. 4 *The 'Manchester Martyrs'. The three Fenians executed at Manchester, following the murder of a policeman there in September 1867. What Irish nationalist symbolism is used in this picture to suggest these men died for their country?*

The attempted rescue of Thomas Kelly from a prison 'van' in Manchester in September 1867, led to the fatal shooting of a police officer and the execution of three of the ringleaders. This time there was no commutation of the death sentence. The three became known as the 'Manchester Martyrs', potent symbols of Irish Nationalism. Details of the trials could be followed in the newspapers, which were enjoying increasing circulation at this time, by a population that was increasingly literate. In Ireland, public opinion was stacking up against Gladstone's government.

However, in England, there was growing anxiety at the continuing Fenian threat. This was reinforced by a bomb attack at Clerkenwell prison in London a few months later. It appeared to be yet another botched attempt by the Fenians to rescue one of their number. Richard Burke, a Fenian arms agent who had masterminded the Manchester prison van rescue, was being held in Clerkenwell. On 13 December 1867, an attempt to rescue Burke was made by blowing a hole in the outer prison wall. Unfortunately, the blast demolished a row of tenement dwellings in the street. Several people were killed and injured. This caused considerable anti-Irish feeling on the British mainland and an expectation that the government would respond with harsh measures.

The Fenian legacy

Although it failed completely in its objectives, ironically the Fenian rising proved to be a turning point in Anglo–Irish politics. A mixture of revulsion and anger led to a call from some quarters for tough government measures to be introduced in Ireland, to suppress the trouble makers. But, in line with the emerging influences of Liberalism and a desire for a more equal society in Britain, others were concerned to identify the cause of the violence and introduce some measure of reform to bring peace to Ireland. The most important person to hold this latter view was Gladstone, who led the Liberal Party into government in December 1868. Gladstone had been shocked by the violence of the movement, but it brought to his attention the urgency of the Irish situation and explains his declaration, at the start of his premiership, of his 'mission to pacify Ireland'.

Activity

Revision exercise

1. Review the section 'The failure of the Fenian rising' on pages 33–4. Copy and complete the table below.

2. From the evidence you present, what conclusion can you draw?

The Fenian rising ended in failure?	
Points that support the assertion	Points that are contrary to the assertion

■ Gladstone's mission to pacify Ireland

Potential problems on several fronts – land, religion, politics

Fig. 5 *A chronological tree showing important dates and events in Irish history. Ireland is represented by a female figure, Erin, with a harp by her side*

As the situation in Ireland deteriorated in the aftermath of the disastrous famine, Gladstone had become aware of the dire social and economic conditions, especially in rural areas. Most of the population lived off the land as there was little industry to take people into the towns. There had been chronic sub-letting of land into small unviable plots earlier in the 19th century when the population had been rising. Any improvements made by tenants attracted a rent increase from the absentee Anglo–Irish landowners. In addition, there was an established Anglican Church that demanded taxes from a largely Catholic population. The Fenian unrest had stirred memories of earlier English interference in Ireland, and the English lack of interest in real problems of the Irish people. What is more, there was a growing desire among the Irish to manage their own affairs. There was much for the ordinary Irishman to feel genuinely aggrieved about and to be persuaded to resort to extremist measures. Gladstone became intensely interested in trying to solve the 'Irish problem'.

What is remarkable and commendable about Gladstone's approach to the situation in Ireland, and the Fenian unrest, is that he took the view that the British government must shoulder some of the responsibility. But perhaps his acknowledgement that the Fenian violence had shocked him into action was also his first mistake in dealing with Ireland.

Gladstone was, as he devastatingly admitted, propelled into positive measures by the activities of the Fenians – a remark that the organisation savoured for years.

3   *Foster, R. F. (1988) Modern Ireland 1660–1972, Allen Lane*

Disestablishment of the Irish Church

Gladstone's religious principles guided him in seeking to achieve basic freedoms and fair treatment for the Irish Catholics. The current situation, in which the Catholics were forced to pay a tax of 10 per cent of their annual income to the established Church, as well as support the Catholic Church, was patently unfair. Out of a population in Ireland in 1861 of 5.8 million, 5.3 million were Roman Catholic. It was a sort of institutional bullying of 90 per cent of the population. There were also a small number of Nonconformists in Ireland who were caught by this existing tax burden.

The Irish Church Bill of 1869 was one of the first measures of Gladstone's new government. The bill proposed disestablishment and partial **disendowment** of the Anglican Church of Ireland, which would mean a compulsory takeover of a proportion of Church property. This, in turn, would reduce the Church's revenue. It was no surprise that the House of Lords initially resisted the change. The established Church was one of the bedrocks of the Tory Party, which dominated the House of Lords. In addition, the Anglican bishops who sat in the Lords were clearly unhappy. For generations, the Anglo–Irish bishops had been appointed from the younger sons of the Irish Protestant landowning families, who dominated Irish society. Queen Victoria was irritated by the proposals, as it had been her right to nominate the Irish bishops. To show her annoyance, she refused to open the new session of parliament. Disraeli, the Tory leader, in the House of Commons, quickly accepted that opposition would be pointless as Gladstone had received a clear majority in the recent general election. Queen Victoria soon saw the wisdom of accepting the inevitable and advised the House of Lords to do the same.

The Irish Church Act, 1869

The act disestablished the Anglican Church in Ireland. It was no longer linked to the State by law, nor was it the official religion of Ireland. There was no longer an obligation on the Irish Catholics to pay the tithe/tax to it. It had become a voluntary organisation on the same level as other religious denominations in Ireland. Its terms included financial protection for life for its existing clergymen and officials. About one-quarter of its property and wealth was removed and the revenues redirected to help the poor by improving schools, hospitals and workhouses.

The Irish Church Act had a number of effects:

- The disestablishment of the Irish Church was the first officially sanctioned dent in the union between Britain and Ireland.
- It created unity among a previously divided and largely Nonconformist Liberal Party.
- It won Gladstone the support of the Roman Catholic leaders.
- It was welcomed by Irish Catholics in general, as it had addressed a major injustice in terms of religious discrimination.
- It raised expectations among the Irish that Gladstone's Liberal government would address other burning issues, such as land tenure.
- It encouraged the hope among many moderate Irish people that Ireland could achieve political independence from Britain by constitutional means. It was perhaps one of several starting points in the quest for Irish Home Rule.

Reasons for the continuation of unrest in rural Ireland

From Gladstone's point of view, he sincerely believed and hoped that his Irish Church reform would be sufficient to settle Catholic

 Activity

Talking point

Gladstone admitted that the Fenian violence had shocked him into action to make concessions and reforms. Why would this admission be an advantage to the Fenians?

 Key terms

Disendowment: when a regular provision or means of support or gift is removed, most often with reference to a church. In this context, it can take the form of money or property.

Cross-reference

The Protestant ascendency in Ireland is discussed on page 41.

■ Cross-reference

John Bright is profiled on page 10.

■ Activity

Talking point

Why did the 1869 Irish Church Act fail to bring an end to the unrest in Ireland?

■ Cross-reference

To recap on the split in the Liberal Party, look back to page 19.

grievances, to calm the unrest in Ireland and draw support away from the Fenians. John Bright articulated the uneasiness in the Liberal Party at the continuing unrest in Ireland in spite of the Irish Church Act. Bright believed there could be no settlement of the land question 'until by some means, and without doing injustice to anyone, the population was placed in larger numbers in possession of the soil of their own country' (*The Times*, 1 May 1869).

Richard Shannon in his biography of Gladstone, picks up the point made by Lord Salisbury (later Conservative PM) that the continuing Fenian agitation was caused by the land problem and was not directed against the Church (Source 4).

> The mass of Irish had little direct concern with the Church of Ireland. But they had an immense concern with what the Church issue seemed to promise in relation to the land issue. A vast swell of excited and deluded hopes and expectations for the disestablishment of the landlords was beginning to build up.

4

*Shannon, R. (1999) **Gladstone, Heroic Minister 1865–1898**, Allen Lane*

■ A closer look

Gladstone's motives behind his Irish policy

Gladstone's move to disestablish the Irish Church at the start of his ministry could be viewed cynically. He knew this reform would be popular with the Nonconformists in the Liberal Party, therefore, it would be a uniting factor for his new Liberal government. Edgar Feuchtwanger refers to this when he says that 'he was acting largely for tactical political reasons. This was the issue that enabled him to pull the warring factions of the Liberal Party together after the split over parliamentary reform.' (E. J. Feuchtwanger, *Gladstone's Irish Policy: Expediency or High Principle?*, 1989)

Marcus Tanner argues against this view:

> When the Church of Ireland Tories accused Gladstone of sacrificing the Irish establishment to unite the Liberal Party behind his leadership, they were wrong. The charge of unprincipled behaviour cannot be sustained. He had lost faith in the Irish establishment almost a quarter of a century before.

*Tanner, M. (2001) **Ireland's Holy Wars; the struggle for the nation's soul**, Yale University Press*

Gladstone first questioned the Irish Church's privileged position in correspondence with Samuel Wilberforce, the Dean of Westminster in August 1845, when he remarked 'title by descent will not uphold her' (i.e. the Irish Church).

Richard Shannon comments on Gladstone's intervention over the voting of the Irish Church Bill in the Commons:

> He (Gladstone) anxiously reinforced the Whips before the first big division (i.e. vote on the Bill). 'Now,' he said, 'that measure will be carried by the unanimity of the Liberal Party and by the commanding character of the majority.'

*Adapted from Shannon, R. (1999) **Gladstone, Heroic Minister 1865–1898**, Allen Lane and from Gladstone Papers 44419,243*

R. F. Foster, in his book *Modern Ireland 1600–1972* (1988), suggests that Gladstone's awareness of the Irish problems and his personal involvement in taking up his mission to pacify Ireland were more strongly motivated by his religious beliefs than his adherence to the Peelite policy of keeping tight control of government spending. In other words, Gladstone was prepared to set aside his principle of retrenchment and accept the financial cost of disestablishing the Irish Church, as he felt so deeply that it was the right thing to do.

Activity

Talking point

There are widely differing views among historians as to Gladstone's motives for his involvement in Ireland. Use the material in A closer look and any other relevant information in the main text to identify Gladstone's probable motives.

In pairs, draw up a list of the motives and put them in the order that you think would be most important to Gladstone. Justify your decision. Share your conclusions in a class discussion.

Irish Land Act, 1870

Fig. 6 *A Punch cartoon from February 1870 referring to the passing of the Irish Land Act. Why has the cartoonist used an image of Gladstone holding the bull's horns to mark this event?*

The land problem

In Ireland, most of the land was owned by Anglo–Irish landlords. Many of these were absentee landlords who rented out their land to tenant farmers. The situation was complicated by casual sub-letting agreements between tenants and there was little security of tenure. The tenant farmers were left in the hands of ruthless bailiffs or land agents, in the absence of the landlord, and they were often turned off the land without just cause or reasonable notice.

The majority of the population depended on making a living from the land as there were few viable industries, except in the north in the province of Ulster. As the population grew in the early 19th century, good agricultural land became scarce and the practice of sub-letting became the norm. The end result was small uneconomic land units. Few improvements were made on the smallholdings and farms, as the rents were raised as soon as the tenants carried out improvements. This naturally discouraged any significant improvements from taking place and the land yield remained poor. This became part of a seemingly unbreakable cycle. The impoverished land failed to provide adequate crops and the Irish peasant farmers were unable to keep up with rent demands from their landlords. This led to many families being turned off the land and ending up in inescapable poverty in the workhouse.

■ Cross-reference

The Ribbonmen are introduced on page 32.

■ Exploring the detail

Ulster Custom

A degree of tenant-right had already been established in Ulster, known as the Ulster Custom. The tenants had security of tenure as long as they kept up to date with their rent payments. They could sell the right to their holding to another tenant as long as the landlord approved of the replacement tenant. As a result, the Ulster tenant farmers became more confident to carry out improvements and this led to greater prosperity among Ulster farmers. However, the weakness was that the Ulster tenant-right was merely a custom and not legally enforceable. In economic adversity, the landlord would ignore the Custom to suit his needs.

The heartless actions of the landowners resulted in a harbouring of deep and bitter resentment, which too often spilled over into violence with arson attacks and sometimes murder. The object of these attacks was often the bailiff or the land agent. The agrarian unrest and sporadic attacks were orchestrated by secret groups who called themselves Ribbonmen. The Irish Tenant League had formed in the 1850s to fight for rights for tenant farmers. They wanted fixity of tenure, fair rents and the freedom for tenants to sell their 'interest' in their holding to another tenant. The demands were nicknamed the 'three fs'.

Gladstone's solution

Gladstone sought to achieve a more equitable relationship between landlord and tenant. He knew that he had to tread a careful path to ensure that his reform did not appear to attack the basic principles of property ownership and alienate the Whig landowners in the Liberal Party. He had a twofold plan: firstly, to give legal weight to the Ulster Custom where it was already adhered to; and, secondly, to increase the security of holding for all other tenants. To achieve this, he proposed that a tenant could claim compensation for improvements made to a property if and when he decided to give up his right to the property. Gladstone proposed heavy financial penalties for landlords who evicted tenants without just cause. They could only evict for non-payment of rent. John Bright, who remained convinced that the land problem could only be solved by offering the Irish peasant the opportunity to own his own piece of land, persuaded Gladstone to include what became known as Bright's clause in the bill – that tenants should be allowed to borrow two-thirds of the cost of their smallholding from the government to buy their interest and repay the loan at five per cent over 35 years.

The Irish Land Act was passed in 1870. This:

- introduced the principle of fair rent
- provided for compensation for tenants at the end of their lease if they had made improvements to their holding
- secured fixity of tenure as long as tenants paid their rent
- made provision for tenants to sell their leases
- arranged for loans to be made available for tenants to purchase land.

Reactions to the Irish Land Act

On the surface, it appeared a sensible and comprehensive reform. However, the Land Act failed to give basic protection to tenants or to satisfy the landlords.

Tenants

The fair rent clause was of limited value as nowhere did it suggest what was meant by a fair rent and, as a result, many unjust evictions still took place. Compensation for improvements was paid to tenants giving up their holdings, but landlords still had the power to raise the rent as they pleased and then evict the tenant for non-payment. There were no compensation payments for eviction if the tenants were in arrears with their rent. The tenants evicted for non-payment were in such dire straits, any system in place via the Land Act could not help them. The cost of buying land was too high for most tenants, even with a beneficial loan scheme. More tenants had been able to buy land under the Church Act, where conditions of sale were easier. The Ulster Custom was too vague to implement with any regularity. Bright's clause to allow sale of leases was not introduced for fear of upsetting the Whig landed interests.

Landlords

There was no incentive to landlords to sell land and allow tenants to become landowners. The landlords understandably resisted attempts by tenants to purchase the land. The land-owning Whigs, who had been traditional Liberal supporters, saw the Land Act as an attack on their property rights, in spite of Gladstone's attempt to be sensitive to their position. They were anxious about the implications for the survival of the union with Ireland and began to express the more conservative opinion of the importance of maintaining the union with Ireland intact.

 Activity

Talking point

Gladstone had tackled the land problem and he had seriously challenged the Anglo–Irish or **Protestant Ascendancy** for the first time in over 200 years. Cardinal Cullen remarked: 'In future the Protestants will find themselves without any privileges. The poor Protestants are all very irritated. They never did imagine England would abandon their cause.'

Discuss the future implications for Irish unity hinted at in Cardinal Cullen's remark.

Aftermath of the Land Act

The Land Act is generally regarded as a failure and caused outbreaks of further unrest among tenants in rural areas. Gladstone's response was to pass the Coercion Act of 1870. This did little to improve the situation. It gave police constables extensive powers to carry out arrests, and brought back a bitter taste in Irish mouths, which destroyed any sweetness of reform. Gladstone had made the classic mistake of following up an act of reform with an act of repression, and succeeded in storing up problems for the future.

The unity within the Liberal Party that Gladstone had achieved over the Irish Church Act was short lived. Each of Gladstone's subsequent reforms alienated different groups within the party, leading to his election defeat in 1874. One of Gladstone's great hopes in his Irish policy had been to give the Catholics their own university. He proposed a new university in Dublin, where both Catholics and Protestants could study side by side. The religious extremists on both sides objected so fiercely that the Irish University Bill of 1873 was thrown out. It was a bitter blow to Gladstone's ambition to bring peace to Ireland.

The emergence of Home Rule

Gladstone's Irish policy during his First Ministry had met with little acknowledged success. But, putting aside any underlying motives he may have had, he was the first British politician to show any interest in or understanding of the Irish problems. He had tackled the problems of lack of equal and fair treatment in religion and land. His reforms were directed at suppressing Fenian demands for the repeal of the union by satisfying Irish grievances. Gladstone was not interested in Home Rule at this point, but the demand for Home Rule (not independence, but the creation of an Irish parliament to deal with domestic issues) could be regarded as the most significant outcome of Gladstone's intervention in Ireland.

Key terms

Protestant Ascendancy: expression used to describe the position of the Protestant landowning class in Ireland that dominated cultural, economic, political and social life. The land had been forfeited from the Catholics by Cromwell in 1650 and redistributed among his Protestant supporters. Cromwell's action against the majority Catholics left a bitter legacy.

Cross-reference

To explore Irish unity further, look ahead to Chapter 5.

Cross-reference

For Gladstone's election defeat in 1874, see page 28.

Activity

Talking point

Review the sections on the Land Act.

Why was there dissatisfaction on all sides as a result of Gladstone's Irish Land Act? What do you think Gladstone could have done to avoid this?

Although Gladstone had won temporary friendships among the Catholic hierarchy with the Irish Church Act, he had not won over the vast Catholic population, for whom disestablishment was never the main grievance. Their dissatisfaction grew with the failure of Gladstone's land reforms. They were still poor and still oppressed by their Protestant masters, and were easy prey for violent extremists who tried to whip up anti-English feeling, especially in the south of Ireland where economic conditions were worse and many landlords disregarded the spirit and the letter of the Land Act. In fact, Gladstone's reforms had succeeded in disturbing the Protestant Ascendancy to the extent that its hold on power and privilege would never be so secure again. This was not altogether clear at the time, but there was a deep sense of unease among the Anglo– (i.e. Protestant) Irish hierarchy regarding Ireland's future.

These disgruntled Irish Protestants lent their support to the Home Government Association (HGA), which was launched in Dublin in 1870 by Isaac Butt. It was the start of the Home Rule for Ireland movement. It had the backing of moderate nationalists, some Catholics and to some extent the Fenians. Support came from both Irish Conservative and Irish Liberal MPs. Butt's involvement with the Fenians and growing acceptance that they had a valid cause, though he disagreed with the means, led directly to his campaign for the repeal of the Act of Union. Butt preferred to call it 'Home Rule'.

Cross-reference

Isaac Butt and the Fenian movement are both discussed on pages 31–35.

Butt believed in achieving political independence for Ireland through peaceful means. He was a constitutional nationalist; that is, he wanted to gain self-government for Ireland legitimately through the Westminster parliament, and aimed for the Irish to have complete control over their domestic affairs. This could mean Ireland enjoying the advantage of a separate parliament without breaking up the union.

By 1873, the HGA was transformed into the Home Rule League. Irish Protestant support began drifting away and was replaced by strong Catholic support backed by the Catholic Church in Ireland. Irish MPs began to voice the grievances of the Catholic tenants against the Land Act in Westminster. In the general election of 1874, 59 Irish Home Rule supporters won seats and this marked the end of Conservatism and Liberalism in Irish politics. It was a victory for constitutional Nationalism and, although the Home Rulers were not in any sense a united political party, they had one common aim, some sort of self-government for Ireland. They agreed to act together on this issue.

The strong Home Rule representation in parliament was a great achievement for Isaac Butt. However, from the start, the Home Rulers lacked the discipline and cohesiveness to bring pressure to bear on the Westminster government. More importantly, they lacked a strong leader. Butt was moderate and spoke good sense, but did not possess the dynamism to keep Home Rule at the top of the political agenda. He believed the Home Rule cause would succeed if they were patient and conciliatory. The 1874 election had brought Disraeli and the Conservatives to power. Disraeli was more concerned with disturbances abroad and appeared indifferent to Irish matters.

Cross-reference

Charles Parnell's career and leadership of the Irish Nationalist Party are covered in detail in Chapters 5 and 6.

The Home Rule movement of Isaac Butt began to give way to a much tougher and less conciliatory group, that sidelined Butt. After Butt's death in 1879, the charismatic and self-confident Charles Stewart Parnell took on the leadership of the Irish party in the House of Commons.

Gladstone's foreign policy to 1873

By 1865, the dynamics between the major European powers was changing. Prussia, the strongest German state, defeated France in 1871 and a united Germany was created in the centre of Europe. This altered the balance of power that had been established in 1815 by the Treaty of Vienna. The new German Empire swiftly took on the mantle of the leading European power and was at the centre of a system of alliances whose main objective was to isolate France.

Britain traditionally held a strong position in European diplomacy, and supported the maintenance of a balance of power between the key states. Britain differed from the other great European powers in its geographical position as an island on the edge of Europe, and also because of its special commitments to its vast overseas empire. The biggest threat to the empire at this time was Russian expansion towards the northwest frontier of India, Britain's jewel in the imperial crown. The Royal Navy was Britain's main military force for the defence of its shores and protection of its empire. Britain's army was relatively small compared with those of the other European powers.

In contrast to Gladstone's intensive activity in his domestic policies and his enthusiasm to solve Ireland's problems, political opponents and public opinion were generally dissatisfied with Gladstone's foreign policy on the grounds that it made Britain appear weak and too ready to back down in the face of any opposition. *The Times* called it demoralising. His apparent inaction and lack of initiative in foreign affairs was probably more to do with the self-imposed constraints of his religious beliefs than indifference. As with all other political activity, Gladstone was driven by a desire to do that which was morally right. In this respect, he believed that it was his moral duty to maintain peace and avoid war at all costs.

Gladstone was a European and believed that the great European powers should act together 'in concert' and preserve peace and maintain a balance of power in Europe. He felt morally bound to respect the rights of other nations, even though this might conflict with Britain's interests. He had disliked Palmerston's aggressive foreign policy, in which he would always act in Britain's interest, regardless of the rights of other countries or the cost in money and human life.

Foreign affairs, 1865–73

Franco–Prussian War, 1870–1

Gladstone judged neutrality to be the best policy in Prussia's war with France in 1870–1. Otto von Bismarck, the powerful and aggressive Prussian chancellor, manipulated a war against Napoleon III of France in order to further his plans for the unification of Germany. France declared war on Prussia and was, therefore, regarded as the aggressor. British sympathies initially lay with Prussia as Britain mistrusted Napoleon. Fears were raised about Napoleon's ambitions to invade Belgium, which was vital to British security because of its proximity across the Channel. Gladstone felt obliged to intervene and secured agreement that both sides would respect **Belgian neutrality** in line with the Treaty of London that they had signed in 1839. Bismarck was happy to agree to this as he had secured British neutrality through diplomacy and so could proceed with his plans to defeat France, annexe French Alsace and Lorraine and declare the creation of a united Germany, which he did in 1871.

Cross-reference

Gladstone's foreign policy during his Second Ministry is discussed in Chapter 4.

Activity

Challenge your thinking

It could be said that Gladstone's was an 'ethical' foreign policy. This was defined by the Foreign Secretary of the New Labour government set up in 1997 when he declared:

'Today's Mission Statement sets out new directions in foreign policy. It supplies an ethical content to foreign policy and recognises that the national interest cannot be defined only by narrow *realpolitik*. It aims to make Britain a leading partner in a world community of nations.'

Realpolitik – 'practical politics based on the realities and necessities of life, rather than moral or ethical ideas'. (Chambers dictionary)

As you read the following section, reflect on this statement. Can Gladstone's foreign policy decisions be described as ethical?

Key terms

Belgian neutrality: an agreement that no country would make alliances with or invade Belgian territory.

Russia and the Black Sea Clauses

In 1870, Bismarck made himself an ally of Russia by encouraging the Tsar to pull out of the Black Sea clauses of the Treaty of Paris, which it had made with Britain at the end of the Crimean War in 1856, and which forbade them from maintaining a naval presence in the Black Sea. The British Foreign Secretary, Granville, called a conference of the Great Powers in London in January 1871. It was agreed that no country had the right to unilaterally withdraw from part of a treaty. This was a face saving exercise on Britain's part, as Gladstone would not contemplate using even the threat of military force and, in reality, there was little he could do. Public opinion went against Gladstone for his inaction over Russia's 'insolent provocation' (R. Shannon, *Gladstone, Heroic Minister 1865–98*, 1999). The new Germany emerged as the strongest European power and with an impressive military machine to back the country up.

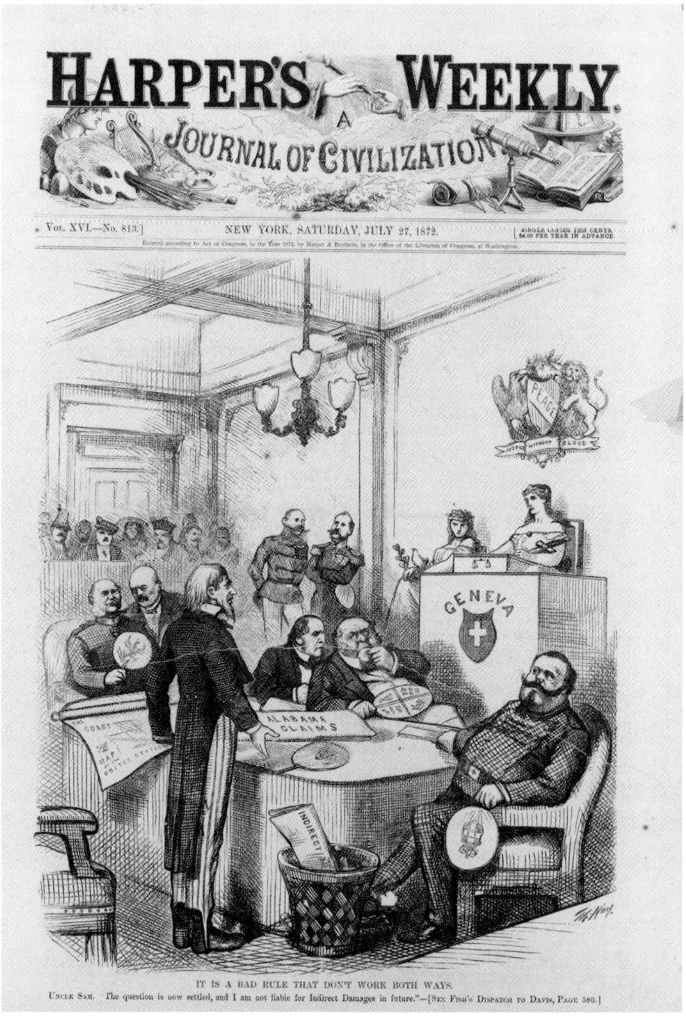

Fig. 7 *America appealing to the international court of arbitration in Geneva for justice over the* Alabama *dispute*

The settling of the Alabama dispute, 1872

The *Alabama*, a Confederate warship fitted out in Britain, had been the centre of a dispute a few years earlier during the American Civil War, when it was used against the Northern States and damaged some of its ships. Britain was deemed to have broken its neutrality promise to stay out of the conflict. Gladstone agreed to submit the American claim to an international court of arbitration, which decided that Britain should pay £3.25m to America. This was a fraction of the original US claim of £9m. Gladstone agreed with the principle of arbitration, rather than an aggressive response to settle a dispute, and so paid the damages, though his detractors still thought it was too much. The British public saw it as a humiliating retreat and this cost the Liberals electoral support.

Popular opinion was gathering momentum against Gladstone's peaceful and ethical foreign policy, which seemed to be giving a free hand to the Russians to move their navy into the Black Sea, giving in to the Americans over the *Alabama* affair, and allowing the new Germany ascendancy in Europe.

Summary questions

1 In what ways did the aims of the Home Rule movement differ from those of the Fenians?

2 Why did Gladstone's Irish Church Act succeed where his Irish Land Act failed?

3 Explain why Gladstone's foreign policy was unpopular with the electorate.

3 Industry, agriculture and social improvement

Fig. 1 *The John Rubery factory was one of a large number of thriving steel manufacturing businesses in Birmingham in 1865. It produced umbrellas, parasols and furniture, which were built on steel frames. Steel was one of the key industries of the industrial Britain*

In this chapter you will learn about:

- progress in industry
- progress in agriculture
- social improvements and rising living standards
- ideas of *laissez-faire*, free trade and self-help
- the onset of economic depression.

The palace and the cottage, the peasant and the prince, are alike indebted for necessaries, comforts and luxuries, to the busy fingers of Birmingham men. The locks and bolts which fasten our doors, the bedsteads on which we sleep, the cooking vessels in which our meals are prepared, the nails which hold together our shoes, the tips of our bootlaces, the metal tops of our inkstands, our curtain rods and cornices, the castors on which our tables roll, our fenders and fire-irons, our drinking glasses and decanters, the pens with which we write and much of the jewellery with which we adorn ourselves, are made at Birmingham. At home or abroad, sleeping or waking, walking or riding, in a carriage or on a railway or steamboat, we cannot escape reminiscences of Birmingham. She haunts us from the cradle to the grave.

> **1**
> *Birmingham, the 'city of a thousand trades'. (New Illustrated Directory (1858)* **Men and Things of Modern England***)*

Source 1 from the Birmingham Directory gives a flavour of the diversity of small businesses that operated during this period in one industrial city.

Fig. 2 *Britain's industrial supremacy supported by pillars of coal, iron and steel*

By 1865, Britain was at the height of its economic and industrial power. In economic strength and industrial output, Britain dominated the world. This unparalleled spurt of economic and industrial growth was evident from around the middle of the century and lasted into the early years of the 1870s. It was accompanied by technological developments in Britain's key industries – coal mining, iron and steel, engineering and the textile industry – and a rapid increase in production across the board. New technology and an increase in scientific knowledge boosted British agriculture during this period, generally referred to as the period of High Farming. British manufactured goods were exported around the globe in British ships. Britain's industrial and economic supremacy was unchallenged by any other power. Governments in Britain adhered to the *'laissez-faire'* principle of limited interference in the workings of the market economy. Taxation was low and free trade was encouraged. These were years of peace and prosperity and many, though not all, Victorians shared in the extraordinary wealth created by the industrial boom. Beneath the material success lay the Victorian virtue of 'self-help' and the belief that good honest hard work brought rewards. The middle classes and the skilled working classes, in particular, enjoyed the rewards of hard work with higher incomes and increased consumption. There was better education and public health. The standard of living rose, but 'the stagnant mass of poverty at the bottom of the social pyramid remained' (E. J. Hobsbawm). After 1873, there were signs of a slowing down in the rate of growth of the economy. Britain was beginning to face competition from newly industrialising nations, such as Germany and America, and needed to adapt to meet the challenge.

Progress in industry and agriculture

Progress in industry

In 1851, the Great Exhibition took place in London's Hyde Park. It show-cased the variety, inventiveness and skill of Britain's manufacturing industries. Exhibits from competitor countries were included to underline Britain's commitment to free trade and to emphasise by comparison the excellence and superiority of British-made

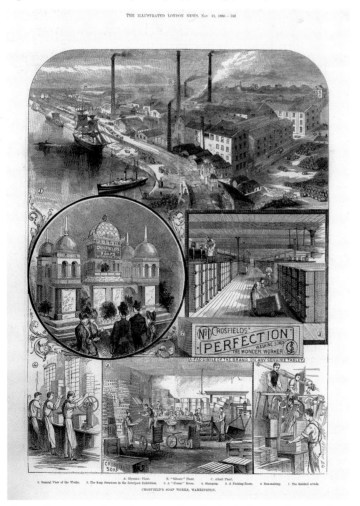

Fig. 3 *This montage shows the stages of production in the manufacture of soap. The increasingly widespread use of soap improved public hygiene*

goods. However, the exhibition also reflected anxiety about Britain's position, free trade and peace, as emphasised by Prince Albert (Queen Victoria's husband) at the opening ceremony. One of the spin-offs from the Great Exhibition had been a rapid increase in export orders, and a growth in overseas markets. One-third of all British goods were exported to the British Empire. Coal was exported to Europe. Many goods went to America because their own industries were not sufficiently developed to cope with the demands of a fast increasing population. It was a period of unprecedented demand for British goods abroad. In every town and city in Britain, producers and manufacturers were working flat out to meet the increasing orders. Britain was justifiably called the 'workshop of the world', importing raw materials, manufacturing the goods and exporting the finished products around the world.

Export figures for the main manufacturing industries between 1860 and 1874, showing consistent and substantial growth.

Table 1 *Annual average per five-year period*

Years	Iron and steel (thousand tonnes)	Coal (million tonnes)
1860–4	1,536	7.38
1865–9	2,027	9.86
1870–4	2,965	12.31

Mathias, P. (1990) The First Industrial Nation, Routledge

There were several reasons for such marked industrial progress. Britain had been the first industrial nation and, by 1865, had far outstripped other countries in establishing markets at home and abroad for its vast range of quality goods. As the greatest colonial power, Britain controlled the vital sea routes to and from its colonies and other overseas markets. Britain had a plentiful supply of natural resources, principally coal and iron ore, which it had the technology to exploit and, by 1865, had been able to forge ahead in design, engineering processes and production. This was against the background of the mid-19th century development of *laissez-faire*, which had given British inventors and entrepreneurs the freedom to develop their ideas. In 1865, Britain's population of approximately 30 million provided a large workforce and an expanding home market. Mobility of the workforce and carriage of goods was made possible by the extensive railway network across Britain, which linked every major town and sea port and facilitated industrial development.

The move towards free trade in the mid-19th century had, by 1865, also encouraged overseas trading and stimulated British industry. The profits from increasing sales and exports of manufactured goods were often ploughed back into existing businesses, and used for further enterprises, such as building railroads abroad. Large amounts of capital were also available for reinvestment as a result of developments in banking facilities, and assured London's position as a world monetary centre.

The key industries in Britain, which were at the centre of the rapidly growing economy, were coal and iron. However, textiles, which had spearheaded the industrial revolution in Britain at the end of the 18th century, still remained a staple and Britain continued to be a major exporter of cotton cloth. Almost all manufactured goods relied to some extent on coal and iron – coal to produce heat or steam and iron to make the machines that manufactured the goods.

Did you know?

During the 1860s the rate of income tax was about 5d (2p) in the £1 and levied on those with an annual income of over £100. This exempted people on low and moderate incomes. Income tax contributed between £6 and £10m of the government's £77m revenue.

Table 2 *Annual average per decade*

Years	Cotton textiles (million yards)	Woollen goods, inc. carpets (thousand yards)
1860–9	2,375	236,267
1870–9	3,573	311,611

Mathias, P. (1990) The First Industrial Nation, Routledge

Activity

Talking point

In which industry was there the highest rate of increase of exports between 1860 and the 1870s? Can you think of a reasonable explanation for this?

As you read the following sections on the progress of industry, you should be able to check whether your explanation is valid.

Cross-reference

To recap on *laissez-faire* and free trade, look back to page 12.

Activity

Talking point

Present the factors that were responsible for Britain's great industrial progress in the form of a diagram. Indicate which factor(s) you believe were the most important.

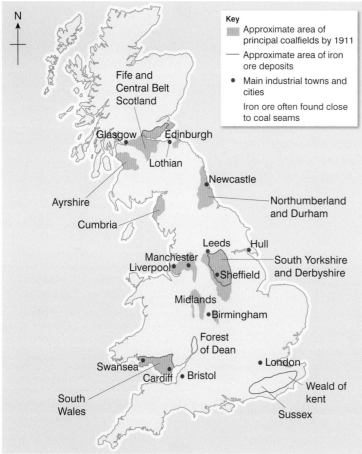

Fig. 4 *Map of Great Britain showing main areas of coal, iron ore deposits and centres of industry*

Coal mining

The growth of the coal industry during this period was immense. In 1865, the output of coal was 98 million tonnes and 10 years later, in 1875, it had risen to 130 million tonnes. A drop in the price of coal, coupled with an increase in demand, helped to stimulate increased production around the middle of the century, after which industry demanded an increasing percentage of the coal produced. The manufacture of iron depended on coke (made from coal) and during the second phase of the industrial revolution iron was needed in greater quantity. By 1870, the iron industry was buying one-third of coal produced in Britain.

Coal was required to power steam engines, which were an integral part of the development of the railways. By the 1860, steam power was generally used in most major industries. The development of iron-hulled steamships demanded coal to fire the ships' engines and iron for their construction. As other countries developed their industries, they imported coal from Britain.

The increasing demand for coal had implications for the organisation and running of the coal mines. All coal mines were privately owned. Landowners who were fortunate enough to have coal seams running under their property made vast fortunes. These fortunes were made largely from the manual labours of the coal hewers. Even in this age of rapid industrialisation, the massive quantities of coal were dug out by hand. This surprising absence of mechanical progress at the coal face could be partly blamed on the continuing of private ownership of the coal mines. There was one serious attempt to develop a coal-cutting machine in the 1860s and this failed (see Exploring the detail). The population growth in Britain meant that there was always a ready supply of labour and the hewers were among the best paid in workers' industry.

There were successful technical developments. The introduction of wire rope and steam-driven winding gear at the top of the coal shaft replaced the hemp rope and the system of the horse gin, and dealt more efficiently with the 600–800-tonne daily haul of coal at some pits. Steam locomotives and iron rails facilitated the transport of coal from the pit head to a wider distribution network and into towns, iron works, factories and sea ports. The railways became the vital link between the mine owner and his customers.

■ **Exploring the detail**

Coal-cutting machines

The first coal-cutting machine, the Gartsherrie, was developed by a successful Scottish mine-owning family, Baird of Gartsherrie, in Lanarkshire and patented in 1864. It worked by using compressed air, but constantly broke down. Consequently, the job of hewing coal remained manual until the early 1900s, when a more sophisticated version of the Gartsherrie came into general use. Until then, the high demand for coal production had to be met by increasing the number of miners. By 1875, about 500,000 men were employed in coal mines. Each miner produced between 200 and 300 tonnes of coal a year!

■ **Question**

Explain why coal production was at the centre of Britain's rapidly growing industry.

Iron, steel and engineering
Iron and steel

Fig. 5 *Painting of a steam hammer at work, by engineer James Nasmyth*

As industry expanded, the demand for high-quality iron increased. Technological developments in the iron industry, earlier in the 19th century, were responsible for the improved quality of the iron and the continuing increase of iron output throughout the 1860s and 1870s. Many engineering projects across the world were dependent on the continuous production of high-quality iron from Britain. Iron ore production jumped from 10 million tonnes in 1865 to over 15 million tonnes by 1875.

> Forty years ago, the air forced into blast-furnaces was cold, and the process of smelting was slow and costly, because of the great quantity of coal that was required. In 1827, Mr J. B. Neilson, engineer of the Glasgow Gas-Works, conceived the idea of heating the air before injecting it into the furnace; and a most successful trial was given to the invention at the Clyde Ironworks. It was found that when heated air was employed the coal might be used raw, and that 2 tons 13 cwt. was sufficient to smelt a ton of iron. This discovery gave an extraordinary impetus to the iron trade.

2 *John Neilson's hot blast. Extract from Bremner, D. (1869)*
Industries of Scotland, Adam and Charles Black

The use of steel in manufacturing developed during this period. Steel is an alloy consisting mostly of iron, with a variable carbon content dependent on the quality of the steel. It is tougher and more versatile than iron. In the 1860s, new processes enabled steel to be produced quickly and cheaply and in large quantities. The most important of these were:

- Henry Bessemer's converter, developed in 1856, which produced semi-steel or mild steel that halved the cost of steel production
- William Siemens' Open Hearth Process, developed in 1866, which allowed the cheap production of mild steel in bulk.

■ Did you know?

Steel production started as far back as the Middle Ages. It was not until the invention of the Bessemer process in the mid-19th century that it became relatively easy and cheap to mass produce. Today, steel is one of the most common materials in the world and is a major component in buildings, tools, motor vehicles and household appliances. The quality of modern steel is identified by a regulated grading system.

One of the results of these new processes was that, by 1870, many rail companies had replaced iron track with steel.

Railways

The developments in transport were intrinsically linked to the expanding coal and iron industries. The most dramatic and far-reaching was the growth of the railways. Britain's well-developed railway industry played a vital role in economic expansion.

> [The railways] enabled economic activity in all other sectors of the economy to expand. (They) were also important as an industry in their own right, creating employment, using capital and demanding economic resources.

3   Mathias, P. (1990) *The First Industrial Nation*, Routledge

From 1860 onwards, development in the railway industry was more to do with expansion of an already established network in England, Wales and the south of Scotland. Laying rail track across the Scottish Highlands presented a challenge because of the difficult terrain and the sparse population. In the end it was a costly exercise, but essential in that it linked remote areas of Scotland to the rest of Britain. Most of the new rail track was to set up branch lines, often linking seaside resorts to larger towns or setting up suburban railways. This development was instrumental in creating an entirely new industry of tourism.

Expansion of the railway network created many jobs, beyond temporary work such as laying new track. Railway companies required permanent staff to run their offices, to drive and maintain their trains and to provide a service to their passengers. In 1870 railway employment was the sixth largest in the country.

The railway companies became concerned with producing better, faster and more reliable engines and this led to the development of precision engineering. Companies were set up to produce more modern rolling stock and locomotives. This side of the industry led to the development of prosperous railway towns such as Crewe, Doncaster and Derby.

In 1865, there were 11,451 miles of railway track in Britain, which carried over 238 million passengers and 112.6 million tons of freight. This earned the railway companies £15.5 million in ticket sales and £18.7 million in freight charges. By 1875 these figures had risen substantially. The 14,510 miles of track carried 490 million passengers and 196 million tons of freight. The revenues in ticket sales were £24.3 million and in freight charges £32 million. (Source Mitchell and Deane, 1962 quoted in Peter Mathias, *The First Industrial Nation*,(1983).

The first London underground line, the Metropolitan, was opened in 1863. This was before the electrification of railway lines. The smoke and fumes from the steam locomotive, together with the sickly smell of oil lamps in the carriages, made for a rather unpleasant ride. In spite of this, the Metropolitan line carried 10 million passengers in its opening year.

The Bessemer steel rails gave a further boost to the railway industry. They cut production costs and, therefore, increased profits and produced more capital for further investment. The profits were often invested in railroad building overseas in India, Canada, Argentina and America. There was no other efficient method of carrying large quantities of heavy bulky goods, or large numbers of people. The railways enjoyed a virtual monopoly until the coming of the motor vehicle at the turn of the 20th century.

Shipping

> An immense amount of capital has been embarked in the steam-shipping trade during the past twenty years. Lines of steamers run to and from all the principal ports of the world, and the most formidable competitors of the railways in this country are the coasting steamers. As the size of the vessels has been increased, a considerable improvement has been made in the matter of speed.

4
*Bremner, D. (1869) **The Industries of Scotland**, Adam and Charles Black*

British shipping dominated the world. Sailing ships still made up the majority of the mercantile marine. Steamships had been built earlier in the 19th century, but were expensive to build and run. The most important stimulus for the increase in shipbuilding in the 1860s was the growth in world trade. This coincided with the massive increase in the production of cheap iron, and later steel, and made it possible for Britain to forge ahead in the development of steamships and monopolise the shipping routes. The Suez Canal was opened in 1869 and drastically cut the journey time from the West to India, China and Australia. The canal was too narrow to pass along in a large sailing ship and this gave a further boost to the British steamship.

In 1866, the Atlantic cable was laid across the ocean between Britain and America, by means of a steamship, so that information could be relayed almost instantaneously using a semaphore system. Telegraph services opened up and they became part of the Post Office in 1868. It was akin to 19th century texting, and was the first step in the gigantic communications industry with which we are so familiar today.

The cotton industry

The factory-based manufacture of cotton provided an impetus for the industrial revolution before 1800. Historian Eric Hobsbawm's remark 'Whoever says Industrial Revolution says cotton' emphasises the key role of cotton in Britain's economy. It remained a major industry after 1865, but its rate of progress was slower. Its share of Britain's export market began to fall in the 1860s, as the exports of other commodities such as coal, machinery, iron and steel goods rose. However, British manufactured cotton cloth still accounted for two-thirds of cotton sold in world markets until just after 1900.

Summary of industrial output

The following statistics give an indication of the enormous and rapid increase in production for the main manufacturing industries in Britain during this period. The fastest growing industries were closely connected to coal and iron.

Activity

Thinking point

1. Using the information above, what deductions can you make about the growth and success of the railways?

2. In pairs, or small groups, carry out some research on the immense social and cultural impact of the railways on the Victorians. Make a short illustrated presentation of your findings to the class. Michael Freeman's book *Railways and the Victorian Imagination* is a good source, but there are others.

- Coal output was almost 100 million tonnes by 1865, and 130 million tonnes by 1875.
- Iron ore production increased at a rapid rate and went from 10 million tonnes in 1865 to over 15 million tonnes in 1874.
- The steel industry was in its infancy, but technical advances raised the output from approximately 100,000 tonnes in 1865 to about 480,000 tonnes by 1874.
- By 1875, the expansion of the railway system accounted for 14,510 miles of track in use (i.e. 19,600 km), and the carriage of 490 million passengers and 196 million tonnes of freight.
- In 1850, the tonnage of sailing ships was approximately 3 million and steamships 100,000. By 1874, the figures had risen to a total tonnage of 5 million, of which nearly 2 million tonnes were steamships.

Employment in all of these industries was substantial. For example, a total of 275,000 workers were employed in the railway industry by 1873; 370,000 in coal mining; 180,000 in iron manufacture; and 482,000 in cotton manufacture. These workers created a demand in the economy because their wages had risen and their newly acquired spending power and desire for consumer goods helped to create further prosperity.

Britain enjoyed a period of exceptional prosperity between 1851 and 1873 by building up the staple industries of coal, iron and steel, engineering, shipping and textiles. These industries produced an annual economic growth rate of about 2 per cent. Their output was far beyond the requirements of home consumption. As a result of growing demand for British goods abroad, these industries created a boom in Britain's export market and accounted for almost all Britain's exports. The profits raised provided capital for further investment at home and overseas.

Progress in agriculture

When the Corn Laws were repealed in 1846, there was a fear in the farming community that the price of home-grown wheat would collapse against competition from foreign imports, and that farmers would be ruined. That did not occur. By 1865, Britain was enjoying of a Golden Age of agriculture, during which harvests produced successive high yields, prices were steady, farmers' incomes increased, there was scientific and technological innovation and improvements were carried out. By 1873, the years of plenty had come to an abrupt end and the farming industry entered a long period of economic downturn.

Fig. 7 *The McCormick reaping machine was shown at the Great Exhibition in 1851 and over the following decades was widely used and adapted to make it more efficient*

A period of prosperity for British farmers

High Farming

Cross-reference

The repeal of the Corn Laws is outlined on pages 4–5.

Fig. 8 *Agricultural stock in animal husbandry in Victorian Britain*

The expression 'High Farming' has been used to describe the farming practices adopted by many farmers during the years after the repeal of the Corn Laws, until the depression hit in 1873. James Caird, a farmer from Wigtownshire in south-west Scotland, is often credited with introducing the term. James Caird called for more intensive farming, taking account of new farming methods and improvements. It is difficult to assess the extent of Caird's influence, but High Farming was popular over the next 20 years and coincided with the Golden Age of British agriculture.

High Farming methods increased productivity. Many farmers moved from purely arable to mixed farming. This meant they hedged their bets by growing wheat and root crops, as well as stocking cattle, sheep and pigs. In this way, they would be cushioned against a sudden downturn in price of either crops or livestock. The surplus crops fed the animals and the animals' manure fed the crops. There was increasing interest in animal husbandry (i.e. stock farming). Some farmers specialised in specific breeds of cattle, such as Herefords and Aberdeen Angus, which produced excellent beef. Much of the profits in farming at this time came from livestock rearing.

With an increase in scientific knowledge, artificial fertilisers, such as superphosphates, were marketed and guano (bird droppings) from Peru was imported in large quantities. The industry was worth £8m a year by 1870. There was also a growing market in animal feedstuffs, made from linseed and cotton seed. These two developments eased the pressure on farmers to pursue mixed farming and made it easier for them to specialise in either arable or livestock.

The problems of poor drainage were met by the manufacture of clay pipes. The government introduced loan schemes for farmers to invest in drainage pipe systems. Improved drainage, together with the use of fertilisers, made substantial improvements in crop yield.

As there was a ready supply of cheap labour – agricultural labourers were among the most poorly paid – the introduction of farm machinery was slow. The gang system continued whereby a gang master would hire out casual labour to farmers, using a group of men, women and children, who depended on him for work. Their pay was pitiful, the hours long and the work seasonal. There were, however, widespread developments in farm machinery. There were better ploughs, seed drills and stream-driven threshing machines.

The steady growth of the population increased the demand for food. The demand for food also rose as a result of the new prosperity brought to Britain from the Californian gold rush. The increased amount of money in circulation led to a general rise in wages and prices, which in turn increased the demand for the produce of the land. The demand was met by agricultural improvements. The development of the railways was beneficial to farming, as food could be transported quickly to the growing towns where there was a ready and ever-increasing market for fresh produce. During the 1860s and early 1870s, farmers benefited from the higher prices of meat, milk, butter and cheese.

Perhaps it was not difficult to achieve success in a market that lacked competitors. In spite of the development of steamships, many mercantile ships remained under sail. Transporting goods by sea was still comparatively slow and there was no real foreign competition at this time. There was an exceptional run of high-yielding harvests between 1860 and 1873, which no one could have predicted and which were attributed to a long cycle of fine dry summers. When the fine dry summers came to an end, the cold winds of competition started to blow in with a vengeance.

Questions

1 What verdict can you reach on the overall state of British farming from 1865 to 1873?

2 What indications were there that the Golden Age of Farming was coming to an end?

Exploring the detail
Standard of living

There are difficulties associated with the concept and interpretation of the phrase 'standard of living'. It is really an economic term and refers to real wages or income, which is the income of an individual after taking prices and costs into consideration. However, 'standard of living' has also come to mean 'quality of life' and is difficult to measure without being subjective. It can include living and working conditions, health, life expectancy, standard of education and amount of leisure time.

Cross-reference

The concept of *laissez-faire* is introduced on page 12.

Rising living standards and social improvement

The growth of industry and agriculture and the resulting buoyant economy; public works of the various municipal authority boards; advances in medical knowledge and treatment; and the social benefits brought by the expansion of the railways all contributed to a rise in living standards in Britain during the 1860s and early 1870s. The growth in the economy created a situation where money was available for social improvements, although *laissez-faire* attitudes made the government reluctant to intervene, to any great extent, in the lives of the people. However, social improvements occurred through limited government intervention in public health legislation, in factory legislation and in the introduction of a State system of education.

Industry and the export trade had expanded rapidly. The staple industries of textiles, coal, iron and steel were all returning huge profits. There had been a massive development in transport in the railway industry and the development of steamships. An entrepreneurial spirit in Britain led to some of the profits going into overseas investments. When these met with success, much of the capital return came back to Britain. The great majority of the profits went to the middle-class manufacturers, and the merchants who organised the buying and selling. The owners of these thriving business concerns and others, who in some way controlled trade and industry, formed part of a growing prosperous middle class. They built substantial houses on the outskirts of industrial towns, such as Edgebaston in Birmingham. They could afford good furniture and furnishings, several domestic servants and the luxury of a carriage and pair (of horses). They limited the size of their families, educated their children privately, ate well and could afford the best medical attention when necessary. This group was a small percentage of the middle class as a whole, who made up approximately 25 per cent of the total population. The upper class accounted for an even smaller percentage (perhaps one per cent) and could always afford to take early advantage of any invention or innovation that would raise their already high standard of living.

The broader definition of middle class was those who could afford to keep a domestic servant. In the 1871 census, there were 1.4 million domestic servants and this offers some sort of guide as to the number of middle-class households in Britain. Among these were shopkeepers, small employers, school masters and clerical workers. An increasing number of the middle classes could afford to move from the old town centres, where houses lacked any 'modern' amenities, to the new suburbs that were being built beyond the smart mansions of their wealthier counterparts. They would not possess their own carriage, but might travel to work on one of the new suburban railway lines that were being built in larger towns and cities, like London, Edinburgh and Birmingham.

Although very real poverty still existed in Britain, the trend by the 1870s was an all-round improvement in standards of living for the working classes. The real value of an average wage rose by 40 per cent between 1862 and 1875, and this gave many workers increased spending power. About 15 per cent of the working class were skilled artisans earning an average income of about £2 a week. Life was less harsh. Membership of the Cooperative society increased and Co-op stores selling groceries and fresh produce began to spread, particularly in the northern industrial towns. Factories were producing cheaper goods specifically targeted at skilled working-class families with spare cash and these goods were available in the rising number of shops.

By 1871, 65 per cent of the population lived in urban areas, where there were plenty of jobs and wages were higher than in rural areas. However, the rapid growth of industrial towns and cities in the preceding decades had created problems in the provision of basic amenities, namely a constant supply of pure water, proper drainage and sanitation, and clean and well-lit streets. In working-class areas, many of the houses were of inferior quality, lacking light, ventilation, running water and decent sanitation.

Some attempts were made to address these problems, but there was still an in-built resistance to centralisation and State intervention. The role of local government in urban areas was important in putting improvements into operation. Although the Municipal Reform Act of 1835 had set the pattern of municipal self-government, by 1870 there were still independent bodies who took responsibility for services such as street cleaning and lighting. In 1871, the Royal Commission on sanitary matters recommended that 'the present fragmentary and confused' Sanitary Law should be made uniform. As a result, the Local Government Board was set up, which reorganised health administration as an office of central government.

Fig. 9 *Growing affluence among middle-class Victorians could be seen in the splendour of their homes and the cultural pursuits that they encouraged in the home. What indications of affluence are there in this picture?*

■ Did you know?

Henry Mayhew, a Victorian journalist, recounts the miserable conditions of many working-class poor and how impossible it was to rise above poverty, in his *London Labour and the London Poor* (1851). Such levels of poverty continued into the 20th century. In the words of one street-seller, who had to rent a barrow to sell his goods:

'I've tried my hardest to get money to have (a barrow) of my own, and to get a few sticks (of furniture). It's no use trying any more. If I have ever got a few shillings ahead, there's a pair of shoes wanted, or something else, or my wife has a fit of sickness, or my little boy ... and it all goes.'

A cholera epidemic in 1866 claimed the lives of 20,000 people and diseases such as smallpox and tuberculosis also took a heavy toll. The Sanitation Act passed in 1866 compelled local authorities to make improvements. One positive result of this was that sanitary regulations were enforced in factories. Gladstone's Public Health Act of 1872 established both Urban and Rural Sanitary Authorities, which were responsible for public health in local areas. It was not a great success because of inadequate funding. There was still not a medical officer of health for every area and there was still a lack of conformity over arrangements for urban sanitation and water supplies. The major step forward in public health did not come about until Disraeli's Public Health Act of 1875.

The Metropolitan Board of Works had been set up in1856 to coordinate public works across London. It was the forerunner of the London County Council. In response to continuing outbreaks of cholera and other water-borne diseases, it organised the construction of a sewerage system for London. The mastermind behind this project was Joseph Bazalgette, the chief engineer. By 1866, most of London was connected to an efficient sewage network. It helped to clean up London's water supply and removed the sight and smell of foul waste along the banks of the river Thames within the city. It reduced mortality rates. The Victoria and Albert Embankments, opened in 1870, were built along the river Thames to conceal sections of sewers, but also reclaimed land for gardens and roads. The construction of the sewers was a major civil engineering project, involving the laying of 82 miles of intercepting sewers below London's streets, all flowing eastwards by gravity. In many ways, Bazalgette's achievement epitomised the 1860s and early 1870s as a period of progress and prosperity.

There was a lack of commitment to improve housing, although the demand for housing exceeded supply. Landlords looked for compensation and so there was little enthusiasm for a programme of slum clearance. In 1866, the Treasury made loans available to local authorities for house building, but there was little interest. The 1868 Torrens Act bound landlords to keep property in a good state of repair. The evidence seems to point to scant action by central government and local authorities to improve the housing stock, except in Birmingham where Joseph Chamberlain carried out far-reaching improvements in both housing and municipal buildings.

For the working classes, life could perhaps be described as less harsh. Trade unions had won legal status (Trade Union Act 1871) and were therefore able to offer their members support over conditions of employment. The Factory Reform movement had successfully campaigned for better conditions and limited hours in many major industries by 1870. Local authorities opened public institutions such as libraries, parks, baths and wash houses in many towns. Simple commodities like soap and matches became more easily available and, more importantly, affordable. Food was also cheaper.

However, in spite of the higher standards of living, there was little security when workers lost their jobs, possibly through being 'laid off' or ill-health. They might have set money aside in the Post Office Savings banks introduced by Gladstone in 1861, or in their Friendly Society; or they might rely on family or neighbours, but they might be in the same predicament. It was the unskilled workers who generally ended up turning to the only State provision available – poor relief and the

■ Activity

Thinking point

In what ways does Bazalgette's achievement epitomise or reflect the progress and prosperity of the 1860s and early 1870s?

■ Did you know?

Almost half of London's sewage sludge is now sold in pellet form as a fertiliser for agriculture. London's sewage has now come full circle, as much of it now fulfils the same functions as the 'night soil' of previous centuries.

■ Question

What brought about a rise in living standards between 1865 and 1873?

■ Activity

Challenge your thinking

What factors helped to keep the standard of living for working-class people high in the late-1860s?

workhouse, with all the humiliation and stigma that brought to a hard-working man and his family.

Ideas of *laissez-faire*, free trade and self-help

Laissez-faire

In 1776, Adam Smith in his economic treatise *The Wealth of Nations* argued that government intervention in trade (i.e. charging duties on goods) would restrict Britain's economic development. His ideas started a new trend in thinking that if governments adopted a *laissez-faire* economic policy, it would encourage growth and prosperity. Adam Smith was, in effect, arguing for free trade. The debate was taken up by leading philosophers and economists, for example Jeremy Bentham and John Stuart Mill, over the following decades.

Laissez-faire was adopted as an economic doctrine in the 19th century. The belief was that there were basic laws of economics that did not change. Therefore, in an orderly market, price equilibrates supply and demand. If goods were in short supply and demand was high, prices would be high. If goods were in plentiful supply and demand was low, prices would fall. The argument was that government regulation would not make any difference.

Adam Smith was referring to exchange of goods when he talked about *laissez-faire*. However, the term gained a wider meaning. It was used as an argument against government social reform. Many manufacturers and mine owners objected to government legislation, such as limiting hours of work, which they saw as damaging their profits. In the early 19th century, *laissez-faire* became the norm and people had little expectation of government interference in economic affairs.

Jeremy Bentham (1748–1832) promoted *laissez-faire* ideas from a Radical viewpoint. His theory was called Utilitarianism. It was based on a view that minimal government interference in the lives of its people would bring 'the greatest happiness to the greatest number'. He saw it as the duty of government to try to achieve this by imposing as few restrictions as possible, but, at the same time, making the administration of government as efficient and as meaningful as possible.

Bentham's ideas of *laissez-faire* suited the new Liberal and Radical political thinking of the mid-19th century, and non-interventionist policy became the favoured economic philosophy of successive governments for much of the 19th century. In terms of Gladstonian Liberalism, *laissez-faire* reinforced their mantra of 'peace, retrenchment and reform'. In carrying out social reform, even Liberal governments tended to limit intervention to basic safety measures in the workplace and some minimal regulation of working conditions. Gladstone was a firm believer in *laissez-faire* and its application to free trade, and efficient administration of government in order to avoid unnecessary expenditure. However, he passed few social reforms that directly improved living and working conditions for the majority of the population, i.e. the working classes. These measures could be described as permissive (i.e. there was an element of discretion in whether or not they were carried out) rather than compulsory, which reflected *laissez-faire* attitudes.

Free trade and self-help

By 1860, almost all trade restrictions had been removed and Britain could call itself a free trading nation. The movement for free trade had gathered strength in the 1850s and, endorsed by the Liberal

Cross-reference

Look back to Chapter 1 for an introduction to *laissez-faire* and self-help, and for profiles of Jeremy Bentham and John Stuart Mill.

Free trade is outlined on page 4.

Activity

Talking point

The *laissez-faire* argument detailed above could be extended to jobs and wages and used against any attempt by the government to fix wages to help low-paid workers.

As a supporter of the *laissez-faire* philosophy, how would you put forward an argument against the government fixing wages for a group of workers?

Cross-reference

Gladstonian Liberalism is discussed on pages 11–12.

The terms 'permissive' and 'compulsory' are dealt with in more detail on page 69.

government, it had become Gladstone's main objective as chancellor of the exchequer. To Gladstone, the logic of free trade was clear. The lower the duties paid by manufacturers, the more cheaply they could produce goods. They could then sell them at a competitive price both in the home market and abroad. The adoption of a free trade policy led to a massive increase in the volume of trade and provided a stimulus for further economic growth.

■ Key profile

Samuel Smiles

Smiles (1812–1904) is best known as a social reformer and author, but he had a successful and varied career. He practised what he preached. Smiles was born in Haddington, near Edinburgh, and was one of 11 children of Samuel and Janet Smiles. His father placed great emphasis on his children's education. Smiles trained as a doctor. He abandoned medicine for a career in journalism, as editor of the *Leeds Times*. He became interested in parliamentary reform and the repeal of the Corn Laws. From journalism, he turned to the railway industry, met up with George Stephenson and became secretary of the South Eastern Railway. Smiles continued to lecture and write on social subjects and campaigned for public libraries and a national system of education. He was well known for his biographies of the great self-made Victorians, such as Stephenson. He was a prodigious writer, but his most popular book remains *Self-Help, with Illustrations of Character and Conduct* (1859). Smiles died in April 1904.

Fig. 10 *Samuel Smiles*

■ Did you know?

In his book *Self-Help*, Samuel Smiles created the idea of the modern 'role model', when he featured the activities of high-achieving men to inspire ordinary young people to overcome disadvantage and adversity and work hard to change their lives. His book, which was read and admired by Gladstone, quickly became a bestseller. Since then, the book has been translated into more than 40 languages – and is still in print.

As part of the general philosophy of *laissez-faire*, there was an emphasis on the importance of the individual. There was a growing belief that everyone should have the opportunity to fulfil their potential. However, they had to take personal responsibility for their actions and be prepared to work hard to achieve their aim, and not blame other circumstances when mishaps occurred. This notion was expressed most clearly in Samuel Smiles book *Self-Help*, which came to epitomise the Victorian values of the mid-19th century of constantly striving to improve oneself and change for the better. Smiles' key virtues for success were a sense of duty, strength of character, thrift and self-help.

To make progress in both material and moral terms was to be admired. There was a clear belief in progress through freedom (*laissez-faire*) and individual effort (self-help). This is linked to the period of progress examined earlier in this chapter – improvement in standards of living, in public health and personal hygiene, and progress in the provision of education. Great strides forward were made in farming and industry. This tangible evidence of progress was taking place against a background of improved communications and during a period of increasing prosperity.

There was a reverse side to this coin. Not everyone aspired to, or could attain, a decent standard of living. Many remained in abject poverty unable to help themselves. Society looked down on individuals who fell into poverty and they were often regarded as feckless, careless and lazy, rather than victims of circumstance in need of State support. In Smiles' words: 'When people live in foul dwellings, let them alone. Let wretchedness do its work.' Contemporary thought was that the best way of addressing social evils was with minimum State interference and a reliance on voluntary activity by middle-class Victorian philanthropists. However, by 1870, the principle and practice of *laissez-faire* and **individualism** was being questioned. Government, society, and the economic framework of Britain were becoming much more complex and the government began to accept the necessity of introducing laws to regulate society and to address the most basic needs of its citizens.

The onset of economic depression

After 1873, the British economy experienced a downturn. Historians are divided as to the causes of the depression and, more controversially, whether there was a depression at all or whether it was simply a myth. It is, however, generally agreed that there were several significant factors that pointed to the start of a period of decline. Industry was still expanding, but at a slower rate and capital was still invested abroad. Production continued to increase, but supply was overtaking demand in both home and overseas markets, and this led to a fall in prices and a reduction in profit margins. In the period after 1870, British trade and industry were facing more competition. There was a continuing increase in imports over exports, most especially in manufactured goods. There were signs of a rise in unemployment.

In many manufacturing firms, especially those that were family owned and run, there was reluctance to consider new science-based industries. Coal and textiles had always made money and many producers believed this would always be the case. They failed to see the necessity for change and began to feel the adverse effects of foreign competition. The British workforce was falling behind those in countries such as the newly united Germany, where the system of education focused on industrial training for some of its youngsters. Most British working-class children left school aged 12 without receiving any training, which would have encouraged innovation. Britain's share of total world manufacture of all types of goods began to decline, as America's increased dramatically by the end of the 19th century.

Economic historian Peter Mathias identifies the onset of depression in British industry in an extract from his book (Source 5).

> Several characteristics about the internal developments in the economy after the 1870s did bode ill for Britain living in an increasingly competitive world. New sectors such as the chemical industry were not coming forward fast enough to replace older industries – or at least to replace them as earners of sterling credits in exports. Secondly the older industries themselves were not accepting innovations, or investing capital for re-equipment on a large enough scale. Thirdly the whole tempo of industrial advance was slowing down.

5   Mathias, P. (1990) *The First Industrial Nation*, Routledge

Challenges to Britain's industrial supremacy came mainly from Germany and America. By the 1870s, both Germany and America had potentially stronger home markets than Britain. A comparison of the coal and iron production of the three countries between 1850 and 1880 highlights the problem for Britain of competing in an increasingly crowded market.

 Key terms

Individualism: the commonly held belief that individuals should take responsibility for their wellbeing and that of their families through thriftiness and hard work. To accept charitable handouts was seen as degrading. It was based on a *laissez-faire* approach that it was not the business of government to interfere in people's lives. It involved the Victorian self-help ethic, promoted by Samuel Smiles and encapsulated in his phrase: 'God helps those who help themselves'.

Question

Can you explain the links between the two ideas that derive from the concept of *laissez-faire*: (a) free trade; and (b) self-help? Pages 4 and 12 will help you with your answer.

 Cross-reference

The depression in industry is explored in detail in Chapter 7.

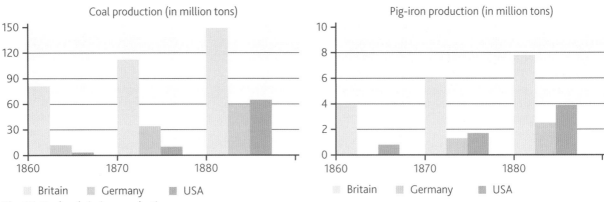

Fig. 11 *Coal and pig-iron production*

Question

Study Figure 11. Are there indications of an economic downturn in Britain from the figures in these production charts or could the figures be used to support the theory of the depression as a myth? Consider the rates of growth to help you with your answer.

Cross-reference

The depression in agriculture is explored in detail in Chapter 5.

A wet summer and a poor harvest in 1873 signalled the end of the Golden Age of agriculture and the start of a severe depression in farming, particularly in arable. There followed several years of wet summers and disappointing harvests. More damaging to the farming industry was the increasing import of cheaper grain from overseas, particularly from North America where the vast wheat fields were opening up for the first time. Ironically, the money that British investors and entrepreneurs had earlier poured into railroad building in America, allowed the transport of large quantities of wheat to be brought to the eastern seaboard and taken in steamships across the Atlantic to compete with the higher priced British wheat. Prices and profits fell and the results were catastrophic for many arable farmers.

One government remedy could have been to introduce tariffs on imported foodstuffs. By the time the agricultural depression occurred, Disraeli was prime minister. Although 30 years earlier he had vehemently opposed the repeal of the Corn Laws and supported Protectionism, times had changed. There had been an enormous growth in the wealth and importance of industry, trade and finance, coupled with an increase in the urban population and decline in the rural population. The influence of the landed interest was weakening, both politically and economically. Disraeli now accepted the policy of free trade and took the political decision not to protect British agriculture. If agriculture was to survive, it would need to adapt and change.

During the years 1865 to 1873, Britain continued to enjoy a period of immense prosperity in both agriculture and industry, which had started around 1850. Its economic progress was undoubtedly sustained by its free trade policy. Gladstone's reduction of taxation allowed individual entrepreneurs and businessmen to build up their private fortunes, as well as the wealth of the nation by investing the large sums of available capital in industrial enterprises at home and abroad. Gladstone's policy of maintaining peace encouraged economic stability, while Britain's potential economic rivals were side-tracked by war – the American Civil War 1863–66 and the Franco–Prussian War 1870–1. The end of Gladstone's first period in office coincided with the onset of depression, but it does not detract from his achievements as prime minister or those of his successor Disraeli, who came to office in 1874. The real causes are more complex, but, in simple terms, the period of sustained growth and unchallenged supremacy in world markets was coming to an end.

Cross-reference

For Gladstone's achievements as prime minister, see page 22.

Learning outcomes

Through your study of this section you have learnt about the nature and status of the two main political parties, the Liberals and the Conservatives, their relevance to the electorate and the un-enfranchised masses, and have developed an awareness of how Britain was governed in the 1865–73 period.

You have considered the impact of parliamentary reform and the major reforms of Gladstone's First Ministry, as well as the importance of these measures in moving Britain towards a modern democratic State. You should be aware of the deep-seated nature of the grievances of the Irish people and the difficulties Gladstone encountered and created in seeking to solve the problem of Ireland. You should also be able to set Gladstone's foreign policy in the context of Gladstonian Liberalism and Britain's status as the world's wealthiest and most powerful nation.

A study of the ideas of *laissez-faire*, free trade and self-help should have enabled you to make a judgement on why its people prospered during the decade between 1865 and 1873 and why this period of prosperity came to an end in 1873.

Practice question

'Successful at home but a failure abroad.'
Assess the validity of this view of Gladstone's First Ministry.

(45 marks)

 Study tip

To answer this question you should begin with a table like the one below.

Policy	Success	Failure
Domestic		
Foreign		

After you have completed your table, you will need to decide what you will argue. Remember, you cannot only agree or disagree with the quotation but agree/disagree with it in part. Since you are likely to have found successes and failures in both policy areas, your essay should involve a weighing up of the evidence. Remember, you should support your ideas with precise examples.

4 Gladstone and Disraeli at home and abroad

In this chapter you will learn about:

- the main features of the new the revival of Conservatism

- the social and political reforms of Disraeli's ministry, 1874–80

- Disraeli's foreign and imperial policy, including his attitude to the problems posed by the Eastern Crisis of 1875–8

- the achievements of Gladstone's Second Ministry, including parliamentary reform

- Gladstone's foreign and imperial policies to 1885.

Fig. 1 *This painting symbolises the wealth and prestige of the British Empire in the late-19th century. How has the artist conveyed impression in his painting?*

When I say 'Conservative', I use the word in its purest and loftiest sense. I mean that the people of England and especially the working classes are proud of belonging to a great country and wish to maintain its greatness – that they are proud of belonging to an imperial country, and are resolved to maintain if they can, their empire – that they believe, on the whole, that the greatness and the empire of England are to be attributed to the ancient institutions of the land.

1   *Extract from Disraeli's speech at Crystal Palace, June 1872*

In his Crystal Palace speech, Disraeli addressed the National Union of Conservative Associations, and therefore used party activists as his channel of communication to a wider electorate. The speech defined Disraeli's own brand of Conservatism or 'Tory democracy'. In Source 1, Disraeli outlines the main principles of Conservatism, belief in Britain and belief in empire.

▣ The revival of Conservatism

The tide turns to the Tories

The general election result of 1874 brought a firm victory for the Conservative Party. The Liberal policies introduced through Gladstone's tireless legislation of the previous six years had alienated most of the

Cross-reference

Disraeli's Crystal Palace speech is discussed on page 64.

Key chronology

British prime ministers (1874–86)

1874–80	Disraeli (Second Ministry)
1880–5	Gladstone (Second Ministry)
1885 (June) to 1886 (January)	Lord Salisbury (First Ministry)
1886 February to June	Gladstone (Third Ministry)
1886–92	Lord Salisbury (Second Ministry)

support that had brought him to power in 1868. He had disturbed the old Whig hierarchy in his army reforms, which brought to an end military privilege. The widespread Nonconformist support was severely dented because of the Education Act, which appeared to give special protection to Anglican schools. He had upset the big brewing interests with his Licensing Bill and infuriated the trade unions with his Criminal Law Amendment Act, which threatened their security. On a more general level, the patriotic British public was unimpressed by Gladstone's foreign policy decisions, which did not reflect Britain's power and might abroad. In 1874, the old Whigs, the merchants and industrialists disappointed at what they saw as Gladstone's wooing of the working class, turned to the Conservative Party and, together with the numerically influential vote of the artisan class (skilled working class), brought the Conservatives to power under the leadership of Benjamin Disraeli.

Disraeli was 70 years old when he became prime minister in 1874 in an election that broke Liberal dominance after almost 30 years. The Conservatives had a secure, if not overwhelming, majority in the Commons. The Tory vote came, as usual, largely from the counties, but English boroughs and some large industrial towns, with a traditional Liberal vote such as Newcastle, Leeds and Glasgow, returned a good proportion of Tory members. Twenty-six out of 33 seats in the industrial cotton county of Lancashire went to the Conservatives.

Disraeli's Cabinet contained a new generation of Tory leaders, although it remained socially exclusive in respect of its landed dominance – only 1 out of its 12 members was not a peer or a landed gentleman. Richard Assheton Cross was the token middle-class man. He came from a Lancashire banking family and had been educated at Rugby and Cambridge, and so was not without means. In some ways, his appointment was a nod to the support Disraeli received from Lancashire, but Cross was a man of considerable talent and fulfilled an important role as home secretary.

Party organisation

The loss of the 1868 election had rankled with Disraeli because it was his Reform Act in 1867 that had extended the franchise to the artisan class in the towns. Disraeli had expected thanks by way of support from these new voters, but quickly came to realise that political parties must improve their organisation in order to reach the new, expanding, better-educated electorate. He appointed John Gorst to overhaul party organisation and set up a Conservative Central Office in London. Gorst, an ambitious barrister and politician who had lost his seat in the 1868 election, was appointed principal agent, with the power to choose the candidates.

> He was methodical, clear-headed, hard-working and efficient. He was a genuine believer in working-class Conservatism, which, not perhaps entirely correctly, he understood to be the essence of Disraeli's creed.

Blake, R. (1997) *The Conservative Party from Peel to Major*, Heinemann

In 1870, the National Union of Conservative Associations, which had been started in 1867 to organise the new working-class borough voters, moved its HQ to Central Office. As a result, Gorst was able to direct its work in the constituencies to improve its electoral organisation. From then on, the National Union grew in importance and became the body to which the constituency groups became affiliated. After Disraeli used it as

Cross-reference

To recap on the events and actions noted here, review Section 1.

Activity

Thinking point

1 Carry out your own research to find out the names of Disraeli's Cabinet members and some background information on each of them.

2 What does the make-up of Disraeli's Cabinet suggest to you about the Conservative Party in 1874?

Cross-reference

Disraeli's policies are outlined on pages 66–67.

Key terms

Tory democracy: the phrase used to describe the policies advocated by Disraeli when he became prime minister in 1874. The Conservative Party maintained its support of established institutions – constitutional monarchy, the British Empire, the Church of England – but at the same time it would support a degree of social reform. This was an attempt by Disraeli to gain working-class support.

his 'sounding board' in 1872 to outline his policies (see below), it became 'an integral part of the Central Office organisation' (Feuchtwanger, quoted in R. Blake, *The Conservative Party from Peel to Major*) and, in effect, its propaganda tool promoting Conservatism in the boroughs. Gorst targeted middle as well as working-class voters and the overall rise in the borough vote was a significant factor in the Conservative victory in 1874.

Disraeli's brand of Conservatism or 'Tory democracy'

For some time after his defeat in 1868, Disraeli kept a low political profile. However, in the period leading up to the 1874 general election, he took advantage of Gladstone's increasing discomfort and unpopularity with several sections of traditional Liberal supporters. Disraeli began to plant the seeds of the idea of a '**Tory democracy**', a new brand of Conservatism, in order to revive the fortunes of the Conservative Party. He did this in two important political speeches in 1872, to the National Union of Conservative Associations at the Manchester Free Trade Hall and the Crystal Palace in London.

In his Crystal Palace speech, in June 1872, Disraeli appeared to be appealing to the working-class vote and using the notion of empire as a unifying force. The ideal of empire was of paramount importance to Disraeli and he saw it as a strong political and economic union, with the monarch at its head. He was interested in the new trends towards democracy and working-class voters, but he strongly believed in maintaining tradition and privilege and knew the party was not ready to abandon the old aristocratic hierarchy. There is also a sense, in the speech, that if the working class placed their trust in the Conservatives, they could share some of the benefits enjoyed by the more prosperous groups in society.

Disraeli's government was responsible for a number of important social reforms and it is tempting to think that Disraeli was also promoting a Tory policy of social reform in the following extract from his Crystal Palace speech (Source 2).

> I ventured to say a short time ago, that the health of the people was the most important question for a statesman. It involves the state of the dwellings of the people, the moral consequences of which are not less considerable than the physical. It involves their enjoyment of some of the chief elements of nature – the air, light and water. It involves the regulation of their industry, the inspection of their toil. It involves the purity of their provisions, and touches upon all the means by which you may wean them from habits of excess and brutality.

2
*Pearce, M. and Stuart, G. (2002) **British Political History**, Routledge*

There is a question mark over Disraeli's sincerity in calling for social reform. It could have been a dig at Gladstone, who had introduced few measures of social reform. It could have been a ploy to pull in the working-class voters. Or was it, indeed, the case that Disraeli was simply outlining the main principles of his new Conservatism?

Whatever the motives behind Disraeli's brand of Conservatism, it is a fact that in the 1874 general election, the working-class votes in the boroughs helped to bring the Conservatives back into power with their first majority government for over 30 years. The electorate as a whole was tired of Gladstone's endless legislation and Disraeli was able to present his party as having a 'broad-based appeal' to the working class as well as property owners – land owners in the country and middle-class business men in the towns.

Differing interpretations of Disraeli's policies

Paul Smith takes the view that Disraeli was being entirely consistent in his 1872 speeches to the National Union and was marking out the future path for the Conservatives in a more democratic era (Source 3).

> Disraeli's proclamation at the Crystal Palace of the 'three great objects' of 'the national party', to maintain the monarchy, the House of Lords and the Church, to 'uphold the Empire of England' and to elevate 'the condition of the people' summed up the Tory doctrines he had been preaching for nearly forty years. The strategy of protecting the institutional and social order by seeking national integration both through the focusing of popular sentiment on the symbols of the crown and empire and through attention to the material bases of popular well-being in the frame of national efficiency would supply the Conservative Party with the major elements of its appeal to the mass electorate for almost a century.

3   *Smith, P. (1996) **Disraeli**, Cambridge University Press*

Historian Robert Blake disagrees with the idea that Disraeli was defining Tory policy (Source 4).

> The nature and effect of these two pronouncements have been to some extent distorted in retrospect. Disraeli did not say very much about empire to the National Union and what he said was vague. He said little more about social reform – the other question in which he is usually supposed to have made a major initiative; and here too he was equally unspecific. But Disraeli did sound a new note when he declared that English people would be idiots if they had not 'long perceived that the time had arrived when social and not political improvement is the object which they ought to pursue'.

4   *Blake, R. (1997) **The Conservative Party from Peel to Major**, Heinemann*

Activity

Pairs activity

Working in pairs and using the information from this section, copy and complete the table below.

Disraeli's Conservatism /Tory democracy

Concept	Your definition of the concept	How the concept fits into Disraeli's idea of Conservatism
Aristocratic hierarchy		
Monarchy		
Empire		
Church of England		
Social reform		
Political reform		

Activity

Challenge your thinking

What do you think Disraeli hoped to achieve when he took office in 1874, and why?

■ The social and political reforms of Disraeli's ministry, 1874–80

Social and political reform

Disraeli's government of 1874 has gained its reputation on the strength of its social reforms. A broad spectrum of reforms, dealing with issues such as housing, public health, trade unions, education and conditions in factories, were introduced in quick succession in 1875 and 1876. These measures appear to be consistent with the idea of Tory democracy. However, Disraeli excluded the Board of Trade and the new Local Government Board ministers from the Cabinet, suggesting that social reform was not a major priority. There is evidence that he had no detailed or coherent programme of reform, and much of the legislation was introduced as a response to pressure from genuine reform groups and from recommendations made by Royal Commissions of Enquiry in a number of areas of concern. The initiative to carry through most of the reforms came from Disraeli's colleagues such as Richard Cross, and not Disraeli.

Housing reform – Artisans' Dwelling Act, 1875

Fig. 2 *An early photograph of poor housing conditions that were to be found in many of Britain's industrial towns and cities*

Too many 'labouring poor' lived in deplorable jerry-built houses, which were insanitary and overcrowded and contributed to major outbreaks of disease. Home Secretary Richard Cross was concerned to improve the state of housing in the large industrial slums, but without creating the precedent that it was the 'duty' of government to provide 'good and habitable dwellings'. The major innovation of the act lay in the power it gave the local authority to purchase, clear and then redevelop slums, financing the scheme with low-interest government loans. The absence in the legislation of a compulsory purchase order reduced its effectiveness and many city councils chose to ignore it. The notable exception to this was Birmingham council, which was led and inspired by Radical MP Joseph Chamberlain. However, its long-term importance was that it established the principle of State intervention with regard to private dwelling houses and marked the beginning of local authority housing.

Key profile

Joseph Chamberlain

Radical Joe (1836–1914) – his political nickname in later life – the son of a prosperous London shoemaker, was a clever, charismatic and talented politician, but also fickle in his political allegiances. He split Gladstone's Liberal Party over Home Rule. As a young man, he successfully reorganised a family business in Birmingham and made a personal fortune. Early influences of Radical and Liberal ideas directed much of his public work. Twice widowed, he turned his considerable energies into local politics. Birmingham town councillor (1869) and mayor to 1875, his extensive improvement programme of public works in Birmingham built his reputation as an pioneering reformer. Chamberlain became MP for Birmingham in 1876, where he enjoyed tremendous popular support. As a Liberal MP, his Radical reform ideas were ignored by Gladstone. After the split from the Liberals, Chamberlain led the Liberal Unionists in parliament, mostly voting Conservative. As Secretary of State for Colonies in Salisbury's government, he was a supporter of the Boer War. He contributed to the downfall of Balfour's government in 1905 with his insistence of reintroducing trade protection. Chamberlain had potential as leader of either party, but neither side fully trusted him. His eldest son, Austen, would grow up to become a chancellor of the exchequer and foreign secretary. His second son, Neville, the first by his second wife, became prime minister in 1937.

Public health

In 1875, the head of the Local Government Board, George Sclater-Booth, introduced an act that pulled together all existing sanitary legislation, which up until then had fallen short of tackling current health problems. His act built on the Public Health Acts of 1866 and 1872. It laid down minimum standards of drainage, sewage disposal and refuse. It made compulsory the appointment of a medical officer of health who was charged with the reporting of all infectious diseases. Public works were established in most districts, to replace private water companies and water sellers. The act was hailed as a great success, although it was a measure of consolidation rather than innovation. Opposition came from the *laissez-faire* brigade, who saw the measure as involving too much State intervention and interference with personal freedom.

Cross-reference

Details of the 1866 and 1872 Public Health Acts can be found in Chapter 1 and Chapter 3.

Richard Cross introduced both the Sale of Food and Drugs Act in 1875 and the Rivers Pollution Act in 1876. The first was an attempt to stamp out the dishonest, and sometimes dangerous, practice of adulteration of food. The most common and least damaging was to add chalk to flour, but more disturbing was the contamination of bread by adding lead. It was a well-structured attempt to regulate the food industry, but a reluctance to make compulsory the appointment of food analysts by local authorities reduced its impact. The second act met with the same stumbling block with regards to control of 'noxious fluids' into rivers. Any suggestion of taking harsh measures against the 'polluters' was opposed and, since prosecutions could only be authorised by the central Local Government Board, few were carried out.

Labour relations and trade union legislation

The 1875 Conspiracy and Protection of Property Act replaced the unpopular Criminal Law Amendment Act that Gladstone' Liberal government had passed in 1871. The act altered the conspiracy laws, so that unions could no longer be prosecuted for doing anything collectively that would be legal if done by an individual. An action by a union during a dispute, which could be legally committed by one person, was therefore legal for a trade union. The act legalised peaceful picketing and, in effect, gave the unions the right to strike. The result of this legislation was to strengthen the position of the trade unions.

The Employers and Workmen Act, 1875, introduced a contract of service, which gave employees terms that were on a par with those of employers. Both sides were to be liable under civil law and this removed the unfair system of employees being liable for breach of contract under criminal law, whereby they could be sent to prison. This legislation was a major step in labour law reform and Disraeli was justly proud of his achievement when he said that he had 'satisfactorily settled the position of labour for a generation'.

Factory legislation

The factory legislation passed in 1874 and 1878 was a consolidation of the previous Factory Acts and set the code of regulations for conditions in factories. The Lancashire MPs, in particular, had campaigned for a maximum nine-hour working day. T. A. Jenkins in his book *Disraeli and Victorian Conservatism* (1996) analyses the Tory thinking on this issue. To get around the inevitable charge of State interference, the government responded by reducing the six-day working week for women and young people to five, with a half day on Saturday, arguing that they were not in a position to negotiate for themselves and therefore required the protection of the law. The maximum number of hours they could work in a week was 56. This had the effect of indirectly reducing men's working hours. The acts brought other industries in line with the textile industry and all factories came under the umbrella of a State inspectorate. This was an important reform as it established the principle of the State offering protection to industrial workers. Pressure from both Conservative MPs and trade unions was brought to bear on the government to introduce this legislation.

The Merchant Shipping Act, 1876

The Merchant Shipping Act is a good example of what could be regarded as 'Tory democracy', but the impetus for this act came almost entirely from the concerns and doggedness of one man, Samuel Plimsoll. There was no legislation in place to protect seamen from the atrocious living conditions on board the ship and conditions of employment at sea. There were no regulations in place to control overloading of ships, which of course put sailors in danger. Plimsoll, Radical MP for Derby, spoke out against the 'coffin ships' in his publication, *Our Seamen*. The merchant seamen's conditions had lagged behind other groups of workers, because there was no merchant seaman trade union.

The findings of a Royal Commission of Inquiry into conditions at sea coincided with Plimsoll's campaign, but the recommendations were initially dropped after strong opposition from shipping interests. Plimsoll persisted and finally, in 1876, an act was passed that introduced regular

■ **Cross-reference**

The Criminal Law Amendment Act is outlined on page 26.

inspection of ships by the Board of Trade officials, better accommodation for sailors on board, and the introduction of the 'Plimsoll Line'. This was the acceptance of the principle of the load-line, which was drawn on the outside of every ship's hull. The position of the line in relation to the waterline was an indication of whether or not the ship was overloaded and whether or not it was safe to go to sea. This hard-fought reform was not compulsory and was not fully implemented until 1890. However, it remains one of the great landmarks of State intervention in helping to secure the safety of a particular group of workers.

Other measures

Lord Sandon's Education Act in 1876 attempted to improve school attendance by setting up school attendance committees, but stopped short of compulsory attendance. Children could not get a job unless they produced an attendance or attainment certificate, and so it became in the parents' best interests for the children to attend school. The responsibility was pushed on to parents to make them answerable by law for non-attendance of children at school. The act could be seen as supporting the Anglican Schools, which were feeling the pressure of falling rolls with the setting up of board schools after 1870.

Assessment of Disraeli's social and political legislation

Cross-reference

For the establishment of board schools, see page 24.

Question

Why was the government reluctant to make some of its new measures compulsory, such as school attendance? Look for other examples in the section on The social and political reforms of Disraeli's ministry, 1874–80.

Fig. 3 *Back view of typical 19th century London artisan terraced housing, with washhouses, privies and yards, all dominated by a railway viaduct built overhead*

Much of the legislation was **adoptive** (or permissive), rather than compulsory; it facilitated change and improvement, rather than insisted on it. Many local authorities shied away from taking action on grounds of cost (e.g. Artisans' Dwelling Act), lack of conviction of the principle of State control and, to some extent, discomfort in imposing restrictions on their own kind, for example imposing fines on factory owners for discharging waste into rivers. It was an indication that Victorian attitudes of *laissez-faire* and self-help prevailed among the upper and middle classes, and there was still a reluctance to accept a too rapid extension of the State's responsibility for the welfare of its people, although the

Key terms

Adoptive legislation: a law that allows organisations or individuals at whom it is directed the choice of whether or not to carry out its requirements. It is sometimes refered to as permissive legislation. Adoptive legislation reflects the *laissez-faire* attitudes of the period.

principle of limited State intervention was accepted. It is most likely that Disraeli's outlook was in line with this thinking.

T. A. Jenkins believes that the motive behind some of Disraeli's legislation was a 'thank you' to groups that had deserted the Liberal Party and helped to bring the Tories to power – for example the Brewing interests, the Lancashire industrialists and the trade unions. Although much of the remaining legislation was directed towards the urban population, there were few constructive social reforms and, with income tax reduced to 2d in the £, there were no surplus funds available. The underlying motive of the Education Act appeared to be to prop up the voluntary Church schools, which thrived on Tory influence in the rural areas. There was also a view that compulsory school attendance could alienate the working classes.

On the other hand, it could be argued that Disraeli established the idea of Tory democracy through his social reforms. The reforms certainly indicated an awareness of the needs of the emergent working class. Their voice was heard more often, and this was as a result of the growing influence and strength of the trade unions and through improved provision of education – both areas of encouragement in the Conservative reforms. The provisions of the Public Health Act were so practical they lasted for over 60 years. The reforms gave credence to the idea of a Tory working-class man and the principle of State intervention was cautiously extended, in spite of the reactionary interests in the Conservative Party.

Disraeli's greatest social achievement was in trade union legislation and labour laws. This did much to make trade unions respectable and encouraged the growth of trade unions. Unionism began to spread beyond the crafts and semi-skilled workers to include unskilled workers. Disraeli's motive was to 'gain and retain for the Tories the lasting affection of the working classes'. But the working class was fickle and by 1880 excitement at what Disraeli had done for them was fading fast.

Activity

Revision exercise

1 Copy and complete the table below.

Disraeli's key reforms

Date	Reform	Benefits	Drawbacks and limitations

2 Working in pairs, using the information collected in the table, assess the success of Disraeli's reforming legislation.

Disraeli's foreign and imperial policy, 1875–8

Foreign policy

When Disraeli took office in 1874, he was faced with similar problems and issues in foreign and imperial policy as Gladstone. Maintaining the balance of power in Europe was of paramount importance, although the balance had changed with the emergence of a strong united Germany in 1871. The German chancellor, Bismarck, created an alliance system that

Exploring the detail

Otto von Bismarck, the powerful German chancellor, had engineered the unification of Germany by 1871. He continued to dominate German and European politics for another 20 years. Bismarck built up a system of alliances, to protect Germany, isolate France and maintain the 'status quo' and a balance of power in Europe. The *Dreikaiserbund* was formed in 1873 as a statement of unity of the three central European Empires: Germany; Austria-Hungary; and Russia. Bismarck's consolidation of the *Dreikaiserbund* kept Germany in a strong position in Europe, France weak and Britain without an ally.

centred on Germany, weakened France and isolated Britain. Disraeli's foreign policy actions were designed to restore Britain's position at the centre of world affairs and uphold the country's interests abroad, particularly those of its empire. To this end, Disraeli pursued an active and interventionist foreign policy.

In his 1872 speech at Manchester, Disraeli had criticised Gladstone's handling of foreign policy and accused him of feebleness in upholding Britain's prestige abroad. Disraeli argued for 'firmness and decision at the right moment' and the maintenance of British power. Disraeli's approach to foreign policy is often compared to the vigorous approach of the Liberal prime minister, Lord Palmerston, in the 1860s. Robert Blake calls Disraeli an 'instinctive Palmerstonian' in that he was intensely patriotic and positioned himself as defender of British interests abroad.

Disraeli's foreign policy decisions were based on expediency and, unlike Gladstone, he did not consider the question of morality in any given situation. This was most apparent in the outcry over the 'Bulgarian atrocities' in 1876, which led to a most bitter confrontation between Gladstone and Disraeli.

Cross-reference

The 'Bulgarian atrocities' are described in more detail on page 73.

The Eastern Question

Fig. 4 *The Eastern Question – the Balkan region, 1878*

The heart of the Eastern Question was the decline of the Turkish Empire (also known as the Ottoman Empire) during the 19th century. The Turkish Empire had once stretched from south-east Europe (the Balkans), through the Middle East and into North Africa. Turkey's decline, especially in the Balkans where Nationalism was bubbling up, could potentially create opportunities for several other European powers. France, Russia, Austria-Hungary, Britain and Germany each became concerned with whether or not they could obtain advantage from supporting or turning their back on a troubled and weakening Turkey. It suited Disraeli to commit himself to a policy of containing Russia's ambitions and to lend conditional support to Turkey to achieve this.

Key chronology

The Eastern Question

1869	Suez Canal opens.
1875	Bosnia and Herzogovina rise against the Turks, followed by Bulgaria.
	Disraeli buys shares in Suez Canal.
	Disraeli agrees to Andrassy Note for Turkish reforms in Bosnia.
1876 April to May	Bulgarian uprising savagely repressed (Bulgarian atrocities).
1876 May	Berlin Memorandum for settlement of Balkan Crisis – no agreement from Disraeli.
1876 June	Serbia and Montenegro declare war on Turkey.
1876 September	Gladstone publishes 'Bulgarian Horrors' pamphlet.
1876 December	Conference of Constantinople called by Disraeli.
1877 April	Russia declares war on Turkey.
1878 January	Disraeli sends British fleet to Constantinople, Carnarvon resigns, Russian–Turkish ceasefire.
1878 March	Treaty of San Stefano, Derby resigns.
1878 April	Disraeli sends Indian troops to Malta.
1878 May to June	Secret agreements between Britain/Russia and Britain/Turkey ahead of Berlin Congress.
1878 July	Berlin Treaty 'Peace with honour'.
1879	Dual Alliance formed between Germany and Austria-Hungary.

The Eastern Crisis, 1875–7

A delicate balance of power existed between Russia, Turkey and Austria. One of the outcomes of the Treaty of Paris, at the end of the Crimean War in 1856, had been to exact a promise from Turkey of better treatment towards the Christians within its empire, while Russia gave up any claim to protect them. The agreement was soon broken and the Balkan Christians again suffered persecution at the hands of the Ottoman Turks. The result of this was a revolt in Bosnia and Herzegovina in 1875 against the Turks, which by the following year had spread to Bulgaria. It later affected Serbia and Montenegro. This was, in effect, a Balkan nationalist rising and offered a chance for European interference. The Great Powers tried to deal with the unrest by diplomatic means, but Disraeli publicly expressed concern as he did not wish the *Dreikaiserbund* to exploit the situation for its own ends. He reluctantly accepted proposals made to the Turkish government, by the Austro–Hungarian minister Andrassy, but these proposals quickly unravelled when Turkey failed to cooperate.

The *Dreikaiserbund* continued diplomatic efforts by issuing the Berlin Memorandum, in June 1876. It was signed by Germany, Austria, Russia, France and Italy, and demanded change and reform within the Turkish government. Disraeli refused to be a signatory on the grounds that he had not been consulted on the terms during the initial discussions. In truth, he was anxious that it would weaken Turkey to the extent that it would not be able to stop Russian expansion into the Mediterranean, which would damage British interests. Disraeli now went his own way and sent British naval vessels to the Dardanelle Straits. The message was clear – Britain could not be marginalised in European decision making. Disraeli's action was seen by Turkey as an indication of British support.

While the European powers were busy wrangling about their perceptions of each other, the new Turkish leader, Abdul Hamid, stemmed the Bulgarian revolt by using a force of irregular troops, the Bashi Basouks, and carrying out hideous atrocities against the Christian population in Bulgaria.

There was strong reaction in Britain from several quarters. The extent of the atrocities was initially minimised by Disraeli, but the scale of the horror was revealed by the *Daily News*. Gladstone made as much political mileage out of it as he could in a violent verbal attack entitled 'The Bulgarian Horrors and the Question of the East'. He proposed to expel the Turks 'bag and baggage' from the Balkans. The relationship between Disraeli and Gladstone was at its most bitter, and Disraeli felt that Gladstone had destroyed British unity at a time of crisis and offered unnecessary encouragement to the Russians. Disraeli appeared to be indifferent to the sufferings of the Christians, which caused moral outrage in Gladstone.

By the end of 1876, Disraeli's foreign policy actions had sabotaged a settlement of the Eastern Crisis, encouraged the Turks to carry out frightful atrocities against the Bulgarians, and caused expressions of deep outrage against him at home.

The Conference at Constantinople, 1876

A conference was called at Constantinople in December 1876, on Disraeli's initiative, to try and stem the worsening situation, but demands for Turkey to reform were rejected by the Sultan. Disraeli refused to pressurise the Turks, going against the advice of his foreign secretary Lord Derby. The Conference broke up and Russia declared war on Turkey in April 1877, justifying it on the grounds that it was acting on behalf of the persecuted Christians.

Disraeli made it clear that Britain would only agree to remain neutral on the condition that Russia did not threaten Britain's position in Egypt and the Suez Canal or enter Constantinople. At this point, public opinion at home turned in Disraeli's favour, with an outburst of '**jingoism**' and anti-Russian feeling. The war was quickly ended the following year with the Treaty of San Stefano, in which Russia proposed doubling the size of Bulgaria, over which it had huge influence. Britain and Austria demanded a European Congress. Disraeli knew that Russia, although victorious, was exhausted financially and militarily and postured by ordering the British fleet to Constantinople and a few weeks later moving Indian troops to the island of Malta. Derby resigned in frustration at Disraeli's brinkmanship. Lord Salisbury was brought in as foreign secretary.

Treaty of Berlin, 1878

The Treaty of Berlin was eventually agreed after a series of secret negotiations. In dealing with Russia, Disraeli's main objective was to keep Russia out of the Mediterranean and reduce Russia's influence in the Balkans. The 'Big Bulgaria' proposed in the Treaty of San Stefano was broken up and a smaller state created and returned to Turkish suzerainty.

An agreement was reached between Britain and Turkey, under which Britain received Cyprus and Turkey promised toleration of Christian subjects in return for Britain guaranteeing

Key terms

Jingoism: the term came from a music hall song that became popular in Britain at the time of the Russo–Turkish war: It had been particularly associated with Palmerston's foreign policy in the 1850s:
We don't want to fight, but by jingo if we do,
We've got the ships, we've got the men,
We've got the money too.

To say 'by jingo' was a mildly threatening oath at that time. Jingoism has since come to mean patriotism.

Cross-reference
Lord Salisbury is profiled on page 78.

Fig. 5 *Congress of Berlin, 1878. Otto von Bismarck, the German chancellor, visiting Disraeli (Lord Beaconsfield), the British delegate at his hotel the Kaiserhof during the Congress. What do you think would be the purpose of such a visit?*

Turkish dominions. Britain could keep a watch on Russian ship movements to the north and south to the Suez Canal.

The agreement between Austria-Hungary and Britain secured Austro–Hungarian occupation of Bosnia and Herzegovina, while the independence of Serbia and Montenegro was guaranteed. Serbia was enlarged.

The Congress of Berlin was a personal triumph for Disraeli. He was successful in that the Congress agreed to limit Russia's gains and the overall results strengthened Turkey in the Balkans and, therefore, the front against Russia. It averted full-scale war, but it placed many Christians under Turkish rule again. Austro–Hungarian occupation in the Balkans weakened the *Dreikaiserbund*. In the nature and the detail of all the agreements lay the seeds of the problems, which led 30 years later to the outbreak of the Great War. Disraeli returned to Britain claiming to have achieved 'peace with honour'.

> Disraeli was the 'Lion of the Congress'. He got all his own way, was the constant centre of attention and very much appeared to dominate both Europe and the world. It was the climax of his career. He had made Britain more completely the arbiter of Europe than ever Palmerston had. And so, weary, ill, but triumphant, Disraeli returned home bringing 'peace with honour'. He received the Garter from the Queen and, for the time being, the Conservative Party and British diplomacy were on the crest of a wave.

5 *Clayton, G. D. (1974) **Britain and the Eastern Question**, Hodder Arnold*

Activity

Thinking point

1 To what extent did Disraeli bring 'peace with honour' in the Eastern crisis?

2 Was he correct in ignoring the plight of the Christians under Turkish rule in order to achieve the best result for Britain?

Imperial policy

The traditional view of Disraeli's imperial policy is that he aimed to pursue the expansion of the empire. More recently, historians such as Paul Smith have concluded that Disraeli wanted to preserve, not expand, the empire. To Disraeli, the empire brought the power and prestige, which gave Britain influence in Europe. There is little evidence to suggest he had any great designs for the empire.

> (Disraeli) had raised the banner of Empire in 1872 on a consolidatory, not an expansionist basis. He used Empire as an inspirational vision and he had a firm confidence in its ability to weigh in the European balance of power, but, as prime minister, he showed little inclination to do anything about it.

6 *Smith, P. (1996) **Disraeli**, Cambridge University Press*

Paul Smith's inference is that Disraeli advertised the importance of empire to increase his popularity (in other words, he was a self-publicist)

Did you know?

In 1879, Germany and Austria-Hungary formed a dual alliance to safeguard them from possible future Russian aggression. The terms were secret, which encouraged an attitude of suspicion among the powers. It was the first of the formal military agreements that led to the system of alliance and counter-alliance, which existed in Europe in the lead-up to 1914 and the outbreak of war.

Cross-reference

For details on the alliance system, see Chapters 6 and 7.

but, in reality, took few initiatives. As with domestic issues, Disraeli left much of the decision making to his ministers or officials abroad.

T. A. Jenkins assesses Disraeli's approach to imperial policy (Source 7).

> ... while Disraeli had in the past publicly asserted the importance of the British Empire, notably in the Crystal Palace speech of 1872, he was not the prophet of a new age of imperial expansion. [His record in imperial matters] confirms the absence of any great imperial vision on Disraeli's part and shows that he responded almost entirely to the initiatives of others.

7   *Jenkins, T. A. (1996)* ***Disraeli and Victorian Conservatism,***
Palgrave Macmillan

South Africa and the Zulu War, 1877–9

In South Africa, in 1877, the Colonial Secretary, the Earl of Carnarvon, put pressure on the Dutch settlers, the Transvaal Boers, to accept the annexation of the Transvaal by Britain, ostensibly to deal with the threat of a Zulu attack. It was meant to be part of a bigger plan to form a South African Federation incorporating British and Dutch settlements, but as part of the British Empire. Carnarvon appointed a rather wayward British high commissioner, Sir Bartle Frere, who disobeyed orders from London and got involved in a war against the Zulus, in which a British force of 1,220 men was wiped out at Isandhlwana

Fig. 6 *An incident during the Battle of Isandhlwana during the Zulu War, depicting Lieutenants Melvill and Coghill (24th regiment) dying to save the Queen's colours, 22 January 1879*

in January 1879. It was several months before the situation could be recovered and the Zulus defeated at Ulundi. Disraeli was furious at the news of the war, but he had given Carnarvon too much of a free hand and, as a result, his own reputation suffered.

Egypt and the Suez Canal

In 1875, Disraeli acted decisively over the purchase of shares in the Suez Canal in 1875. The government of the **Khedive** of Egypt was on the verge of bankruptcy and needed £4m to avoid insolvency. Disraeli moved quickly and consulted Queen Victoria, who gave the purchase her blessing. Money was raised through a loan with the Jewish bankers the Rothschilds. It was a smart move by Disraeli. Once Britain was able to exert influence over the Suez Canal (though it never had a controlling interest), there were huge advantages in terms of the development and control of Britain's Empire:

- Britain negotiated a low rate for British shipping to pass through the canal, and this helped to achieve cheaper imports and exports and so stimulated trade.
- The deal helped to establish a solid British interest in Egypt.
- It reduced the travelling time to India and the Far East.

Key terms

Khedive: a Turkish word meaning 'Lord', and signifying a high-ranking position as a ruler's representative, or governor in an outlying province of an empire. It became the term used to describe Turkish viceroys who ruled Egypt between 1867 and 1914. The title Khedive was first used in Egypt by Muhammad Ali Pasha, regarded as the founder of modern Egypt, in 1805. The Turks still retained authority (suzerainty) over Egypt and would not accept the use of the title Khedive until 1867.

It provided an easy and speedy means of increasing military and naval forces in the Far East and more especially in India, where security concerns were growing.

Disraeli and British India

Fig. 7 *Disraeli offering the crown of India to Queen Victoria. She was proclaimed Empress of India on 1 May 1876. What political point is the cartoonist trying to make with his portrayal of Disraeli?*

The trouble spot was the Indian north-west frontier with Afghanistan, and it became a battle of wits between Russia and Britain as to who could gain control of Afghanistan first. Disraeli thought it expedient to encourage good relations with the Amir of Afghanistan, Sher Ali, so that he would be sympathetic to British concerns rather than Russian ambitions. The Colonial Secretary, Lord Carnarvon, was in charge of British policy in India. Lord Lytton was appointed as Viceroy with the remit of setting up a British mission in the Afghan capital Kabul. Lytton supported a forward or expansionist policy in India. There were reservations from Salisbury, Secretary to India, and Derby, foreign secretary, about Lytton's suitability for the job.

Salisbury had had to warn Derby that 'Lytton is burning with anxiety to distinguish himself in a great war'. Derby expressed 'grave doubts as to the fitness of the man for the place!' But Disraeli who liked a bit of bluster and brag, kept Lytton on, only to discover once Salisbury's restraining hand was removed, that Derby had been right.

8

Charmley, J (1999) **Splendid Isolation***, Hodder*

In 1878, the Tsar sent a mission to Kabul, the capital of Afghanistan. Lytton was ordered to take no action until all diplomatic channels had been tried. In spite of this, Lytton sent troops into Afghanistan and chased the Russians out and deposed Sher Ali. A British mission was established in Kabul. However, in September 1879, resentment against the British spilled over into a massacre of the entire mission. A strong force of British troops was immediately despatched, but order was not restored until after Disraeli had left office in 1880.

There was much criticism of Disraeli's lack of control of Lytton and his aggressive policy towards Afghanistan. But soon after, a stable and lasting relationship with Afghanistan emerged, which could be attributed to Disraeli's policy.

Fig. 8 *Disraeli's foreign policy*

The achievements of Gladstone's Second Ministry, 1880–5

The general election of April 1880 brought victory for the Liberals. Gladstone was riding high on a successful election campaign in his new Midlothian constituency in Scotland, where he defeated the sitting Conservative member, the Earl of Dalkeith. Mounting anger and impatience at Disraeli's foreign policy decisions had drawn Gladstone back into frontline politics. Gladstone's campaign against the Bulgarian atrocities became a crusade against 'Beaconsfieldism'. Gladstone's pamphlet 'The Bulgarian Horrors and the Question of the East', published in September 1876, was the starting point of his successful campaign.

In 1880, there was a noticeable division in the Liberal Party. The old Whigs were led by Lord Hartington who feared Gladstone's radicalism. The Radical Liberals were led by Joseph Chamberlain, who was at odds with Gladstone over the need for increased taxation to pay for an extensive programme of social reform. Chamberlain had designs on the leadership of the party. At the same time, the Irish Nationalist Party, under the inspirational leadership of Charles Parnell, was now strong enough to make its presence felt in the political arena.

The leadership of the Tory Party was taken over by Lord Salisbury who sat in the Lords and by Sir Stafford Northcote in the Commons. Northcote

Activity

Challenge your thinking

How accurate is Paul Smith's assessment of Disraeli's imperial policy that he used empire as an 'inspirational vision' but 'showed little inclination to do anything about it'?

Question

Why did Disraeli's imperial policy lead to increasing unpopularity of the Conservative government?

was so ineffectual that a group nicknamed the Fourth Party emerged under the leadership of Lord Randolph Churchill and took responsibility for attacking Gladstone's policies in the Commons.

Key profiles

Robert Cecil, 3rd Marquess of Salisbury

The political career of Cecil (1830–1903), 3rd Marquess of Salisbury, spans 50 years. Prime minister three times, 1885–6, 1886–92 and 1895–1902, he dominated British politics in the closing years of the 19th century. In foreign policy, Salisbury lifted Britain's power and prestige to new heights. His reputation as a heavy-weight political leader has suffered by comparison with his predecessor Disraeli and his political opponent Gladstone, although he wrecked Gladstone's plans for Home Rule. The character of Salisbury's Conservatism was profoundly pessimistic, religiously inspired and reverential towards traditional institutions such as the monarchy and parliament. He protected the privileges of property and the Anglican Church. Salisbury was against change in a rapidly changing world in which middle-class influence was increasing, as the aristocracy to which he belonged was losing political control. He was against extension of democracy, but pessimistically accepted it would happen and was pragmatic enough to work on the 1884 Reform Bill to ensure advantage for his own party. Salisbury was prepared to compromise to accommodate the Liberal Unionists after their split with Gladstone in 1886. His humour and tolerance in dealing with colleagues contributed to his success in holding together a ministry for most of the years 1886–1902.

Lord Randolph Churchill

Third son of the 7th Duke of Marlborough, Churchill (1849–95) came to political prominence in the 1880s with outspoken attacks on Gladstone's government and weak members of his own Conservative Party. He was supported by three young, progressive Conservatives, who became known as the Fourth Party. Churchill believed in 'Tory democracy' and wished to popularise the party by introducing social reforms. He was a popular figure among rank-and-file and seen as a potential future leader. Chancellor of the exchequer in Salisbury's Second Ministry, Churchill had made too many enemies to survive in post. He died aged 45 from degenerative brain disease which, according to his son Winston Churchill, was syphilis.

Domestic policy

Much of Gladstone's Second Ministry was taken up with the problems relating to Ireland. However, he was responsible for some other far-reaching political reforms and actions that moved Britain towards greater democracy.

Electoral reform

Three important pieces of electoral legislation were passed by Gladstone, which brought Britain much closer to democracy: the Corrupt Practices Act, 1883; the Franchise Act, 1884; and the Redistribution of Seats Act, 1885.

The Secret Ballot Act of 1872 had succeeded in getting rid of intimidation in elections, but not corruption, and Gladstone introduced the Corrupt

Cross-reference

Joseph Chamberlain is profiled on page 67.

Practices Act to close the loopholes that allowed corruption to continue. This measure ensured that a candidate's election expenses were set to a specified limit, and made clear what campaign money could be spent on. Election agents had to produce accounts. The act clearly defined illegal and corrupt practices and introduced stiff fines and prison sentences for anyone breaking the law. It meant that politicians now had to win support by promoting better policies. This was reinforced by a growing working-class electorate.

The real impetus for electoral reform came from Joseph Chamberlain. It was part of his strategy to take control of the Liberal Party and replace its ageing leadership with his own younger, more radical and dynamic package. Chamberlain believed that electoral reform could produce more Liberal voters from the labouring population in the rural areas who still did not have the vote. These were mainly agricultural labourers and a large number of miners. There was no logical argument against extending the franchise. At the time, Gladstone's ministry was running into trouble over Ireland and he agreed to electoral reform as a means of winning back his popularity. In the event, Chamberlain had underestimated Gladstone's amazing constitution and tenacity. Gladstone took the credit for the reform.

The effects of electoral reform

The franchise reform removed discrimination over voting – it was no longer tied to property. A uniform franchise for both counties and boroughs now existed. Agricultural labourers and miners in rural areas were brought into the voting system. The electorate doubled from nearly 3 million to 6 million out of a total population of 35 million. Two out of three men now had the vote. The act enfranchised the working classes and substantially reduced the influence of the landed classes. It was a great step towards democracy in Britain.

The redistribution of seats brought an end to the over-representation of the rural areas and under-representation of the industrial towns and cities. Most constituencies were now single member and equally sized in terms of population, so that the system of constituencies was tied in with the distribution of the population. For the first time, this meant fair representation across Britain. The increased electorate encouraged the two main political parties to improve their organisation and the efficiency of their party machines. This brought Radical Liberals into contact with the new rural voters, while the Conservatives strengthened their support in the boroughs. This act introduced a recognisably modern system of electoral representation.

The new Irish voters consolidated the position of Parnell and the Irish Nationalist Party and strengthened them for the Home Rule fight. The Liberals had lost much necessary old Whig support by the abolition of so many seats. The Radical Liberals, led by Joseph Chamberlain, took on a more influential position in the Liberal Party. It marked the beginning of the end of Gladstonian Liberalism.

Gladstone's administration achieved little else in terms of reform. It was distracted by crises abroad and problems over Ireland. Tensions between various factions in the party also impacted on a cohesive programme. Gladstone, now over 70, was increasingly difficult to work with. Joseph Chamberlain's ambitions were harder to contain. However, Chamberlain's plans for social reform, although ignored by Gladstone and feared by the old Whigs, attracted the voters who gave the Liberals a majority in the 1885 election and Gladstone a short-lived third term in office. The Liberal Party, however, was, severely weakened.

Exploring the detail

Terms of the Franchise Act, 1884

- In the counties, the vote was given to all male householders over 21 and £10 lodgers.
- A £10 occupier franchise was created for those living in shops or offices.
- The older franchises still applied.

Terms of the Redistribution of Seats Act, 1885

- Boroughs with a population under 15,000 lost both their MPs.
- Boroughs with a population under 50,000 lost one MP.
- 142 seats were redistributed.

Cross-reference

Parnell and the Irish Nationalist Party are covered in more detail in Chapters 2 and 5.

Exploring the detail

Election of working-class MPs

An important development with future implications for the two-party system in Britain was that working-class MPs were elected for the first time, with financial support from the trade unions. MPs still did not receive a salary.

Did you know?

Gladstone passed legislation that extended women's legal rights. His 1870 legislation on married women's property rights had been a largely ineffective attempt to give women more control of their property. He responded to the lobbying of educated, middle-class ladies by passing the Married Women's Property Act, 1882, which ended a husband's automatic right to claim his wife's property as his own and equalised the property rights of married and unmarried women. Gladstone did nothing, however, to extend the right to vote in local elections, which was given to single women ratepayers in the Municipal Franchise Act, 1869, to include married women. This did not occur until the Local Government Act of 1894.

Activity

Revision exercise

Gladstone's reforms suggest that he was highly principled and believed in equality, fairness and democracy. Copy and complete the table below, indicating how his reforms demonstrated all of these qualities.

Gladstone's qualities	Actions/legislation which demonstrated them
High principle	
Equality	
Fairness	
Democracy	

Gladstone's foreign and imperial policies to 1885

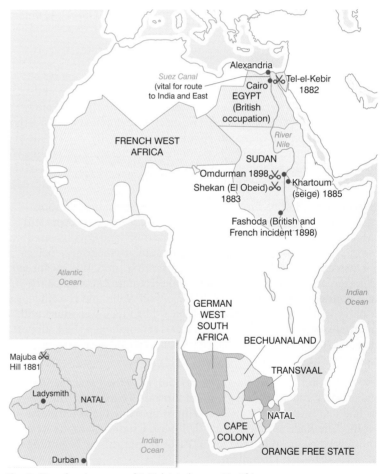

Fig. 9 *Map showing areas of British involvement in Africa*

In his Midlothian campaign, Gladstone had made clear his fierce opposition to Disraeli's foreign and imperial policies. He criticised Disraeli's policies on the grounds of aggression, immorality and cost, and all but promised to undo his legacy. It was difficult to work out where Gladstone stood on foreign and imperial affairs. In his First Ministry, he had been severely criticised for being almost disinterested. During Disraeli's government, Gladstone had argued vehemently from an anti-imperialist position, but, once in office, he appeared to turn around to a pro-imperial stance.

Major areas of foreign policy

Egypt

By 1878, Egypt was on the verge of political and economic collapse. Britain had considerable investments in Egypt and in the Suez Canal. There had been gross misuse of funds by the Khedive Ismail Pasha that had been earmarked to build up the infrastructure, for example roads, rails and docks. The Khedive was deposed in favour of his son and an Anglo–French Dual Control Commission was put in place to restore financial stability and look after foreign investors. It gave itself the power to pass reforms and cut expenditure, however, not surprisingly, this stirred up nationalist feeling. In 1881, Arabi Pasha, an Egyptian army officer, led a nationalist rebellion, seized power, formed a government and banned foreign intervention in Egypt.

To protect British investments in Egypt, Gladstone sanctioned the navy to join France and send warships to Alexandria. The Egyptians prepared defences against the Anglo–French fleet. At the last minute the French withdrew. Confused orders led to an attack on Alexandria by the British fleet and there was a general breakdown of law and order. Gladstone's Liberal government had little alternative but to invade Egypt alone, ironically establishing Britain as a land power in the Middle East for the first time. Arabi's nationalist rising was short-lived. He was defeated, at Tel-el-Kabir, by British troops under General Sir George Wolseley, captured and deported.

Gladstone had intended to sort out the problem and withdraw from Egypt as quickly as possible. He justified his un-Gladstonian decision to overthrow the nationalist movement, as he believed Britain's interests and the strategic position of Egypt, vis-a-vis the Suez Canal, to be of greater importance. A further justification was to bring order and stability to Egypt. To this end, he appointed Sir Evelyn Baring (later Lord Cromer) as Consul-General, a position he maintained with great efficiency for the next 20 years. While a Khedive continued to rule over Egypt in name, Egypt's freedom became little more than symbolic and ultimate power resided with the British Consul-General.

The Sudan, 1883–5

The Sudan was under the control of Egypt. Sudan's authority had been undermined by actions of a religious extremist, the Mahdi. In 1883, the Khedive of Egypt sent a force into the Sudan under a British officer Colonel Hicks to suppress the Mahdi. At the Battle of Shekan, Hicks was killed and the Khedive's army ambushed and trapped. Gladstone expressed some sympathy for the Mahdi's position and his right to fight for his people's freedom and a right to self-government. It was a view that had little sympathy in 'Empire England'. Control of the Sudan by the pro-European Egyptians, rankled with the Sudanese, many of whom supported the Mahdi.

The army of Egypt, containing a number of British officers, civil servants and their families, was in a perilous position marooned in various garrisons within the Sudan. Gladstone had two choices: either to attempt a complete conquest of the Sudan; or a complete evacuation. The decision was made to send General Gordon, who knew the Sudan well, to the capital Khartoum to carry out the evacuation. There was a view in British government circles that Gordon had his own agenda, to refuse to withdraw until he had taught the Mahdi a lesson. At first, Gordon held the Nile valley against the Mahdi. When he was pushed back into Khartoum, Gordon requested

Fig. 10 *The army of Egypt, which contained many British officers, in action against the Mahdi in the Sudan, 1883–5*

Fig. 11 *The death of General Gordon (1833–85) at Khartoum when the city fell to the Mahdi on 16 January 1885*

relief troops. There was an unnecessary delay and the reinforcements arrived on 28 January 1885 – two days too late to save Gordon. He was seen as a national hero, who had been badly let down by the British authorities. Gladstone continued his policy of withdrawal from the Sudan, leaving the Mahdi in control. Gladstone reached the peak of his unpopularity in Britain.

Transvaal and the Boers

The Zulus were defeated in 1879 and Sir Garnet Wolseley was made high commissioner of the Transvaal, making it a crown colony instead of giving it the self-governing status as promised. Gladstone had strongly criticised the annexation of the Transvaal in 1877 by Disraeli, and so there was an expectation from the Boers, once the Zulu threat had been dealt with, that they would have independence. In 1881, Gladstone stalled on the issue of Transvaal independence as he was considering setting up a South African Confederation. As a result, fighting broke out between the British and the Boers and the Boers inflicted a humiliating defeat on the British at Majuba Hill in 1881. Gladstone could either send more troops to sort out the Boers, or accept their point of view and grant independence. He chose a compromise of independence with the British crown maintaining sovereignty. This was soon dropped after the Boers' angry reaction. In 1884, the British government finally recognised the South African Republic.

Afghanistan

Gladstone's intention was to withdraw from Afghanistan, but he was dissuaded by the Indian Viceroy, Lord Ripon, who was anxious not to create unrest on the border and allow the Russians to take advantage. Gladstone agreed to continue the defence of Afghanistan, although he felt the policy carried risks as the British did not have the necessary control in Afghanistan to ensure success. In 1885, the Russians seized the Afghan town of Penjdeh, which lay close to the Russian border. Given Gladstone's handling of the Sudan crisis, the Russians expected to get away with it. Gladstone surprisingly threatened force and the Russians withdrew and agreed to arbitration.

Summary of Gladstone's foreign and imperial policies

In his policy towards Egypt, Gladstone had to consider British interests first. His occupation of Egypt surprised many and was greeted with approval by the general public. However, it caused his old friend, John Bright, to resign from Cabinet saying his actions were 'simply damnable – worse than anything ever perpetrated by Dizzy'.

Concerted European action over Egypt failed. The situation caused friction between Britain and France into the 20th century. Turkey was

■ **Activity**

Research task

General Gordon of Khartoum (1833–5) was already a well-known public figure before the fateful siege of Khartoum brought a heroic end to his colourful life.

Carry out your own research on Gordon using the following title to direct you: What made General Gordon an extraordinary Victorian?

Present your findings to the class.

■ **Cross-reference**

Disraeli's annexation of the Transvaal and his actions in Afghanistan are outlined on page 75.

annoyed at being side-lined. France and Germany, jealous of Britain's powerful position in East Africa, looked for colonial opportunities for themselves. Gladstone appeared to be on the back foot and pulled out of areas of informal British control, for example the Congo basin, to make way for other European interests.

Gladstone was against interference with nationalist movements, as he believed they had a right to express themselves. At the same time, he was up against the pro-imperialist positions held by the majority of MPs. In the Transvaal, Gladstone hesitated before ordering a withdrawal. This became a costly mistake in terms of the defeat at Majuba Hill. He was seen as giving way to force. He might have been better sticking to his principles and awarding the Transvaal independence in the first place. In the long term, the Boers thereafter regarded the British as weak.

The Sudan was a mistake in the choice of Gordon, who was known for his obstinacy and pro-Imperialism, but Gladstone handled the whole incident badly from start to finish. Gladstone was pilloried by the British public who were angry at the abandonment and needless death of a national hero, and Britain was humiliated by Gladstone's withdrawal from the Sudan, leaving the Mahdi victorious.

There was little sympathy or understanding of Gladstone's foreign policy actions, which often appeared contradictory. Therefore, even his successes met with criticism and created divisions in the party between the Radical anti-imperialists and the Whigs who often supported a pro-imperialist position.

Cross-reference

The effects of Gladstone's policies in the Transvaal can be seen on page 126.

Did you know?

Such was the public fury over the death of Gordon that Gladstone's nicknamed changed from the affectionate GOM (Grand Old Man) to MOG (Murderer of Gordon).

Question

What inconsistencies were there in Gladstone's foreign and imperial policies?

Summary questions

1. How significant were Disraeli's social reforms?
2. Did Disraeli bring 'peace with honour' in his foreign policy?
3. Assess the importance of Gladstone's electoral reforms in terms of developing democracy.

5   Conflict and trouble – in Ireland and at home

Fig. 1 *Charles Stewart Parnell encircled by other prominent men in Irish politics and government. This picture was published in 1881 and underlines Parnell's leadership of the Irish Nationalists and the high esteem in which he was held at that time*

That as the land of Ireland, like that of every other country, was intended by a just and all-providing God for the use and sustenance of those of his people to whom he gave inclination and energies to cultivate and improve it, any system which assigns its ownership and control to a class of landlords, to be used as an instrument for political self-seeking, demands from every aggrieved Irishman an undying hostility. Such action is a flagrant breach of human principles.

1   *Adapted from a speech by John Ferguson at the tenants' rights meeting in Irishtown, Co. Mayo on 20 April 1879*

This extract from a speech by John Ferguson, land reformer and Home Rule advocate, at the start of the Land League and the Land War, could be said to encapsulate the 'Cause of Ireland' and the injustice felt by the Irish people over generations.

The history of Ireland during the latter decades of the 19th century is one of conflict, and failure to achieve any acceptable solution to the governing of Ireland. Ireland was under economic as well as political pressure. The movement for Home Rule gathered momentum during the 1870s against the background of the Great Depression in Britain. One of the reasons British industry and agriculture experienced difficulties was fierce competition from overseas. Ireland was particularly badly affected by depression in agriculture as it was the country's main industry. The glut of cheap American corn coming on to the market drove down prices and profits. When tenant farmers, no longer able to pay their rent, faced eviction, violence erupted. This was encouraged by the activities of the Land League, which campaigned for reform.

When Gladstone came to office in 1880, he sought to repress disorder, as well as remove agrarian discontent in Ireland with a policy of coercion and conciliation. He faced up to the challenges presented by the emergence of a strong Irish Nationalist Party led by the dynamic Charles Stewart Parnell. In 1886, Gladstone's introduction of a Home Rule Bill split the Liberal Party and brought Unionism into the political melting pot. During this period, the Irish problem was on the agenda of three prime ministers, all with very different approaches: Gladstone's commitment to finding a lasting solution was unquestioned; Disraeli lacked interest in Ireland; and Salisbury tried to deal with Ireland with firmness on one hand and 'killing Home Rule with kindness' on the other.

All three prime ministers had to steer Britain through the so-called Great Depression, which descended on the economy after 1873. Historians argue as to whether or not the depression in industry existed or whether it was merely a myth. In agriculture, the economic downturn was dramatic and caused real hardship in rural communities. It also made farmers adapt and diversify and this eventually brought about a recovery.

Key profile

Charles Stewart Parnell

Parnell (1846–91) was the son of an Anglo–Irish landowning father and educated at Cambridge. He had an anti-English American mother and he seems to have adopted a deeply held dislike of the English, otherwise he was an unlikely Irish Nationalist.

In 1875, Parnell won the Meath by-election for the Home Rule Party and embarked on an obstructionist policy in parliament, to bring attention to the cause. He became president of the Home Rule Confederation in 1877, replacing the more constitutionally minded Isaac Butt. Parnell led the Home Rule Party in the House after Butt's death in 1879.

He had a ruthlessness and authority that gave him massive support in Ireland. He condoned the actions of the Land League and was imprisoned in 1881. He maximised the position of the Irish National (i.e. Home Rule) Party in parliament, withdrawing and then returning support for Gladstone when he introduced a Home Rule Bill in 1886. His reputation was under scrutiny over a false accusation of complicity in the Phoenix Park murders. In 1890, the country was scandalised by a divorce case in which he was named as co-respondent. The Irish Nationalists were split, but abandoned Parnell when their alliance with the Liberals was threatened. He died the following year from rheumatic fever, aged 45.

Cross-reference

Previous developments in Ireland are discussed in Chapter 2.

Key chronology

Events in Ireland, 1874–86

1874	59 Irish MPs elected under Home Rule banner.
1875	Charles Parnell becomes MP for Irish constituency of Meath.
1879	Formation of Irish Land League by Michael Davitt.
1880	Charles Parnell becomes leader of Irish Nationalist Party.
1881	Land Act.
1882	Kilmainham Treaty agreed between Gladstone and Parnell.
	The Phoenix Park murders.
1885 November	General election gives balance of power to Irish Home Rule Party in Commons.
1885 December	News leaks of Gladstone conversion to Home Rule.
1886 June	Home Rule Bill defeated. Liberal Party splits.

■ The Irish Land War

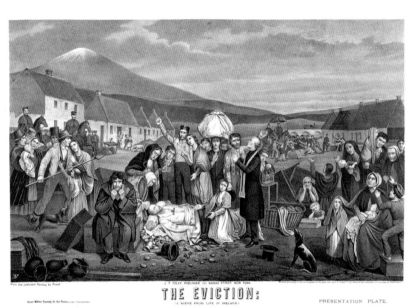

THE EVICTION:
[A SCENE FROM LIFE IN IRELAND]

PRESENTATION PLATE.

Fig. 2 *Irish tenants with their belongings after being forcibly evicted from their homes on land often owned by British absentee landlords*

Cause for unrest in Ireland

The effects of the agricultural depression were being felt in Ireland by the late-1870s. Up until that time, profits in agriculture were increasing and the Irish tenant farmers were enjoying a degree of prosperity and a rise in the standard of living. Between 1877 and 1879, unusually wet summers, disastrous harvests and the arrival on the market of cheap American corn changed all that. It brought a combination of low crop yields and a fall in the price of British wheat. This meant a fall in profits for farmers.

The Irish were particularly hard hit. The majority of them were tenant farmers. When they could no longer meet the rent demand, they were evicted. In addition, many landowners reacted by organising their land into larger units to make them more viable. This resulted in the eviction of smaller tenants. The provisions of Gladstone's 1870 Land Act did not offer sufficient protection. The response of the Irish peasants to the economic crisis was to conduct a land war demanding reductions in rent and, in more radical areas, redistribution of the land. The movement started in the impoverished west of Ireland, where the failure of the potato crop had caused great distress, but soon spread across the country.

Fig. 3 *Parnell addressing a meeting of the Irish Land League*

■ Cross-reference

The 'three 'Fs' are first mentioned on page 40.

The Land League

The Land League was founded in October 1879 by Michael Davitt, a member of the Fenian (Irish Republican) Brotherhood, or IRB, and recently released from prison for his part in the earlier Fenian outrages. The League had connections with the Irish American revolutionary secret society Clan na Gael, founded in 1867, as well as links to the IRB whose headquarters were in Paris. The League was funded by money from America and quickly opened branches throughout Ireland. The hard-pressed tenant farmers flocked to join. The aim of this new pressure group was to reform the land tenure system and gain security for tenant farmers and smallholders, although 'peasant proprietary was the objective of the more politically conscious central committee' (H. C. G. Matthew, *Gladstone 1875–1898*, 1995). The League's programme was based upon the 'three Fs': fair rent; fixity of tenure; and free sale of the right of occupancy.

Davitt invited Charles Stewart Parnell to preside over the League. Parnell was a rising star in the parliamentary Home Rule Party and this linking of the land reform movement with parliamentary activity constituted a 'New Departure' of cooperation in the Irish national movement. Irish revolutionaries had previously refused to work with Irish parliamentarians, but the League won the support of John Devoy of Clan na Gael and the Fenian Brotherhood and, in Parnell, found a champion, who, in 1880, became leader of the Home Rule Party in parliament.

Key profile

Michael Davitt

Davitt (1846–1906) was the son of an evicted Catholic tenant farmer from Co. Mayo. The family moved to Lancashire, where young Davitt lost his right arm working in a cotton mill. He joined the Fenian movement and served a seven-year prison sentence for gun running during the Fenian outrages in 1869. Davitt had a genuine social conscience and made agricultural land reform his main objective. In 1879, he founded the National Land League, but was prepared to use violence and intimidation to achieve his aims. He was elected MP for Co. Meath while in prison in 1882.

A closer look

Landlords and tenants – historiography

The previously accepted view that the Land League supported the demands of an impoverished peasantry against exploitative landlords has been discredited by several historians.

Michael Winstanley, *Ireland and the Land Question, 1800–1922* (1984), points out that the motive of the League was more likely to be coercing the landlords to reduce rents so that the prosperity gained by the tenant farmer during the boom years of the previous two decades would not be eroded.

H. C. G. Matthew refers to Gladstone, querying whether non-payment of rents was 'due to "distress" or to "conspiracy". The Compensation for Disturbance Bill assumed it was "distress": the denouement, as the Land League gained support and confidence in the second half of 1880, suggested to Gladstone that it was both.' (*Gladstone 1875–1898*, 1995).

R. F. Foster disagrees with the notion of the landlord as simply a 'coroneted ghoul' and maintains there were a wide variety of landlords. Rent levels were generally 25–40 per cent of the tenants' gross incomes. But on a subsistence level holding in the impoverished west, any rent was too high. On a large farm in a more prosperous area, rent fell far behind price levels to the advantage of the tenant. Foster agrees that some rents were high and some landlords evicted ruthlessly when they were not paid. However, when the crisis of the late-1870s came, many landlords were already on the point of insolvency and this coincided with their tenants looking for a reduction in the rent (*Modern Ireland 1660–1972*, 1988).

Activity

Talking point

Conspiracy or distress? There are clearly two sides to the argument as to the motives of the Land League. Re-read the previous section of this chapter. Working in small groups, draw up possible motives for one/or the other side of the argument. Debate the issues as a whole class.

Violence and coercion

To achieve what he regarded as justice for tenant farmers, Davitt's Land League organised demonstrations using perfectly legal methods such as mass meetings often to the accompaniment of brass bands. The demonstrators centred their demands on fair rent, fixity of tenure and free sale of the right of occupancy. To back up the demonstrations with action, the League encouraged the tenant farmers to withhold their rent. In some areas, the agitation spilled over into intimidation and violence, particularly in Connaught in the west, where distress was most keenly felt. It was also part of a long tradition in Ireland to settle agrarian disputes with violence and 'direct action', especially during times of economic stress.

Neither Davitt nor Parnell wholly condemned the violence, though both advised members not to get involved in criminal activities. According to Donald Jordan in *Land and Popular Politics in Ireland* (1994): 'there is no doubt that the purposefully legal land movement stimulated the wave of agrarian crime that accompanied it'.

Gladstone was returned to office in the general election of April 1880. H. C. G. Matthew maintains that Gladstone was surprised at the level of distress in Ireland, but quickly accepted there was a problem as the number of evictions rose. He immediately turned his attention to finding a solution. The Bessborough Commission was set up in June 1880 to investigate the working of the Land Act 1870, but was not due to report until the following year.

To increase the pressure on the government, Parnell called for decisive action against the Irish landlords and a revival of the campaign of obstructionism or filibustering to delay legislation – used as a tactic in the Commons during Disraeli's time in office, This practice was used at every opportunity.

In Ireland, violence flared as the worst effects of the agricultural depression were felt and the number of evictions spiralled. Evicted tenants were supported by gangs carrying out acts of reprisal against the landlord. At the lower end, it was burning hayricks or injuring livestock. Incidents of attacking the landowner or his agent and of bombing and burning his home were more serious.

An intentionally non-violent but unnerving tactic encouraged by the Land League was ostracising or **boycotting** landlords who had been guilty of 'abuses' such as unfair evictions or rack-renting. Once the finger of the Land League was pointed at these landlords, the entire community was organised to refuse them all goods and services, including labour to work the farm. The same treatment was meted out to so-called 'land grabbers', who took over the farms of evicted tenants and land agents. Any opposition to the boycott was met with further threats and intimidation.

Gladstone regarded the Land League as a criminal conspiracy. He was willing to accept that the non-payment of rents was due in part to genuine 'distress', but that the rest was 'conspiracy' on the part of the Land League. Gladstone was frustrated that an attempt to prosecute Parnell, in Dublin in December 1880, for conspiracy to obstruct the payment of rent failed because it proved impossible to get anyone to testify against him.

Lord John Browne, an Irish landowner and chairman of the Mayo grand jury, expressed the view of many when he justified his refusal to cooperate (Source 2).

Key terms

Boycotting: the term came into use during the land war in Ireland meaning to shun or ostracise anyone taking over land from an evicted tenant. The origin can be traced to the treatment given to Captain Charles Boycott by the Land League. Boycott was agent to a wealthy absentee landlord in Co. Mayo and had evicted tenants. He was mercilessly targeted by Land League supporters and needed almost permanent police protection.

> I am not willing to give evidence against Mr Parnell for many reasons. Though I don't mind the risk of being shot, I do most decidedly object to having my hay burnt, my livestock maliciously injured, my herdsmen prevented from acting for me and the public prevented from purchasing my sheep and cattle: all of which I regard (to say the least) the possible result of giving offence to the only real government in the country – that of the Land League.

2   *Jordan, D. E. (1994) **Land and Popular Politics in Ireland**, Cambridge University Press*

The escalating unrest and acts of lawlessness persuaded Gladstone to pursue a policy of coercion, although he was reluctant to take this course of action. W. E. Forster, the Chief Secretary for Ireland (1880–2), urged him to do so, convinced that coercion was the only way of destroying the Land League and ending the Land War. Gladstone accepted the need to introduce another Land Act to outweigh the negative effects of coercion. His strategy appears to have been to deal with the demands of the Land League by introducing a new Land Act and dealing with the methods employed by the Land League with coercion. In this way, Gladstone hoped to restore order.

In 1881, a Coercion Act (the Protection of Person and Property Act) was pushed through parliament, which allowed anyone suspected of involvement in illegal activities to be imprisoned for indefinite periods without trial. It was, in effect, the suspension of **Habeas Corpus**. The legislation was held up by excessive filibustering of the Home Rule MPs, one session lasting 41 hours! To prevent a repeat of this obstructionism in the future, the Commons' rules on debating and voting were changed.

Gladstone hoped that his Land Act, passed in tandem with the Coercion Act, would successfully address the contentious issues surrounding land tenure in Ireland. But Parnell saw the Land Act as a victory for his tactics of incessant protest and was even more determined to continue to apply pressure until Home Rule was established. He encouraged the tenants to continue to withhold their rent and to boycott the new land court set up by the Land Act.

Parnell and his followers were arrested under Forster's Coercion Act and held in Kilmainham gaol and the Land League was proscribed (outlawed).

> Gladstone was as ruthless a wielder of power as any contemporary when he saw a necessity or a benefit, as Parnell found in 1881. The benefit was the working of the Land Act and the weakening of the League, and in this Gladstone was successful.

3   *Matthew, H. C. G. (1995)* ***Gladstone 1875–1898****, Allen Lane*

Key terms

Habeas Corpus: this term comes from Latin meaning 'you have the body'. It exists to preserve the right of the individual not to be detained illegally. It takes the form of a writ to a jailer to produce the person in court, to establish the legality of the detention. It has a long history, stretching back to before the Magna Carta in 1215, at which time it was common law. Very occasionally it is suspended by the government during social unrest.

There was still popular support for Parnell and continuing violence, though Parnell feared losing control while in gaol. Gladstone sent Joseph Chamberlain to reach a compromise with him, without reference to Forster. The resulting Kilmainham Treaty agreed that the government would settle the current arrears of rents of all tenants on condition that Parnell denounce the violence and end the rent-strikes. As part of the bargain, Parnell was released in May 1882. Forster resigned, convinced that further coercion, rather than making concessions and doing deals with the 'trouble makers', would have been a better course of action.

The Phoenix Park murders, which occurred a few days later, set back the prospect of cooperation between Gladstone and the Home Rule Party. Sir Frederick Cavendish, the new Chief Secretary for Ireland and Thomas Burke the Permanent Under Secretary were attacked and brutally murdered while walking in Phoenix Park in Dublin. The assassinations were carried out by an extremist group, the 'Invincibles'. Parnell denounced the murders immediately, but the vicious attacks continued and it seemed as if Parnell had indeed lost some of his power.

A tougher Coercion Act, the Prevention of Crimes Act, was passed. The Phoenix Park murderers were arrested and hanged. Gladstone and Parnell entered secret talks and the 1881 Land Act began to work

IN MEMORIAM.

𝕷𝖔𝖗𝖉 𝕱𝖗𝖊𝖉𝖊𝖗𝖎𝖈𝖐 𝕮𝖆𝖇𝖊𝖓𝖉𝖎𝖘𝖍

AND

𝕸𝖗. 𝕿𝖍𝖔𝖒𝖆𝖘 𝕭𝖚𝖗𝖐𝖊.

Foully Murdered in Phœnix Park, Dublin, on May 6th, 1882.

As blameless as the flowers which borrow stain
From the spilt ruddy life-stream of the slain,
    When battle rages 'midst the fields of Spring :
As bravely fallen as the few who mount
The dread death-breathing breach, nor pause to count
    The shot's quick crashing, or the steel's swift swing :
Rest, while the whole land's voice lifts to the blue,
In grief and praise, Pæan and Requiem too !

Fig. 4 *Phoenix Park murders 6 May 1882. A memorial notice to Lord Frederick Cavendish, Chief Secretary for Ireland and Thomas Burke, Under Secretary*

The 'three 'Fs'

The terms of the Land Act in 1881 introduced the 'three 'Fs':

■ Fair rents to be decided through special land courts.

■ Free sale of leases would be acceptable if a tenant wanted to give up farming before the lease expired.

■ Fixed tenancies were to be arranged between landlord and tenant.

■ Activity

Thinking point

Parnell commented on the Land Act that 'while it has not abolished landlordism, it will make landlordism intolerable for the landlords'.

1 What did Parnell mean?

2 Why would the landlords dislike the Land Act?

3 What implications would it have for them in the future?

■ Activity

Revision exercise

Re-read the previous section and the information about the 1870 Irish Land Act on page 39.

1 Why was there unrest in Ireland in the late-1870s?

2 How successful was Gladstone in dealing with the Land League?

3 Why was Gladstone's Land Act of 1881 better received by the Irish than his 1870 Act?

■ Cross-reference

The key events and political figures in Ireland before 1874 are discussed in detail in Chapter 2.

The 1800 Act of Union is outlined on page 4.

as it was intended and rents were set at a more affordable level. One further concession by Gladstone, an Arrears Act, was passed in 1882, which effectively cleared the rent arrears of all tenant farmers that had built up during the Land War. The Irish problems had been resolved by Gladstone's doggedness and determination – but the solution was only temporary!

The Land Act, 1881

For Gladstone, the 1881 Land Act was a direct response to the Land League's demands for fair rent, fixity of tenure and free sale. When the Bessborough Commission reported in December 1880 it strongly recommended the introduction of the 'three 'Fs' and this formed the basis of Gladstone's act. There was much opposition in parliament and Gladstone persisted through 58 sittings in the Commons and called on the Queen's help to get it through the Lords.

Special Land Courts were set up to establish a fair rent and both landowner and tenant were to be bound by the court's decision. The rent was to be fixed for 15 years. The tenant was safe from eviction as long as he paid the rent and the rent could not be raised against a tenant's improvements. The main weaknesses of the act were that it did not help the thousands of tenants already in arrears and on the point of eviction, and there was no definition of what was a fair rent. In the event, the rents were on average 20 per cent lower and this brought down the price of land, which made it easier for tenants to buy land, assisted by government loan schemes. After a cautious start, tenants flocked to the land courts. The great achievement of the act was to turn around the prospects of the disadvantaged Irish peasant by helping them to achieve ownership of the land they farmed.

■ The question of Home Rule

The Home Rule movement

There were several factors that brought the question of Irish Home Rule on to the political agenda and made it increasingly difficult for the Westminster government to ignore.

■ **The influence of Isaac Butt**: In many ways the Home Rule movement stemmed from the initiatives of Isaac Butt when he set up the Home Government Association (HGA), in May 1870. This worked towards a federal solution with a separate parliament in Dublin, so that Ireland could run its internal affairs. By 1874, Butt had replaced the HGA with the Home Rule League, which had a sufficiently wide-based support among the Irish to be a truly national organisation. The 1874 general election had returned 59 Irish MPs on a Home Rule platform. Although there were divergent opinions as to how Ireland should be governed, the group formed the nucleus of a strong Irish Nationalist or Home Rule Party, whose actions directed Irish politics for the next decade.

■ **The consequences for Ireland of the Ballot Act of 1872**: One of the reasons for the success of the Home Rulers in the 1874 election was the ability of the Irish voter to express himself freely at the ballot box without fear of reprisal or eviction from his generally Protestant pro-Union landlord.

■ **Gladstone's failure to satisfy Ireland during his First Ministry, 1870–4**: Gladstone had made himself unpopular among many of his own supporters with his Irish legislation, and there was a view in

Britain that Ireland had been dealt with rather generously. Gladstone's legislation had been bold and innovative in that it challenged Protestant Ascendancy. However, in practical terms, it did not satisfy the Irish people. The 1870 Land Act, in particular, was a failure. It left an increasing number of tenant farmers with the feeling that independence from Britain was the only satisfactory solution.

The Great Depression: There was an increase in economic and social distress as the effects of the depression began to be experienced, particularly in the rural south and west of Ireland, and there was an increase in the number of evictions. This caused seething resentment among the tenant farmers against British dominance and the system of land tenure. At the same time, opportunities for itinerant Irish immigrant workers in England and Scotland had dried up. The return of many of these disgruntled men to Ireland increased anti-British feeling and a desire for separation. Many joined Michael Davitt's Land League.

Impact of pressure groups: The agitation of the Irish tenants against eviction and refusal to pay rents, directed by the Land League, brought considerable pressure to bear on Gladstone's new government in 1880 to introduce land reform. It was strengthened by the Land League's loose alliance with the Home Rule League, now led by Parnell. Parnell agitated in the House for redress for evicted tenants. The pressure contributed to Gladstone's major reform of the Land Act in 1881.

The Parnell factor: Charles Parnell emerged on the Irish political scene shortly before Butt's death, and just at the time the Home Rule movement needed a leader with his strength of purpose and dynamism. His decision, as leader of the Home Rule League, to cooperate with the Land League was inspired and gave great momentum to Home Rule. His skilful management of the Irish MPs led to a strong Irish Nationalist Party, which held the balance of power in parliament. Parnell's leadership was a major factor in finally persuading Gladstone to support Home Rule. Parnell became the undisputed leader of Irish Nationalism.

Fig. 5 *Irish peasant girl guarding the family's last few possessions after eviction for non-payment of rent*

Gladstone's conversion to Home Rule

In June 1885, Parnell and the Irish Nationalists, disenchanted with the Liberals' lack of progress over Ireland, voted with the Conservatives over a budget amendment. Gladstone's government was defeated and Gladstone resigned. Robert Cecil, Marquis of Salisbury, formed a minority Conservative government, which could only survive with the support of the Irish Nationalists. Salisbury was quick to introduce two concessions to the Irish and then call an election in November 1885. The policy of coercion was ended and a Land Purchase Act was introduced, which set aside £5m to assist tenants to buy their holdings from the landlord. Parnell called on the Irish immigrant population in England and Scotland to vote for the Conservatives in the general election, as he believed Salisbury might support Home Rule.

Cross-reference

The Great Depression is covered on pages 98–100.

Activity

Challenge your thinking

Re-read the section on Gladstone's Irish policy in Chapter 2 on pages 36–42.

Why do you think Gladstone was surprised at the level of distress in Ireland when he returned to office in 1880?

Cross-reference

Minority government is explained on page 14.

Table 1 *General election results, November 1885*

Liberals	335
Conservatives	249
Irish Nationalists	86

Did you know?

The Hawarden Kite

The leak to the press about Gladstone's conversion to Home Rule was made by Gladstone's son, Herbert. It became known as the 'Hawarden Kite'. Hawarden was the name of Gladstone's home. A 'kite' is a small long-tailed bird of prey or a light frame covered with cloth for flying in the air. It can also mean to start a rumour and see test reactions to it – sometimes referred to as 'seeing which way the wind blows'. It has been suggested that Gladstone was 'kite flying' to see how the rumour of supporting Home Rule would be met both in political circles and in the country.

Activity

Source analysis

Read Source 4.

 What is H. C. G. Matthew's explanation for Gladstone's support for Home Rule?

2 Does this tie in with Gladstone's 'mission to pacify Ireland'? Explain your answer.

3 What conculsions can you draw about Gladstone's commitment to solving the Irish question?

Exploring the detail

In the general election following the defeat of Gladstone's Home Rule Bill, the Conservatives won 316 seats, the Gladstonian Liberals 191 seats, the Liberal Unionists gained 78 seats and the Irish Nationalists 85. Lord Salisbury took office as prime minister of a Conservative government in August 1886.

It is worth noting that, in Ireland, not one Liberal won a seat; there were 16 Ulster Conservatives, who formed the nucleus of the future Irish Unionists. Every Irish Nationalist supported Parnell. Ireland had, in effect, voted for Home Rule.

The election produced an interesting result. Although the Liberals had a majority of 86 over the Conservatives, the Irish Nationalists returned with 86 seats and again held a powerful position between the two main parties. Salisbury continued as prime minister of a minority government until January 1886, when the Conservatives were defeated on a vote on the Queen's speech. Salisbury resigned, but did not call another election. Gladstone formed a new Liberal government.

Prior to these events, in December 1885, Gladstone dropped a bombshell (the 'Hawarden Kite') – it was leaked to the press that he had altered his position on Ireland and now supported Home Rule. It proved to be one of the most momentous political decisions of the 19th century.

Gladstone's apparent sudden change of mind needs an explanation. He believed the government should remain consistent in its Irish policy and the sudden ending of coercion by Salisbury had led to new outbreaks of violence and uncertainty. He was aware there was a feeling among government officials in Dublin that some form of devolved government would bring stability. It is possible that he feared the Conservatives might introduce Home Rule under his nose, if the ambitious, charismatic Randolph Churchill, sympathetic to the Irish, was in the Cabinet. Some historians believe that Gladstone would have preferred that to happen and thus avoid the inevitable split in his own Liberal Party.

> Gladstone was prepared reluctantly, to meet violent disorder in Ireland with coercion, but the more he had to do so, the more he sought a long term political solution which would pacify the Irish, achieve civil order, and restore the norms of liberal civil society. Pacification and the absence of the forces which made coercion necessary were the goals Gladstone sought through the 'trilogy' of social order, a complete land settlement, and Irish autonomy in Irish affairs.

 Matthew, H. C. G. (1995) **Gladstone 1875–1898**, *Allen Lane*

By February 1886, Gladstone was back in office and prime minister for the third time. He almost immediately introduced a Home Rule Bill. Lord Hartington, leader of the Liberal right, declared his unwavering opposition to Home Rule. Gladstone drove forward undeterred, but he did so without first securing the support of Joseph Chamberlain, the heir apparent to Gladstone and the leader of the Radical wing of the Liberals. Gladstone disliked Chamberlain and had failed to take him into his confidence over his Home Rule plans.

The First Home Rule Bill proposed that Ireland should have its own parliament in Dublin, to take charge of all internal affairs. Foreign affairs, defence and external trade would be left under the control of the government at Westminster. There would be no representation of Irish MPs at Westminster. The bill was met with opposition on all sides. The Hartington faction opposed it. Randolph Churchill led the Conservative attack by stirring up divisions between the Protestant Irish in Ulster in the north and the Catholic-dominated south. Chamberlain resigned his post and led a devastating attack on the bill that was defeated 343 votes to 313.

It was a personal blow for Gladstone and split the Liberal Party. The defecting Liberals, led by Chamberlain, called themselves Liberal Unionists and, in future, voted with the Conservatives. It put the Conservative Party in power for 20 years. In Ireland, and in Irish politics, it created the conditions for an increasingly bitter divide between those who wanted independence from Britain and those who wanted to stay in the union.

The growing divide between Nationalism and Unionism in Ireland

Question

What was Parnell's contribution to Irish Nationalism?

Fig. 6 *Map of Ireland showing concentration of Nationalists and Unionists*

The strong position of the Irish Nationalist Party at Westminster, and Gladstone's shift in policy to accepting the desirability of Home Rule, caused consternation among those Irish who wished to preserve the union with Britain. The Unionists were mainly Protestant and centred in the Province of Ulster in the north. There were also Unionist pockets in the south among the old Anglo–Irish aristocratic families, the few wealthy industrialists like the Guinness family and Trinity College academics in Dublin. Although they allied themselves to the northern Unionists, their geographical isolation denied them any political clout.

Ulster had traditionally enjoyed more economic prosperity than the largely poor agricultural south of Ireland, and particularly after the great industries of the industrial revolution – textiles, iron foundries, shipbuilding and engineering – came to Belfast. Their close trading links with the empire gave them a British rather than Irish identity. They feared that Home Rule would overwhelm Ulster's special relationship with Britain and dilute prosperity. As a result, the Unionists hardened their hearts against any compromise over Home Rule and this, in turn, led to a polarisation between Unionists in the north east and Nationalists in the rest of Ireland.

PUNCH, OR THE LONDON CHARIVARI.—September 18, 1886.

A WAITING GAME.

H-rt-ngt-n. "HULLO, RANDOLPH! WHAT'S YOUR LITTLE GAME *NOW?*"
R-nd-lph (*Aside—sotto voce*). "ALL RIGHT! WANT HIM TO SHOW HIS HAND!"

Fig. 7 *Randolph Churchill trying to make Lord Hartington (Liberal Unionist) show his hand after the general election, in August 1886, as the Liberal Unionists held the balance of seats in the Commons*

A closer look

Randolph Churchill and the Ulster Unionists

It had been argued that Lord Randolph Churchill's (now Conservative leader in the Commons) vehement opposition to Home Rule in 1886, fanned the flames of the Nationalist/Unionist division in Ireland. It is fair to point out that the spark of antagonism between the two sides was already there. James I had granted land to Protestants in the north in the early 17th century. In 1690, Protestant William of Orange defeated James II's Catholic army at the Battle of the Boyne in Ireland. The loyalty of the Orangemen in Ulster to the British crown was assured from that day. Churchill maintained that the interests of the Ulster Protestants would be ignored if there was Home Rule, and that Nationalist Catholic interests would be served. On a visit to Belfast, which was more about his personal political ambitions than Irish unity, Churchill encouraged the slogan: 'Ulster will fight and Ulster will be right'. After 1886, the Ulster MPs left the Liberals and joined the Conservatives. In the 1886 general election, the alliance of Liberal and Conservative Unionists won most of the Northern Ireland seats.

Cross-reference

Randolph Churchill is profiled on page 78.

Question

Why was there a growing division between Nationalists and Unionists?

The contrasting attitudes of Disraeli, Gladstone and Salisbury to the Irish question

Fig. 8 *Disraeli, Gladstone and Salisbury on the Irish question*

Disraeli and the Irish question

Disraeli was never very interested in Ireland or Irish politics. He never visited Ireland. As prime minister, he avoided the question as much as he could. He was involved in dealing with the Fenian outrages for a short time in 1868. He strongly opposed Gladstone's disestablishment of the Irish Church, declaring that Gladstone had entered into an unholy alliance with the Pope. Historian T. A. Jenkins is an authority on Disraeli and has made several references to Disraeli's attitude to the Irish question.

In 1874, Disraeli's election address contained a reference to Gladstone's policies in Ireland:

> in which he warned that the existence of the United Kingdom was being jeopardised by the disreputable conduct of the Liberals, who had (allegedly) aligned themselves with the Parnellite Home Rulers. In Disraeli's view, Liberal (flirting) with Irish Nationalism was part of a wider, sinister design to 'enfeeble our colonies by a policy of decomposition'.

> *Jenkins, T. A. (1996) **Disraeli and Victorian Conservatism**,*
> *Palgrave Macmillan*

The address was designed to be alarmist, but reveals Disraeli's concern for empire rather than Ireland. When Disraeli formed his government in 1874, he did not give the Irish Secretary a place in the Cabinet.

In 1880, Disraeli strongly opposed the Liberals' Irish Compensation for Disturbance Bill, which penalised Irish landlords who evicted tenants. Disraeli took the view that Gladstone was trying to 'victimise the landlord class' and that it would set a precedent for English landowners. In this instance, Disraeli appeared more anxious for the longer-term survival of the landed classes rather than the Irish peasants.

Disraeli:

> *had tried to focus public attention on the threat to the United Kingdom from the Home Rule movement at the time of the 1880 General Election. His warning was not heeded then, but the policy of resistance to Irish Nationalism proved to be a potent political issue for the Conservatives within a few years of Disraeli's death.*

> *Jenkins, T. A. (1996)* **Disraeli and Victorian Conservatism***, Palgrave Macmillan*

Gladstone and the Irish question

During his first term of office (1868–74), Gladstone introduced a major legislative programme for Ireland, involving Church, land and education, because he sincerely wished to remove Irish grievances. He believed that all people had the rights to basic freedom and justice. He believed his legislation would rectify religious and economic disadvantage and reduce Protestant Ascendancy, which was the cause of so much bitterness. His Ballot Act of 1872 gave Irish Nationalists a voice in parliament for the first time, and allowed them to become a major political force, although this was probably not his deliberate intention. At that time, he did not see any necessity for introducing Home Rule.

■ **Cross-reference**

Pages 36–42 gives details of Gladstone's Irish policy during his First Ministry.

By the time of his Second Ministry in 1880, Gladstone was forced to be proactive on Ireland, as Nationalism and the activities of the Land League were firmly on the political agenda. This was partly in response to economic hardships in Ireland and continuing grievances, which the economic depression magnified, but partly because Irish demands were changing and becoming more extreme.

The historian H. C. G. Matthew comments that Gladstone was aware of the escalating scale of the problems in Ireland with evictions by the landlords and retaliatory outrages by the tenants against the landlords. However, he 'held out against a "radical" solution' until it became unavoidable and then he acted swiftly and authoritatively to address the issue by passing the 1881 Land Act.

In deciding whether to strengthen tenant rights rather than supporting the more revolutionary option of peasant proprietorship, Gladstone probably based his decision to strengthen tenant rights on his belief in social hierarchy and carrying out measures that would be of least cost to the State.

Gladstone had to introduce tough coercive measures to deal directly with the violence and to try and restore law and order. He was uncomfortable with coercion and sought to balance it with concession and conciliation. When his reasonableness was met with deliberate sabotage and lack of cooperation, e.g. by the Land League and the Nationalists, over applying the 1881 Land Act, Gladstone was shocked and angry and could be tough. When he lost patience with Parnell, he had him arrested and imprisoned in Kilmainham.

By 1885, Gladstone was obliged to reassess his strategy on Ireland when Parnell withdrew Nationalist support from the Liberals.

When Gladstone finally introduced a Home Rule Bill in 1886, it was generally accepted as a genuine conversion and a response to growing pressure in Ireland. Some historians, however, such as D. A. Hamer, have suggested that it was an attempt to reassert Gladstone's control over the Liberal Party. In a sense this worked, as the party split and the Liberal Unionists joined the Conservatives and so Gladstone was able to maintain authority over the majority pro-Home Rule Liberals.

A positive interpretation of Gladstone's reason for accepting the necessity of Home Rule is given by F. L. S. Lyons in Source 5.

> There was a moral imperative involved in this decision [which he arrived at] by asking himself what was the right, ultimately Christian, solution. It was a central tenet of his faith as a Liberal that enlightened self-government was the highest stage of political evolution that man could reach. Holding this view, he had been in the past the champion of Italian and Balkan Nationalism. Was he justified in denying Ireland the right to travel the same road?

5   *Lyons, L. S. (1985)* **Ireland Since the Famine***, Fontana*

Once Gladstone committed to Home Rule, he never wavered, even though it split the party he had built up and sent the Liberals into the political wilderness. Home Rule became his sole ambition and his obsession in what remained of his life.

Salisbury and the Irish question

Salisbury maintained a ruthless attitude to the whole Irish question throughout his long political career. His biographer, Andrew Roberts, comments on Salisbury's views on the Irish question in Source 6.

> Salisbury blamed Britain's ceaseless attempts at political and financial initiatives, which constantly raised Irish expectations and thus helped cause the very problems they were intended to solve.

6   *Roberts, A. (1999)* **Salisbury, Victorian Titan***,*
Weidenfeld & Nicolson

Salisbury referred to the Irish as 'the ignorant peasantry of Ireland' and their 'amiable practice to which they were addicted of shooting people to whom they owe money'. He was in fact referring to the Land War and attacks by tenants on the landlord. He believed the Land League was made up of a group of trouble makers and referred to them as 'malcontents'.

When Salisbury took office in June 1885, with a minority government, he appeared to consider some form of Home Rule for Ireland. However, he was only playing along in order to gain Parnell's support in the coming general election in the hope of achieving a majority.

Roberts explains Salisbury's arguments against Home Rule in Source 7.

> Issues of Ireland's own economic good and of Britain's security should Ireland ally herself with an enemy, were considerations. Salisbury's most fundamental sticking point was a profound disbelief in any long- term safeguards which would protect the (Ulster) Protestants planted in Ireland in the 17th century. He believed the Ulster Protestants would fight a civil war rather than submit to majority Catholic rule from Dublin.

7   *Adapted from Roberts, A. (1999)* **Salisbury, Victorian Titan**, *Weidenfeld & Nicolson*

Salisbury was typical of his generation of Conservative politicians and, like Disraeli, was more concerned with the British Empire and the impact that Home Rule might have on it. It was important to strengthen British control over the vast empire if the country wished to maintain its world power status against growing challenges from America and Germany.

After Salisbury became prime minister again in June 1886, he had no intention of introducing Home Rule and appointed a tough and able Chief Secretary for Ireland, his nephew A. J. Balfour. During his second and third ministries, Salisbury's pragmatism led him to pursue three main policies in Ireland:

1 Firmness.
2 Attacking Parnell's reputation.
3 'Killing Home Rule with kindness'.

Cross-reference

To read about changing government policy towards Ireland under Salisbury, look ahead to page 119.

Activity

Revision exercise

Copy and complete the following table summarising the attitudes of Disraeli, Gladstone and Salisbury to key issues of the Irish question. Bear in mind that Disraeli died in 1881.

	Disraeli	Gladstone	Salisbury
Violence			
Coercion			
Irish peasants			
Land Act 1881			
Nationalism			
Unionism			
Home Rule			

The Great Depression and its impact

The period between 1873 and 1896 is often described as the 'Great Depression'. Agriculture certainly went through the economic doldrums, but the overall state of the economy is seen by some historians and economists as going through a period of 'readjustment' rather than depression. S. B. Saul, as the title of his highly regarded book *The Myth of the Great Depression* (1969) suggests, argues against this. To the Victorians it was a reality. Their confidence was rocked by falling prices, narrowing profit margins and foreign competition in a sphere in which they had been dominant for a century and they feared national decline.

The onset of depression followed a period of outstanding economic growth and prosperity. It is true that the economy was still growing, but at a slower rate. The rate of production in the major industries of coal, cotton and steel was increasing, but more slowly. There was a fall in prices, which meant smaller profit margins for the manufacturers, and workers were laid off more frequently. There were periods of unemployment during these years, but they were not sustained. While the depression in agriculture continued, there was a recovery in industry by 1880, followed by another less-severe slump in the mid-1880s and another in the mid-1890s.

Table 2 *The Rousseaux price index, 1874–86*

Year	Index of total agricultural and industrial products; average of 1885 = 100
1874	121
1875	117
1876	115
1877	110
1878	101
1879	98
1880	102
1881	99
1882	101
1883	101
1884	95
1885	88
1886	83

Adapted from Mitchell, B. R. and Deane, P. (1962) **Abstract of British Historical Statistics**, *Cambridge University Press*

Table 3 *Average wheat prices 1874–86 (per imperial quarter)*

Year	s. d.
1874	55 9
1875	45 2
1876	46 2
1877	56 9
1878	46 5
1879	43 10
1880	44 4
1881	45 4
1882	45 1
1883	41 7
1884	35 8
1885	32 10
1886	31 0

Mitchell, B. R. and Deane, P. (1962) **Abstract of British Historical Statistics**, *Cambridge University Press*

It is generally accepted there was an economic downturn and there are a number of theories as to the causes. Certainly, the fall in prices (which was apparent in 1873 and continued over the next 25 years) appears to mark the start of the depression. The reason for the falling prices is not so clear. Some historians/economists have favoured a single-cause explanation. One of these is that there was a shortage of gold to support currency. There were no new discoveries of gold after the 1850s, until it was found in huge quantities in the South African Transvaal, in the late-1880s. Another reason offered is simply that Britain had come to the end of a long period of economic growth that could no longer be sustained. A combination of these, and the factors outlined below, probably accounts for the economic problems of the period.

Causes of the Great Depression

Overseas competition

Britain was dependent on its export trade to maintain its position of economic supremacy in the world markets, and had enjoyed almost a monopoly of the production and export of coal, iron and steel, the key industrial commodities. For the first time, Britain was experiencing a serious challenge to its position as a result of the rapid industrialisation of America and Germany. America

■ Exploring the detail

The amount of currency (money) in circulation was based on the value of gold held in the Bank of England. This was known as the gold standard. Since the Bank could only issue currency up to the value of the gold in its vaults, when there was less gold, there was less currency in circulation and this caused a slow-down of economic activity and depression.

■ Cross-reference

Overseas challenges are covered in more detail on pages 125–127.

was rich in natural resources and in manpower from European immigration, and raced ahead in economic development. By 1890, it had overtaken Britain in the production of both iron and steel and Germany was not far behind. Britain did stay ahead in the production of coal, but only until 1900.

Tariff barriers

The **tariff barriers** set up by Britain's new competitors to protect their industries, presented another problem for Britain's economy. Germany introduced trade tariffs in 1879 and America followed in 1890, while Britain clung on to its long-held belief in the policy of *laissez-faire*. The Fair Trade League established in 1881, pressed the government for some form of protection against British competitors without success. However, it has been suggested by several historians that, in the 'scramble for Africa' during the 1880s, one of Britain's underlying motives in securing colonial territories was trade protection. Colonial expansion in Africa would give Britain access to a new supply of raw materials and markets for British goods.

Out-dated technology

It could hardly be avoided that other countries would eventually industrialise and challenge Britain's monopoly. As the first industrial nation, Britain had fallen behind the latest technology and its machinery was either old or obsolete. There was a reluctance to invest new capital. This was especially so in the steel industry where the up-to-date British Gilchrist-Thomas method of steel manufacture was adopted by the Germans.

Absence of entrepreneurial drive

There is a view, held by some, known as the Third Generation Syndrome, that the entrepreneurial spirit of earlier industrialists was lost as the management of family firms was handed down to less-capable or less-interested successors. There was little engagement with future development of new industries such as chemicals and electrical engineering or practical knowledge of what changes might be needed to maintain a successful business.

End of railway boom

The boom in railway building had ended by 1875, as most major towns and cities already had good rail links. This reduced the demand for iron and steel and led to job losses.

Average levels of unemployment rose from 1873 until they hit a peak of 11.4 per cent in 1879. They fell away again to 2 per cent during 1882–3, but reached 10 per cent in 1886. This is where the impact of the depression was truly felt. Periods of unemployment were experienced by large numbers of the respectable, hard-working, thrifty, artisan classes who had prospered in the middle years of the 19th century. The support of trade unions and friendly societies was not enough to alleviate their straitened circumstances and there was no State welfare scheme to save them from the worst effects of losing their income and their livelihood. The majority of unemployed unskilled labour had no unions until the late-1880s, and they were forced to rely on the support of family and friends or resort to the workhouse. However, falling prices meant cheaper goods in the shops and a rise in real wages, as long as workers were in a job.

Keith Robbins acknowledges the dilemmas surrounding the reality and myth of the Great Depression (Source 8).

Key terms

Tariff barriers: taxes on the import of goods and materials from another country, which, if they were cheaper than the home product, could inhibit the growth of the home country's manufacturing industry.

Exploring the detail

The succeeding generations of early 19th century entrepreneurs often enjoyed the material benefits of their grandfather's or great grandfather's success. The sons were sent to public schools, where tuition was dominated by the Classics and the ethos was based on aristocratic values of gentlemanly pursuits. Such establishments had no tradition of promoting entrepreneurial skills or preparing pupils for a career in industry.

If we mean by (depression) a failure to sustain previous rates of growth then the description is accurate, but there was no general decline. If unemployment did rise, for those still in work the fall in prices and the growth in real wages produced a continuing sensation of real improvement. [We need to bear in mind] the absence of comprehensive 'unemployment statistics' and the incompleteness of statistical information on production during these decades. However, the appointment of Royal Commissions to consider the agricultural depression and also trade and industry bears witness to contemporary disquiet about the state of the economy.

8   *Robbins, K. (1994) The Eclipse of a Great Power, Modern Britain 1870–1992, Longman*

Question

What conclusion does Keith Robbins draw as to the myth or reality of the Great Depression?

The problems of agriculture and the rural communities

The Golden Age of farming came to an end quite suddenly in the 1870s. At this time, British farmers were producing about 50 per cent of the home consumption of wheat and about 90 per cent of meat. Dairy farmers also supplied the home market with butter, milk and cheese. Farmers had made huge profits, built themselves solid, spacious farmhouses and enjoyed a comfortable lifestyle. Not all areas in Britain had benefited from this prosperity. In the remote north and west of Scotland, farming was under-resourced and ploughing and harvesting was still carried out by hand with the old Scots foot plough (caschrom) and the scythe. But, for most of the country, the accessibility of good, cheap, home-produced food helped to improve general health and raise the standard of living in Britain.

There were several reasons for the depression in agriculture. During the 1870s, there was a run of cool wet summers, with consequently low-yielding harvests. The summer of 1879 was the wettest on record. Crops rotted in the ground, there was a shortage of animal feed, and there were outbreaks of disease among livestock, such as 'foot and mouth' and swine fever. It was difficult enough for farmers to get back on track without such unwelcome disasters. With agricultural immunity already low, recovery was made more difficult with the onset of foreign competition.

Fig. 9 *The development of the steamship enabled large quantities of grain to be transported quickly and cheaply from America to Britain, undercutting British markets*

During the 1870s, the mid-west prairies of North America opened up, with the cultivation of the rich soil for the first time and the production of great quantities of wheat. Railways that had done so much to contribute to British farmers' prosperity earlier in the century, were now assisting the US farmers to transport their wheat thousands of miles to the ports on the eastern seaboard. The irony, of course, was that it was British money and expertise that had developed the rail system in America, and indeed in many countries across the world. The rapid development of steamships meant that the grain could be transported cheaply in huge quantities to Britain and Europe and undercut their markets.

Advances in farm machinery, particularly the combine harvester in America, revolutionised the process of harvesting. It had first been used in 1839, but had to be pulled by a team of horses, was hopelessly inefficient and largely ignored. With the coming of steam (and later mechanisation), this changed and the combine became popular because it carried out the actions of reaping (cutting the crop) and threshing (beating the ears so that the grain separates from the chaff) simultaneously. It was ideal in the vast American wheat lands.

The development of the canning process in the 1880s meant that beef from the large cattle ranches in Argentina and Uruguay could be put into tins to preserve it and export it to Britain. Methods of refrigeration developed at this time – previously perishable goods (mainly lamb) could be transported from as far afield as Australia and New Zealand, and could compete with British goods in terms of price, if not quality!

The decision by Disraeli (1874–80) to continue Gladstone's free trade policy meant there was no tariff protection from foreign competition. It was an indication of the weakening influence of the landed interests in parliament.

The result of these innovations and advances meant fierce competition for the British farmer and prices fell heavily. The price of wheat fell from 55 shillings a quarter in 1874 to 31 shillings in 1885. The hardest hit areas were the wheat and cereal counties of the south and east. Farmers went bankrupt; many out-of-work agricultural labourers deserted the countryside and settled in the towns. Life was not much easier for them there, as the depression in industry made finding regular work difficult. Many workers sought a better life by emigrating to America and Canada. According to the census returns, the number of agricultural workers fell from 1 million in 1871 to 600,000 in 1901.

The pattern of British agriculture changed as a result of the depression. No part of the country was unaffected and British farmers had to diversify in order to survive. Farmers in the south of Scotland, Warwickshire and Lancashire were less badly affected, as these areas already concentrated on mixed farming. In some areas there were successful new developments and in others there was less scope for change. Some farmers were slow to spot the need to change. Many farmers moved into dairy farming as milk could not be easily imported, and yet it could be quickly transported some distance within Britain by rail. Poultry farming became popular. The development of market gardening as an alternative to farming met with great success, especially in areas like the Vale of Evesham and the Thames Valley where fruit, flowers and vegetables grew well. In Britain as a whole, the area under cultivation fell, while the area turned over to pasture increased.

The depression in farming was one cause of the violent unrest in Ireland. Irish farmers, who were mostly tenant farmers, were equally hard hit by the rising wheat prices. It left many of them unable to keep up their rent payments and they were forced out by their landlord. The tradition among Irish labourers to find seasonal work on English and Scottish farms came

Did you know?

Meat canning introduced corned beef to Britain and it became a staple of the British diet by the early 20th century. The best-known brand name was Fray Bentos, the name of the town in Uruguay where it was processed. Corned beef was used for soldiers in both world wars. It remained popular in Britain until the 1980s.

Cross-reference

More on the weakening influence of the landed interests in parliament can be found on page 12 and page 64.

Cross-reference

The effects of the Great Depression in Ireland, including the Irish Land War, are described on pages 84 and 98.

to an end and they swelled the ranks of the poor, hungry, discontented peasants who needed someone or something to blame for their ills.

Historians have identified a decline in the rural way of life that coincided with the agricultural depression, although not all agree that this was the main cause. T. C. Smout argues that it was the lure of urban living, 'as the city rose, the countryside ultimately declined' (*A Century of the Scottish People, 1830–1950*, 1967). Rural living offered fewer economic and employment activities and a less-attractive lifestyle, especially for the younger generation.

The loss of jobs on the land, through mechanisation of agricultural processes and the creation of larger farms from smaller units, added to the fallout from the agricultural downturn and encouraged the exodus to the towns. The effect on rural communities is poignantly expressed by H. C. G. Matthew in Source 9.

Table 4 *UK wheat and flour imports (average per decade)*

Years	Thousand cwt.
1860–9	33,697
1870–9	50,406
1880–9	70,282
1890–9	85,890

Mathias, P. (1990) *The First Industrial Nation*, Routledge

> All this left rural society demoralised and neglected, with the passivity characteristic of communities in decay. Thomas Hardy's novels, whose span of publication (1872–96) covered almost exactly the years of agricultural depression, captured magnificently the uncontrollable and distant forces which seemed to determine the fate of the country communities and their inhabitants. The 'general drama of pain' which (Hardy's) novels depict was the disintegration of a civilisation.

9   *Matthew, H. C. G. (1986) 'The Liberal Age 1851–1914' in **The Oxford Illustrated History of Britain**, Oxford University Press*

THE COTTAGE.

Mr. Punch (to Landlord). "YOUR STABLE ARRANGEMENTS ARE EXCELLENT! SUPPOSE YOU TRY SOMETHING OF THE SORT HERE! EH?"

Fig. 10 *A satirical* Punch *cartoon, in which Mr Punch is urging a country landowner to raise the standard of housing for his labourers at least to that of his horses!*

The movement of so many people to the towns created a kind of nostalgia for the life left behind in the countryside and an idea that rural life was idyllic. The reality was very different. For those who remained, conditions were tough. Standards of housing were generally poor.

Families lived in small two-roomed thatched cottages, with no running water or indoor sanitation. In Scotland, on large farms, a dozen or more unmarried male farm workers would share a 'bothy', where communal living conditions were at their most basic. Improvements came much more slowly than in the towns.

Mine workers formed part of the rural community, as mine workings were situated in the country areas. They lived in rows of single-storey houses, which were sometimes reasonable, but again lacked sanitation and were overcrowded by today's standards.

Agricultural labourers were the lowest paid workers and they worked longer and more irregular hours. Few dared to be members of a union for fear of losing their livelihood and, until 1884, they had no vote and therefore no political voice. There were few public amenities in villages. There was a social backwardness as they remained cut off from many modern developments. Education was often chaotic as many children were kept away from school during busy times in the farming calendar, such as harvest time, as farm work involved the whole family. In most rural areas, however, there still existed close family bonds, a strong sense of community, measured deference to the local landowner, reverence for the Church and respect for each other.

Exploring the detail

The first trade union for farm workers, the Agricultural Labourers' Union, was formed by Joseph Arch in 1872 to seek better pay and working conditions. In Scotland, the Scottish Farm Servants Union was formed, but it made little progress.

Activity

Revision exercise

1. Draw a spider diagram to illustrate the causes of the Great Depression in: (a) industry; and (b) agriculture.

2. Identify the impact of the Great Depression on: (a) workers in urban areas; and (b) farm workers.

3. Explain why there is historical controversy over the existence of a 'great' depression.

Learning outcomes

Through your study of this section you should be aware of the conflicts and difficulties that beset the British governments at home, in Ireland, across the empire and in relations with Britain's European neighbours, and how each government sought to deal with them with varying degrees of success.

You should be able to understand the impact on the pattern of party politics through the revival of the Conservative Party and the split in the Liberal Party over Home Rule for Ireland. You should recognise Joseph Chamberlain's role in this. You should be aware of Gladstone's motives in his Irish policy and the reasons he converted to the idea of Home Rule.

As well as assessing the importance of domestic reforms, you should understand the impact of foreign policy for Britain, especially with regard to the Eastern question. From your study of foreign policy in the 1874–86 era, you will have begun to identify how the seeds of the First World War, which broke out in 1914, were sown.

Finally, you should understand the effects of the Great Depression in industry and agriculture on both the British people and politics.

Practice question

To what extent was British policy in Ireland between 1874 and 1886 an utter failure?

(45 marks)

Study tip To answer this question, you will need to be aware of the different policies applied to Ireland by Gladstone, Disraeli and Salisbury over this period and judge the degree of failure of each of them. You will need to consider the Land War, the 1881 Land Act, the Home Rule movement under Butt and then Parnell, the Kilmainham Treaty and the Phoenix Park murders. You should decide whether the policy of coercion was justified and whether it was an indication of failure or toughness.

Try to reflect on failure and success from different points of view, e.g. Parnell and the Nationalists as opposed to the Unionists, the peasants as opposed to the landlords, and be careful not to judge the past from a present-day standpoint. You should also use the differing viewpoints of historians to support your argument.

Before you start, draw up a plan, so that your answer unfolds in a logical order and carries an argument through to a conclusion. It may be the case that you will wish to argue that policy was a failure, but it is more likely you will wish to qualify this position, and examine the phrasing of 'utter' in the question.

6 Conservative dominance: political developments

Fig. 1 *This cartoon of Gladstone, Lord Hartington and Chamberlain represented the three elements of the Liberal Party in 1886 at the time of the split over Home Rule. Gladstone remained as leader of the party, while Hartington led the Liberal pro-Union right wing and Chamberlain the pro-Union Radical group*

In this chapter you will learn about:

- the extent of the decline of the Liberals and the dominance of the Conservatives between 1886 and 1901

- the development and spread of the Labour movement

- the emergence of the Independent Labour Party

- the significance of the Labour Representation Committee

- the impact of the Home Rule issue

- the changing government policy towards Ireland.

The extent of Liberal decline and Conservative dominance, 1886–1901

Liberal decline

Gladstone, the 'Grand Old Man'

By 1886, Gladstone's powers were diminishing. He had been leader of the Liberal Party for 20 years. He became party leader at the time when the main ideas of 19th century Liberalism, individualism, *laissez-faire*, and free trade appealed to many sectors of society. Between 1868 and 1874, he had presided over one of the great reforming governments of the 19th century. Gladstone's insistence on introducing the Irish Home Rule Bill in 1886 caused a cataclysmic split in the Liberal Party and for the following 20 years they were out of office. Many thought it was time for a change at the top. However, there were more who had a deep and unwavering sense of loyalty to the 'Grand Old Man' and, for that reason, continued their support of Gladstone and, by association, Home Rule. In Source 1, Robert Rhodes James gives an assessment of Gladstone's later years.

Both in Parliament and in the country he was an outstanding and dominating figure, and he enjoyed an immense personal following in the Liberal Party. But it cannot be seriously denied that this amazing longevity and energy were a source of deep misfortune for the party which he had in effect created, and whose character and policies had been so notably shaped by his towering personality, sincerity, political skill and passion. He was thus at one and the same time the Liberals' greatest asset and their most grievous liability.

1   *James, R. R. (1976)* **The British Revolution**, *Hamish Hamilton*

Key chronology

Prime ministers, 1886–1901

1886–92	Lord Salisbury (Second Ministry)
1892–4	Gladstone (Fourth Ministry)
1894–5	Lord Rosebery (Liberal)
1895–1902	Lord Salisbury (Third Ministry)

Gladstone had become convinced that Home Rule would once and for all solve the Irish problem. He appeared to ignore all the danger signs that many Liberals were as set against it as he was for it. More damaging to his reputation was that his obsession with Ireland led to his neglect of any meaningful programme of social reform. This was short-sighted as, by his own hand, Gladstone had extended education (1870) and then the franchise (1884) to the 'masses'. With knowledge and a political voice they would surely look for a party that would represent their interests. It is perhaps not surprising that at the end of the period of Liberal decline and Conservative domination a new political party had emerged, the Labour Party. It would present the most damaging challenge to the revived 20th century Liberal Party, long after Gladstone's death.

Liberal Party split

Gladstone's conversion to Home Rule was a staggering blow to the Liberal Party and one from which it was unable to recover for 20 years. Joseph Chamberlain, the brilliant and talented Radical 'heir apparent', left the Liberal Party over the Home Rule Bill. Lord Hartington, former Secretary for India, and a group of Whigs also voted against Home Rule and split from the Liberal Party. The defecting Liberals called themselves Liberal Unionists, as their objective was to keep Britain's union with Ireland. At first, Chamberlain held himself apart from the Hartington Whigs, intent on seeking his own political advantage. By 1895, all these Liberals, including Chamberlain, were absorbed into the Conservative Party, which became the Conservative and Unionist Party.

The Liberal Party split over the Home Rule issue was the one that 'grabbed the headlines', but there were already other equally fundamental differences brewing within the party. Liberal policies over colonial expansion caused dissent within the party and created a rift between imperialists and anti-imperialists. There were ideological tensions rising between the older *laissez-faire* Liberals and Radical Liberals, like Joseph Chamberlain, who favoured a stronger social reform programme. Before the 1885 election, Chamberlain had put together a programme of radical social reform known as the 'unofficial programme'and, in doing so, had won the votes of the new rural labouring electorate and secured a Liberal election victory. His programme was based on the concept of greater State intervention and included ideas such as free education, graduated income tax, reform of local government and land reform, granting smallholdings to agricultual workers. He feared that his programme would be sidelined with the introduction of Home Rule. Chamberlain believed that Gladstone was out of touch with the electorate and that the time was ripe for a welfare policy to tackle the immense problem of poverty among the unskilled working class.

Cross-reference

Imperialism and the rift between Imperialists and anti-Imperialists is dealt with in detail under Liberal Imperialism on page 124.

Activity

Challenge your thinking

The Conservatives taunted the Liberals that it was impossible to support Home Rule and be an Imperialist. What were the contradictions between supporting Home Rule and being an Imperialist?

The antipathy between Gladstone and Chamberlain, although brought to the surface by the Home Rule issue, was deep seated and as destructive to the Liberal Party as any other issue. Anthony Wood defines this antipathy when he explains that Gladstone 'could not bring himself into close touch with a man, whom he regarded as a cold-blooded careerist'. If Gladstone had overcome his personal prejudices and rewarded Chamberlain with a good Cabinet position and taken him into his confidence over Home Rule, the outcome might have been different. But perhaps Gladstone recognised something of his own character in Chamberlain – formidable intellect, ambitious and fiercely energetic, and 'the most … compulsive figure in British Affairs'.

Gladstone's Fourth Ministry

Fig. 2 *This cartoon depicts the strong opposition led by Lord Salisbury to defeat Gladstone's Home Rule Bill in 1893. Can you explain the symbolism of the Roman soldiers and their battering ram? Notice the anxious figure of Gladstone peering from the castle window*

The Liberal Party narrowly won the 1892 election. Gladstone's government was weak and entirely dependent on which way the Irish Nationalists voted. Once again, Gladstone introduced a Home Rule Bill for Ireland and was defeated. He resigned for the final time in 1894. His successor was Lord Rosebery, keen and clever, but inexperienced in the Commons, and to be Gladstone's successor was an almost impossible task. Rosebery's aristocratic background counted against him at the Radical, Nonconformist end of the party. His attempts to introduce legislation were deliberately thwarted by the House of Lords. Rosebery hoped to have public support over the Lords' undemocratic behaviour, but in the 1895 election the Liberals suffered a crushing defeat. It seems they had little of interest to attract the mass of working-class voters to whom they had given a political voice only 10 years earlier.

Did you know?

When Gladstone took office as prime minister for the fourth and final time in 1892 at 83 years of age, he was the oldest person to do so.

Cross-reference

Sir Henry Campbell-Bannerman's political career is covered in detail in Chapter 8.

Question

Why did the Liberal Party decline after 1886?

In 1898, the Liberals appointed a rather dull and largely unknown party leader, Sir Henry Campbell-Bannerman. It was hoped that the Liberals could set aside their differences, achieve a degree of unity and win a general election. However, Campbell-Bannerman was no match for the accomplished Conservative leader, Lord Salisbury.

Conservative dominance

Fig. 3 *Lord Salisbury addressing the House of Lords. He was the last British prime minister to sit in the Lords*

Conservative election successes

In the election after the defeat of Gladstone's Home Rule Bill in 1886, the Conservatives did not win an overall majority and were dependent on Liberal Unionist support to keep them in power from 1886–92. They retained the support in parliament of most of the 79 Liberal Unionists, although there was no formal alliance (or coalition) between the two parties at this stage. Lord Salisbury became prime minister for the second time and gathered around him an intellectually indifferent Cabinet apart from Randolph Churchill, who became leader in the Commons and Chancellor of the Exchequer. Within a few months, Churchill fell foul of Salisbury and left the government.

The Conservatives remained in office except for a brief interlude during Gladstone's last term of office between 1892 and 1894. In the 1895 election, Salisbury and the Conservatives won an astonishing victory with 341 seats over the Liberals' 177 seats, with additional support from the 70 Liberal Unionists. The 82 Irish Nationalists were ineffective. The alliance between the Conservatives and the Liberal Unionists became more formalised, with the inclusion of Chamberlain in the Cabinet. The Conservatives were in an unassailable position.

Salisbury's domestic policies

The vital character of the 1886 electorate was its increased size and altered composition. There were nearly 3 million new voters, mostly rural workers, agricultural labourers and miners, out of a total of 6 million. They had yet to develop voting habits and party allegiance, but welfare issues were high on their agenda and so it would seem logical that to capture their vote would assure a majority for either political party.

Neither the Liberals nor the Conservatives had much to offer in terms of social reform, except 'unauthorised' schemes from the Radical Chamberlain and the ambitious Churchill. Yet Salisbury's modest domestic programme of his Second Ministry appears to have been sufficient to increase his majority in 1895. This is more surprising given Salisbury's dislike of democracy and disapproval of too much education for the working classes. Andrew Roberts, Salisbury's biographer offers an explanation in Source 2.

> Although Salisbury generally did not like change, and thought it usually for the worse, if established interests were not too badly damaged he was willing to countenance it for specific, verifiable (obvious) public benefit, and also occasionally, of course, for electoral advantage.

2

*Roberts, A. (1999) **Salisbury Victorian Titan**, Weidenfeld & Nicolson*

In spite of this, Salisbury's domestic policies can be viewed in the light of a widening democracy in Britain. Salisbury was shrewd enough to keep the Liberal Unionists on side and it is their influence that can be detected in the beneficial measures passed by Salisbury's government.

A Local Government Act (1888) created county councils and set up the London County Council. This gave the new rural voters a degree of control over local affairs. Reforms in education were introduced. A Board of Education was established. Fees for children attending board schools were abolished in 1892. Responsibility was given to local councils for technical education, an area in which Britain lagged far behind its industrial rival Germany. Government grants were given to universities for the first time.

The Housing of the Working Class Act (1890) allowed local councils to identify uninhabitable dwellings and replace them with council-built houses. A Factory Act (1890) put an end to children under the age of 11 working and set a maximum of 12 hours a day for women workers. The Allotment Act and Smallholdings Act (1892) attempted to set up agricultural labourers with their own plot of land. They achieved little, but indicated government awareness of high rural unemployment. Meanwhile, the Royal Commission on Labour (1892–5) reported that almost 50 per cent of the labouring classes earned about 75 pence a week, while the survivable rate was £1.25. These findings were largely ignored by Salisbury's government.

Reasons for Conservative domination

The Conservative domination of the political scene for so long has some curious aspects and it is difficult to draw a clear conclusion as to why it occurred. Although the Home Rule crisis cost the Liberal Party the election and gave the Conservatives a clear majority, some historians now 'minimise its importance' (according to Blake) and yet it appears to be the starting point for 'Conservative Ascendancy'. The split in the Liberal Party was shattering and appeared to be the direct result of Gladstone insisting on introducing Home Rule against the wishes of about one-third of his existing parliamentary party. The resulting defection of the Liberal Unionists undoubtedly strengthened the Conservative position in parliament and left the Liberals considerably weakened.

Another factor seems to have been at work to strengthen the Conservatives. The middle-class vote had been moving gradually to the Conservatives, seen as the party that 'resisted' too much change. In 1865, no Conservative was returned for London borough. In 1900, 67 out of 75 London seats were scooped by the Tories. These were known as the 'Villa Tories' because their substantial dwellings created the smart suburbs of Britain's towns. There is a view that Salisbury's shrewd move to

---

■ Did you know?

The London County Council was the forerunner of the Greater London Council (GLC), which was set up in 1965. In 1986, Most of the powers of the GLC were devolved to the London boroughs. In 1997, the Blair Labour government was committed to bringing back London-wide government. In 1999, a referendum approved by two to one the establishment of a new London authority and elected mayor. The new Greater London Authority (GLA) was established in 2000.

■ Key chronology

Social reforms of Salisbury's Second Ministry, 1886–92

1888 Local Government Act

1889 Technical Instruction Act

1890 Housing of the Working Class Act
    Public Health Act
    Factory and Workshops Act
    Shop Hours Act

1892 Free Elementary Education
    Smallholdings Act

negotiate a Redistribution Bill as the price for the Lords allowing through Gladstone's 1884 Franchise Act, increased the number of 'Villa Tories'.

> Thus the Tories were able to use a Liberal reform to create a political structure of single-member, middle-class urban and suburban constituencies on which the basis of their subsequent political success has consistently rested.

*Matthew, H. C. G. (1986) 'The Liberal Age 1851–1914' in **Oxford Illustrated History of Britain**, Oxford University Press*

The position of the two parties on Imperialism worked in the Conservatives' favour. While the Liberals had no consensus, the Conservatives trumpeted the 'Age of Imperialism'. The popular sentiment and enthusiasm for Imperialism and pride in nation helped to sustain the Conservative vote.

The Conservative Party organisation came under the control of Richard Middleton, an ex-naval officer, who was the Conservative national agent and secretary of the National Union from 1885 to 1903. These dates coincide well with Conservative success at the polls. Middleton was sensitive to the slightest changes in political mood and climate and his advice, especially on timing of elections, was of great value to Salisbury. He increased the number of constituency agents and organised them on a regional basis. He revamped the National Union and promoted the activities of the Primrose League.

Overall, the legislative record of Salisbury's second government was more sympathetic to the needs of ordinary people than expected, although it ignored the growing gap between the wealth of the middle and upper classes and the poverty of many working families. The spread of Trade Unionism among the unskilled workforce and the appearance of **Socialism** led to mass meetings and demonstrations and there were protests against Balfour's Irish policy. The government's reaction was always swift, as in the Trafalgar Square incident, and any incitement to violence was prosecuted. But this firm approach did not damage their electoral appeal.

Salisbury's Third Ministry, in 1895, had the advantage of a talented front bench, and yet it produced little constructive legislation. An Agricultural Ratings Act and a Diseases of Animals Act were passed off as measures to help farmers, as agriculture was still in the doldrums. Chamberlain pushed through a Workmen's Compensation Act (1897) but failed to interest the Conservatives in the idea of old-age pensions. In spite of their 'legislative paralysis', the Conservatives won the election in 1900 with another huge majority, possibly on a wave of patriotism over success in the Boer War. It was nicknamed the 'Khaki Election'. In 1902, Salisbury gave up office through ill-health and not defeat at the hands of the electorate.

Randolph Churchill had advocated 'Tory democracy' as a means of capturing the vote of the enlarged electorate after the 1884 Reform Act. He had proposed a raft of reforms in public health, housing, introduction of National Insurance, public amenities, etc. His sudden departure from government, in 1886, could have jeopardised the Conservatives' electoral chances. This was not the case. There were reforms and, whilst these were not enough to satisfy the demands of Socialism, the package was better than any on offer from a discordant and directionless Liberal Party. To some, the Liberal Party had become a one-issue party with little appeal

Activity

Research task

Find out what you can about the Primrose League – its origins and purpose. To what extent did it have an impact on Conservative electoral success during this period?

Key terms

Socialism: 'a system under which the wealth of a country and the means of production are owned and managed by the state'. Socialism is the opposite to the Victorian ideal of *laissez-faire*, in which the State leaves the people as free as possible to manage their own affairs. The idea of Socialism is that the State controls the nation's affairs, to make sure that everyone has a share of the good things in life, to try and achieve equality for all.

Exploring the detail

Bloody Sunday, 13 November 1887

A large socialist gathering in Trafalgar Square in London got out of hand when demonstrators fought with police. Troops were brought in and, although they did not fire on the crowd, two people were killed and many injured.

Did you know?

The term 'Khaki' is used to describe an election that takes place immediately after a war and the results are affected by wartime attitudes. The Boer War was the first in which British soldiers wore a khaki (dust-coloured) uniform.

Activity

Challenge your thinking

What did the Conservative and Liberal parties stand for? How much appeal do you think they had to the working-class voters?

As you read the following section, think about the threat posed by the development of the Labour movement to both the Conservative and Liberal parties.

Key chronology

1874 Trade unionists, Thomas Burt and Alexander McDonald, are the first working-class men elected to parliament.

1881 Social Democratic Federation formed.

1884 Fabian Society set up by Sidney and Beatrice Webb.

1892 Keir Hardie and John Burns become first Independent Labour MPs.

1893 Independent Labour Party formed through efforts of Keir Hardie.

1900 Setting up of the Labour Representation Committee.

to either working or middle-class voters, and this sufficed to keep the Conservatives in office for almost two decades.

The development and spread of the Labour movement

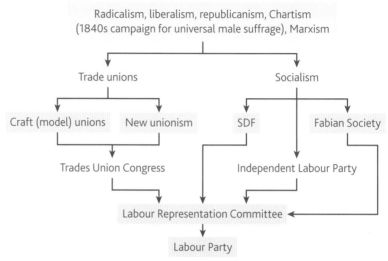

Fig. 4 *Diagram showing the key elements in the development and spread of the Labour movement*

In the latter half of the 19th century, the Labour movement gained in strength. The movement grew firstly out of the enormous political, social and economic changes of the period and, secondly, from the development of Trade Unionism. It signified the struggle of working people to achieve a common objective of creating a fairer, more just and more equal society. The process of industrialisation, especially the factory system, brought many working men and women together for the first time. The factory floor was where opinions were exchanged and discussions took place on unacceptable working conditions, long hours and poor financial reward for the workforce, when set against the huge profits that the factory owner was making. The working classes realised they could start to change and improve their conditions if they were well organised enough to negotiate with their employers. It was from the factory floor that working-class organisations started to emerge, particularly in the form of trade unions.

Political reform and the Labour movement

The extension of the franchise to include the working classes became one of the main focuses of the trade union movement during the 1860s and 1870s. Trade union political activists helped to set up the Reform League in 1865 to put pressure on the government for franchise reform, while the Junta, formed from the London Council and who had influence over the unionist movement as a whole, continued to lobby members of parliament directly. The granting of the vote in the second Reform Act of 1867 to working-class men, albeit a small select group of artisans and members of the craft unions, was a crucial step towards the Labour movement attaining some political influence. In 1867, far-sighted politicians, such as Robert Lowe, predicted the day when the elite members of the working class, newly educated, prosperous and enfranchised, would seek to form their own party.

In the election that followed the 1867 Reform Act, there were no still no working-class candidates, in spite of the fact that there was no longer a property qualification for MPs. This, in theory, should have made it easier for working-class candidates to stand for parliament, but it was still completely impossible in terms of both time and money. The Ballot Act in 1872 had increased working-class voters' confidence, as they were no longer subject to pressure or intimidation at election time and could vote freely for their candidate.

It was the extension of the franchise, in the 1884 Reform Act, to unskilled labourers that really strengthened the political status of the working classes. After this, it became more important for the Conservative and Liberal parties to go out and seek supporters. They could no longer afford to displease the large working-class electorate with hostile trade union legislation or ignore their social needs. By the late-1880s, political reform was stimulating the development of a Labour movement increasingly motivated to form a political party for the working class.

Contribution of the New Unions and the spread of the Labour movement

The reputation of the old craft unions had been raised by their preference to bargain and not strike. They had established a policy of mutual cooperation between the different unions and they had gained considerable political influence. But rather than attempt to form a separate political party for working men, they continued to support the established politics of *laissez-faire* and self-help. The Craft Unions had little sympathy with the mass of poorly paid, poorly housed, unskilled working people, whose struggle to survive increased during the 1880s and 1890s with fluctuations in trade and periods of high unemployment.

At this time, unions emerged representing the large unskilled and low-paid worker force. They distinguished themselves from the older unions, as membership was not dependent on belonging to a particular trade. They became known as New Unions. It began to make more sense for the New Unions to use their funds to help Labour candidates win a seat in parliament. This encouraged the leaders of the unskilled unions to cooperate in the formation of a working-class political party.

The spread of socialist thinking and ideas

The spread of socialist thinking and ideas, during the later years of the 19th century, led to the formation of several socialist societies in Britain. They were formed by middle-class intellectuals, rather than working-class people. They referred to themselves as socialists. One of the most influential of these societies was the Fabian Society set up by Sidney and Beatrice Webb in 1884. Their prolific socialist writings were designed to persuade the government to introduce social reform. They believed Socialism would come about gradually and not through revolution.

The Webbs were part of the socialist movement that recognised a certain kinship between Socialism and Liberalism, along with Labour leaders such as Keir Hardie and Ramsay MacDonald and (New) Liberals such as Charles Trevelyan. There was a sense that Socialism was the evolutionary next step on from a Liberalism that had performed its historic mission of extending political freedom.

Exploring the detail

Lib-Labs

In the 1874 election, two miners' leaders, Thomas Burt and Alexander MacDonald, became the first working-class MPs. They were known as Lib-Labs. They stood in working-class areas and were not opposed by Liberal candidates by agreement, and so cannot be classed as Independent Labour representatives. They were generally members of the craft unions. They believed in self-help and *laissez-faire* and were not particularly concerned with issues of poverty and social reform. They voted with the Liberals in parliament. Their numbers grew slowly until the early 1900s, but they made no real impact on the Labour movement.

Cross-reference

For a detailed account of the growth of the New Unions, see page 132.

Fig. 5 *This 1886 Punch cartoon depicts the fear of the establishment that Socialism was spreading among the British labour force*

Key terms

Marxism: the theories of Karl Marx (1818–83), the German philosopher, were concerned with the conflict between capital and labour. He put forward ideas that encouraged others to believe in the destruction of Capitalism in order to establish a classless society.

Did you know?
The Fabian Society

The Fabian Society, which still exists today, took its name from a Roman general Fabius, who achieved victory in war by slowly wearing down his enemy, rather than engaging in a pitched battle.

Cross-reference

For details of the formation and importance of the Labour Representation Committee, see page 114.

The writings of the German philosopher Karl Marx, for example the *Communist Manifesto* (1847) and *Das Kapital* (1867), which expounded the evils of Capitalism and the value of a classless society, interested British socialists, like Henry Hyndman, but **Marxism** was never very influential. The Social Democratic Federation (SDF) formed by Hyndman, and the Socialist League started up by the poet and artist William Morris, were more extreme but their membership was always small.

British socialists did not wish to bring about change by violent revolution. They preferred to work on the theory that if they made socialist ideas respectable, then the public would come to accept them. They wanted to create a separate socialist party that could come to power legitimately through the ballot box.

The socialist societies gave Labour some of their basic beliefs when they argued in favour of public ownership of institutions such as industry and transport. They were also important in encouraging working-class education. The rising influence of Socialism was an important stage in the development of the Labour movement. Socialists held open-air meetings, or stood and preached outside the factory gates to spread the message that the workers were entitled to a better life. They started to organise the unskilled workers to strike for better conditions. They ultimately had limited influence on the Labour movement and the formation of the Labour Representation Committee in 1900.

The needs of the working classes

Neither the Liberal Party nor the Conservative Party satisfied the needs of the recently enfranchised working classes. Gladstone believed in reforms to a limited extent, but he was too preoccupied with Ireland and did not agree with the State making provisions for the poor. Gladstone still held to the principles of *laissez-faire*, self-help and philanthropy and had refused to accept Chamberlain's plan to tackle social problems in the 1880s. Salisbury had little direct interest in social reform and was too interested in foreign affairs. The growing problems of poverty, caused by unemployment, ill-health and poor housing were largely neglected. Historian K. Laybourn is of the opinion that the Liberal Party was complacent about any serious threat from the Labour movement and that the formation of a Labour Party took them by surprise.

The emergence of the Independent Labour Party

Even as late as 1890 the Labour movement was a weak vehicle for the political aspirations of the working class. Trade Unionism was patchy and Trade Councils were only just beginning to emerge in many areas. In truth, the Liberal Party had little to worry about and was confident in its estimation that at least two-thirds of the working-class voters would continue to vote Liberal in the future. It was the almost endemic weakness of organised labour which deluded the Liberal Party into thinking that it could stand still in the face of the 'little breezes' of discontent that occasionally emerged. What the national Liberal Party had failed to appreciate was the seething discontent which had erupted among trade unionists from the late-1880s onwards. This neglect combined with working-class anger and frustration to produce an Independent Labour movement.

4   *Laybourn, K. (1988) **The Rise of Labour, the British Labour Party 1890–1979**, Edward Arnold*

The Independent Labour Party (ILP) first emerged in Bradford in January 1893. Keir Hardie, a Scottish miners' union organiser, was its chief instigator. His early political ambitions had been thwarted. In 1888, he failed to secure support from the mid-Lanark Liberal Association to stand as a Lib-Lab candidate. Undeterred, he stood as the first Scottish Labour candidate, but failed to win the seat. As a result of this experience, he founded the Scottish Labour Party. This spurred on other working men (usually union leaders) to form local Labour groups across the country – mostly in the north of England, the Midlands and central Scotland. In 1892, Hardie and John Burns, the Dockers' leader, became the first Independent Labour MPs, gaining seats in two by-elections.

In 1893 Hardie helped to form a new socialist group, the ILP. At the opening conference, Hardie was elected chairman and leader. He was determined the ILP would stand on its own and not be treated as the 'poor relation' of the Liberal Party and be used to keep the Liberal Party in office. The ILP stood for practical reforms that would benefit working people. It demanded the end of child labour, an eight-hour working day, a national scheme of unemployment and sickness insurance and a tax on unearned income.

In the 1895 general election, not one of the 28 ILP candidates won a seat; this included Hardie and Burns. It was a major set-back for the ILP, but, against the odds, Hardie continued to attempt to broaden the appeal of the ILP by cooperating with the trade unions, recruiting new members and promoting women's movements. The Conservatives returned to office with a huge majority. It seemed they had no need to show interest in social reform or labour politics.

Keir Hardie's vision was to extend the political influence of Labour. As a union delegate, he sought endorsement of the ILP from the TUC, at their Annual Conference. The TUC was still dominated by the craft unions, whose members clung on to the self-help ethic and regarded the socialist ILP with suspicion and so refused endorsement for several years running. The future of the ILP looked unpromising. It was small, under-funded and lacked essential union support.

Cross-reference

For more on John Burns, look ahead to pages 135–6.

Key profile

James Keir Hardie

Keir Hardie (1856–1915) was born in Scotland, the illegitimate child of a domestic servant. He received no schooling and was working in a coal mine at the age of 11 years. He taught himself to read and write by attending night school. He set up a union at his colliery, but was sacked after leading a strike. In 1886, Hardie became the secretary of the Scottish Miners Federation. He edited a paper, *The Miner*, and used it to give the miners an understanding of politics. He abandoned Liberalism when he realised there was no offer of social reform in exchange for working-class support. He became a socialist. When Hardie took his seat in parliament as an Independent Labour MP, he broke convention by turning up dressed in tweeds, rather than formal morning dress. He was a founder member of the Independent Labour Party in 1893. He played a part in the setting up of the Labour Representation Committee, which became the modern Labour Party. In 1900, Hardie became MP for Merthyr Tydfill and Aberdare, representing Labour.

Fig. 6 *Keir Hardie*

The Labour Representation Committee

By 1899, there were changes in the trade union movement as it became increasingly dominated by the big new mass unions, whose main aim was to improve the conditions of the workers. These unions, most of whose members were low-paid unskilled workers, had become well organised with a network of branches and their numbers grew rapidly, helped by a low subscription rate of 1d a year. The expanding membership kept the funds in a healthy state.

At the same time, the craft unions, which had always dominated the trade union movement, watched the growth of the new mass unions with anxiety, realising that they could lose control of the TUC. Even their members were affected by the bouts of unemployment, which came during the slumps of the 1880s and 1890s, and they began to fear for their own job security. They decided to adapt to meet the changed circumstances. They allowed the recruitment of unskilled members at a lower subscription and they were prepared to be more militant. They were also starting to come around to socialist ideas and recognise the need for the government to put in place a plan for social reform. They appeared to acknowledge that the self-help philosophy was not practical in times of depression and it weakened their faith in *laissez-faire*.

For a long time, Keir Hardie had believed that the various trade unions and the different socialist groups should join forces and form one large political party. In spite of the changes in the trade union movement, there was still opposition among the old craft union leaders to the idea of a separate working-class party. In 1899, the Annual Conference of the TUC voted by a slim majority to hold a conference of labour groups and societies and union representatives to discuss how to increase parliamentary representation. Negotiations began immediately and the following year a meeting took place in London that resulted in the formation of the Labour Representation Committee (LRC), a political organisation whose purpose was to represent working-class interests in parliament.

In February 1900, the LRC was formed from union representatives; the ILP; local Labour parties; the cooperative society and members of the socialist societies such as the Fabians, the Socialist League and the SDF. Ramsay MacDonald was appointed its first secretary.

Several craft unions refused their support. They were still not convinced by the socialist arguments. This left the LRC short of much-needed funds, and the additional organisational skills and leadership talents of the influential craft unions. The Taff Vale Judgement of 1901 and the Conservative government's refusal to introduce legislation to protect the unions finally convinced the craft unions that they needed a working-class party in parliament to protect their interests, and they finally joined the LRC. The LRC was renamed the Labour Party in 1905.

■ The impact of the Home Rule issue and changing government policy towards Ireland

When Charles Parnell emerged from Kilmainham gaol in 1882, he turned his attention directly to a campaign to fight for Ireland's right for some measure of political independence. The Home Rule movement, led by Parnell and operating against a background of severe economic depression, was a powerful political force that had dramatic and far-reaching repercussions on a variety of aspects of British and Irish political, social and cultural life.

■ Exploring the detail

The Taff Vale case

In 1900, an unofficial strike of railway workers on the Taff Vale Railway in South Wales received the backing of the Amalgamated Society of Railway Servants. The strike left the Taff Vale Railway Company out of pocket and they sued the union for £23,000 damages and won the case. The implication was that unions were liable for damages to employers, and so in future would be afraid to strike to improve conditions or wages. Also, the financial penalties could break the union. The immediate result was that the union saw the necessity of Labour representation in parliament to protect the legal rights of trade unions. This strengthened the LRC.

■ Question

Why did the Taff Vale case increase the craft unions' interest in the LRC? How important was this to the LRC?

■ Cross-reference

To recap on the Home Rule issue, and the role of Charles Parnell, revise Chapters 2 and 5.

The new Irish National Party, led since 1880 by Charles Parnell, quickly gained the majority of Irish seats that had previously been held by Liberals or Conservatives and created a third party in parliament. An examination of the election results of this period easily demonstrates the disproportionately powerful position held by Parnell and the Nationalists. At crucial moments, Parnell was able to make or break governments. This created a short period of political instability with long-term effects. In 1885, both Liberal and Conservative parties were dealing with radical challenges from within the party ranks – Joseph Chamberlain's 'unauthorised programme' of social reform in the Liberal Party and Lord Randolph Churchill's 'Tory democracy', his version of Disraeli's ideas on social reform. In Source 5, historian Anthony Wood indicates the subtle but powerful impact of the Home Rule issue on British politics between 1885 and 1886.

> It was the Irish Home Rule question that played the dominating part in the very complicated negotiations which ensued during the next twelve months. To the official leaders (Gladstone and Salisbury) it was becoming clear that some new policy was required that would restore unity and perhaps steal the thunder of these break-away groups (led by Chamberlain and Churchill). The Irish vote was an obvious prize, and Parnell only had to remain in touch with both sides, watching eagerly for the highest bidder.

5   *Wood, A. (1969) **Nineteenth Century Britain**, Longman*

Parnell's irritation with Gladstone's lack of movement on the Home Rule issue had led to the Irish National Party voting with the Conservatives to bring an end to Gladstone's Second Ministry in 1885. When Parnell realised that Salisbury would not go as far as Home Rule, he switched allegiance back to Gladstone. The Liberals won the 1886 election, but could be held to ransom by the Irish Nationalists who held the balance of power in parliament. On each of the two occasions the Home Rule Bill was defeated, in 1886 and in 1893, Gladstone had no option but to resign. Home Rule was dictating the frequency and outcome of elections and potentially the stability of parliament.

Home Rule dominated the career of one of the 19th century political giants, William Gladstone. Once Gladstone had committed to Home Rule it became an accepted part of the Liberal creed and when the Irish Nationalists once more held the balance of power in the Commons, as they did more than two decades later, in 1910, the Liberal prime minister, Asquith, dutifully introduced another Home Rule Bill. It is difficult to understand how a man of such prodigious talent as Gladstone allowed the Irish question to overwhelm the majority of his time as prime minister. But for Gladstone 'if an action seemed right and necessary, he would perform it, even though he might break his party, as he did over Home Rule' (A. Wood, *Nineteenth Century Britain*, 1969).

As a result of the Home Rule issue, the Liberal Party failed to focus on the serious problems of poverty that were causing real distress among many ordinary families. This damaged the Liberals' reputation among working-class people, who began to look towards the emerging Labour Party to cater for their needs.

Gladstone's insistence on pushing ahead with the Home Rule Bill in 1886 caused a deep and long-lasting split in the Liberal Party, which allowed an Imperialist Conservative government to dominate British politics for two decades. The Liberal Party lost one of its most gifted politicians, Joseph Chamberlain. The group of Liberals that followed

Cross-reference

A full discussion on Irish Nationalism in the early 20th century is provided on page 168.

Chamberlain called themselves Liberal Unionists, as their objective was to keep Britain's union with Ireland. They were eventually absorbed into the Conservative Party, which became the Conservative and Unionist Party. Some historians believe the Liberal Party was irrevocably damaged by the split and that this contributed to the rise of the Labour Party.

When Gladstone returned to power in 1892, Home Rule was still at the top of his agenda. His majority was so small against the Conservatives that he was entirely dependent on the Irish Nationalist support, again. His bill proposed an Irish parliament at Dublin as before, but this time provided for 80 Irish MPs to sit at Westminster. The question of Ulster was again ignored. The bill aroused fierce debate in the Commons for weeks on end. It eventually passed the Commons, but was thrown out by the Lords.

The defeat of Gladstone's 1893 Home Rule Bill raised the question of the constitutional position of the House of Lords and its ability to veto reforms passed by the Commons. The impact of the Home Rule issue could have been more severe at this point. Gladstone wanted to dissolve parliament and call an election on the question of the revision of the powers of the House of Lords, but he was overruled by his Cabinet. The House of Lords' hereditary composition made it almost a second chamber for the Conservative Party. It laid down a marker for the successful Liberal challenge to the House of Lords in 1910, and a fundamental change in the constitution, which brought Britain a step closer to democracy.

The Home Rule issue created a deep animosity between Nationalists in the south and the Unionists in the north. This 'bitter polarisation' on the question of Home Rule culminated in an armed uprising in 1916 and ultimately the permanent division of Ireland into Ulster and the Irish Free State in 1922.

The Home Rule issue also brought religious tensions to the surface. For the Ulster Protestants Home Rule meant Roman Catholic rule from Dublin. The religious hatred between the two sides in some parts of Ireland intensified and left a terrible legacy for the future.

The campaign for Home Rule was severely disrupted in 1890 when Parnell became involved in a divorce scandal. It rocked his party to its foundations and, although the majority thought he should resign, he clung to power, but died suddenly the following year, leaving his Irish Nationalist Party broken and divided.

There was sustained support for Home Rule from the Irish Nationalists throughout the period 1880–1901, regardless of Salisbury's 'killing Home Rule with kindness' policy and Parnell's disgrace. In many ways it epitomised the struggle for Irish identity against the authority of the British government, which had existed since the Act of Union in 1800. Parnell acknowledged its significance in a speech to an Irish gathering when he was at the height of his powers (Source 6).

Cross-reference

The events of 1910 are discussed on page 155.

> No man has the right to set a boundary to the onward march of a nation. No man has the right to say 'Thus far shalt thou go and no further'.

> **6**   *Extract from speech given by Charles Parnell in Cork.*
> *The Times, 22 January 1885*

It was inevitable that the impact of the Home Rule issue would reverberate for years to come.

The aftermath of the Home Rule defeat

Violence was never far away with Ireland. Charles Parnell had suffered disappointment over the defeat of the Home Rule Bill in 1886, but when he put forward proposals to parliament to ease the distress of the Irish tenants, who were suffering from the continued effects of the agricultural depression, he was rebuffed by Salisbury. In Ireland, a 'plan of campaign' was seized on by two Nationalist MPs, John Dillon and William O'Brien. All the tenants of one landlord would act together to refuse to pay the high rents demanded and give support to anyone who was evicted as a result. It was almost a rerun of the Land Wars.

Salisbury and Ireland

Salisbury entered office in June 1886, determined to give Ireland 'resolute government' and limit the power and influence of Parnell. Gladstone had dealt with Ireland with coercion and conciliation hand-in-hand. Salisbury thought the government had become too soft on Ireland and he adopted a hard-line policy from the start, by planning to use tough action to deal with the perpetrators of the violence and unrest. Only then would it be appropriate to address Irish grievances.

He appointed his nephew, Arthur Balfour, as Secretary for Ireland in 1887. Balfour was keen to prove himself, to deflect the criticism of **nepotism**. He first introduced a generous Land Act (July 1887) to demonstrate to the Irish tenants the government's desire to address their main grievance. It improved on Gladstone's Act and allowed for further rent review. Balfour's next move was to outlaw the plan of campaign and follow this up with a new Crimes Act, which gave police and magistrates special powers to deal with trouble makers. When violence escalated with a riot at Michelstown in September 1887, the police shot and killed three of the demonstrators. Balfour was unmoved and earned the nickname 'Bloody Balfour'.

> **Cross-reference**
>
> The Land Wars are described on page 86.

> **Key terms**
>
> **Nepotism:** showing favour to one's relatives or close friends.

◼ Key profile

Arthur James Balfour

Balfour (1848–1930) was born into an Anglo–Scottish aristocratic family. His mother was Lord Salisbury's sister. Balfour's father died when he was eight and Salisbury took a keen interest in his young nephew's political career. He was given a post in Salisbury's Cabinet in 1887 and, as Chief Secretary for Ireland, was given the nickname 'Bloody Balfour' for his tough policies. He was leader of the Commons and, uniquely, first lord of the treasury, though not prime minister, 1895–1902, while Salisbury was prime minister and foreign secretary in the Lords. This meant one family had unprecedented influence over the government for 20 years. As prime minister 1902–5, Balfour ran into trouble over tariff reform, which helped bring down his government. From 1906 to 1911, he led the Conservative Party in opposition, but took less interest in politics until he reignited his career in 1916 as foreign secretary in the wartime coalition and held a Cabinet post between 1925 and 1929. He died a year later. Balfour was a great intellectual and philosopher, with a keen interest in the relationship between science and religion, which was hotly debated during that era.

Fig. 7 *A. J. Balfour, from a photograph published c.1890*

Balfour never flinched from carrying out the tough measures he had introduced. There was shock at the imprisonment of a well-known Irish poet, Wilfrid Blunt, for flouting the new law. Balfour's stock rose.

Did you know?

The phrase 'Bob's your uncle' is believed to have originated from Lord Salisbury's frequent appointment of his relatively inexperienced nephew A. J. Balfour to high office, culminating in Balfour taking over as prime minister from his uncle in 1902. Lord Salisbury's first name was 'Robert'!

Exploring the detail

Crimes Act, 1887

- Boycotting, intimidation and resisting eviction were illegal.
- Incitement to commit an act was illegal.
- Examinations by magistrates could be made in private under oath.
- Trial could be held away from area where acts were committed.
- Any organisation could be made illegal with immediate effect.
- Punishment was six months' hard labour with right to appeal.

Cross-reference

The Phoenix Park murders are outlined on page 89.

Activity

Thinking point

Parnell was named as the correspondent in Captain O'Shea's divorce. This was a legal way of saying Parnell had an affair with Kitty O'Shea.

When a story about a politician's private life breaks in the media today, how does the public react? Should someone lose their job over a revelation in a newspaper about their private life? Can you find any recent examples to compare with Parnell's case?

The levels of violence subsided and rents were paid. In 1890, Balfour relaxed the Crimes Act and tried to inject a rescue plan to deal with distress and unemployment by introducing Public Works. A Congested Districts Board was set up that gave grants for industrial development in overpopulated western areas. Light railways were constructed opening up remote parts of the country. Balfour rewarded the Irish peasantry with further financial assistance for the voluntary land purchase scheme. In 1891, £33m was set aside to guarantee tenants' loans for buying land. By the 1890s, prices were rising again and, with lower rents and more peasant proprietors, conditions were improving in rural Ireland. Andrew Roberts draws the following conclusion on this period in Ireland's history: 'For all Gladstone's boasts of his mission to pacify Ireland, it was Balfour and Salisbury who actually achieved it, at least in the medium term.'

A closer look

Charles Parnell: triumph and tragedy

It is suggested that part of Salisbury's Irish policy was to discredit Parnell, leader of the Irish Nationalists at Westminster. In May 1887, *The Times* made reference in several articles to Parnell's involvement in inciting violence in Ireland. This culminated in *The Times* printing a forged letter supposedly written by Parnell, implicating him in the Phoenix Park murders. Parnell vigorously denied the accusation, but it was not until early in 1890 that a special commission investigated the case and the forger was uncovered. Parnell was cleared.

Parnell's time of triumph was short lived. A few months later he was named in Captain O'Shea's divorce from his wife Kitty. Parnell and Kitty had lived together, discreetly, for several years and had children together. It was inconceivable that O'Shea was unaware of the relationship and, in any case, the O'Sheas had lived apart before Parnell and Kitty met. O'Shea's motive appears to have been to get a share of his wife's fortune. The public knew nothing of Parnell's private life. When the news broke, the Victorians, with their high moral attitudes, were scandalised. Parnell was ruined. His health was broken and he died in October 1891.

The Home Rule campaign was seriously jeopardised by the scandal over Parnell's involvement in the O'Shea divorce case. The case upset the Catholic Church and weakened its support for Home Rule. Gladstone refused to work with the Irish Nationalists as long as Parnell stayed on as leader. The Irish Nationalist Party was split throughout the 1890s, between the Parnellites and the majority who followed a new leader, Justin McCarthy.

Summary questions

1. What factors led to the Conservative domination of government from 1886 to 1901?
2. Why did the Labour movement develop in the late-19th century?
3. How successful was Salisbury in dealing with Ireland?

7 | Imperialism, the economy and the unions

■ Key terms

Splendid isolation: the term used most often by historians to describe Britain's position in relation to other nations in the late-19th century. It refers to Britain's reluctance to become involved in the complex system of European alliances, which other countries formed to safeguard their own interests and security. In a way, the term is a compliment, as Britain was perceived as being strong enough not to need friends. Lord Salisbury is the politician most closely associated with conducting an isolationist policy, between 1885 and 1902, though this view is now challenged.

Imperialism: when a State adopts a policy of extending power and dominion over another country or region, usually by territorial acquisition or by taking political or economic control. Because it always involves the use of power, whether military force or some subtler form, Imperialism has often been considered morally reprehensible. The term is frequently used in international propaganda to denounce and discredit an opponent's foreign policy.

Fig. 1 *Map showing the extent of the British Empire in 1886, immediately prior to the 'Scramble for Africa'. How much of the symbolism and the figures depicted around the map can you relate to Britain and empire possessions?*

■ The issues surrounding Britain's Imperial position and 'splendid isolation'

Britain's Imperial possessions

■ Key chronology

Foreign affairs, 1886–91

1885	The Berlin Conference
1887	Britain signs Mediterranean Treaty with Italy
1895	Opening of the Kiel Canal in Germany
1895 December	Jameson Raid
1896	Kruger Telegram
1897	Chamberlain's Colonial Conference held in London
1898	British conquest of the Sudan
	Kaiser approves German Navy Laws to build up German navy
1899	Start of the Boer War

The late-19th century is often seen as the age of **Imperialism**. Britain ruled over the largest empire in the world. Britain possessed India and South Africa and had extended its claim over the whole of Australia by 1830 and New Zealand by 1840. Added to British possessions were Ceylon, Malta, Mauritius and the Seychelles, and some Caribbean Islands. Britain acquired Singapore, Malacca, Hong Kong, Burma and Sarawak and many more smaller territories.

Cross-reference

For Gladstone's foreign policy to 1873, see Chapter 2. For his foreign and Imperial policies to 1885, see Chapter 4.

Did you know?

Expansion of the British Empire

Between 1885 and 1900, Britain acquired approximately 6 million km^2 of overseas territories, with a total population of between 50 and 60 million people.

In the late-19th century, Britain, in common with several of its European neighbours, made what seemed a mad dash for what was left of vulnerable underdeveloped territories, which would bring more resources and markets and new outlets for capital investment. Between 1882 and 1900, most of Africa was divided up among European Imperialist nations.

Britain made the greatest gains of all in Africa, controlling Nigeria, Kenya, Uganda, Northern and Southern Rhodesia, Egypt and the Sudan, Somaliland and Bechuanaland. In the Pacific, Britain took Fiji, parts of Borneo and New Guinea and other islands. Eighty-eight million subjects were added to the empire and, by 1900, Britain exercised authority over a fifth of the world's land surface and a quarter of its peoples.

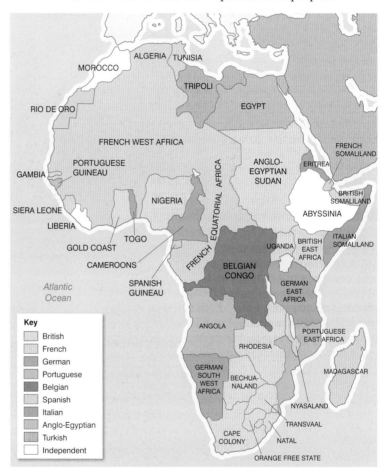

Fig. 2 *Map showing the division of Africa among the European nations in the late-19th century*

Britain and the British Empire

During most of Salisbury's 20-year premiership, the 'Scramble for Africa' was in progress. Salisbury saw the value of possessing colonies, but he did not wish to expand the empire any further. Britain had occupied Egypt in 1882 to protect British trading interests, but Salisbury regarded Britain's occupation of Egypt as a burden – 'a disastrous inheritance'. One serious outcome of this had been a souring of relationships with France over their interests in the Suez Canal. Salisbury was reluctant to spill British blood over any territorial disputes, but he too found it necessary to intervene in order to protect British interests in Egypt and the Nile valley.

Exploring the detail

Imperial legacy

Salisbury had an Imperial legacy to contend with. Disraeli had encouraged a pride in empire. He had also imposed a new burden on British Imperial policy by underlining the responsibility to impose the white man's code of conduct, religion and ethics on the colonised territories, to 'civilise the natives'. This assumed that Britain knew what was best for primitive indigenous populations and also that the British were superior. Gladstone spoke out against Imperialism. One of his basic beliefs was that national groups had the right to determine their own form of government and Imperialism went against that.

The Berlin Conference was held in 1884 and 1885 to monitor European countries' land acquisitions in Africa, and to avoid disputes breaking out. Salisbury took a very pragmatic view and was signatory to several crucial agreements, which decided on borders that were often difficult to define because of the inhospitable terrain and remoteness. The Italians and the British agreed a border between the Sudan and Eritrea. The British and French came to an agreement on control of Zanzibar and Madagascar respectively. The Germans acknowledged British control of Zanzibar, Kenya and Uganda in exchange for British recognition of the Cameroons, Tanganyika and German South West Africa.

European empire building in Africa had begun peacefully, but by the 1890s blood was shed to secure what little unclaimed territory remained. Although Salisbury rarely sought confrontation, he agreed to British conquest of the Sudan in order to remove a French threat. Sudan was controlled by the Dervishes, who constantly threatened Egypt, but more upsetting to Britain was the suspected French interest in the Sudan. In September 1898, General Kitchener decisively defeated the Dervishes at Omdurman and secured the Sudan for Britain. Within a few days the French made claims on the Upper Nile (south Sudan). Kitchener rapidly moved towards the French troops at Fashoda and threatened action. Humiliated, the French withdrew. Their ally Russia could do nothing to help and the British navy was in a strong position in the Mediterranean.

Joseph Chamberlain – colonial secretary

Salisbury's colonial secretary was Joseph Chamberlain, who had defected from the Liberals over Home Rule for Ireland in 1886. It was Chamberlain's vision of the empire that was most responsible for the fashion for Imperialism in the last two decades of the 19th century. He believed that the way to overcome Britain's economic problems was to build up existing colonies and expand into new territory. By increasing trading opportunities with the empire, there would be more jobs and less unemployment.

Chamberlain encouraged **joint-stock companies** to invest in undeveloped areas of the empire. He organised government loans to finance irrigation projects and railways. He organised a Colonial Conference in 1897, where he expressed his desire to establish an empire customs union. This was not a success, but many of his other policies were. He was in tune with public opinion of the day and he inspired a sense of British pride and confidence in their empire.

Salisbury allowed Chamberlain considerable freedom in dealing with Imperial issues. Chamberlain oversaw the final conquest of the Sudan in 1898, the expansion of influence in China and the involvement of Britain in the Boer War from 1899 to 1902.

Splendid isolation

Salisbury acted as foreign secretary during most of his three periods in office (1885, 1886–92 and 1895–1902). Salisbury was responsible for conducting what became known as the policy of 'splendid isolation'. The expression is misleading. Salisbury did not set out to separate Britain from any potential allies; it was more to do with his cautious policy of not getting involved in alliances that could lead Britain into a war. It was maintaining this position that gave Salisbury the reputation of being isolationist. Salisbury's biographer, Andrew Roberts, challenges this perception (Source 1).

Cross-reference

Omdurman and Fashoda can be located on the map of Africa on page 80.

Fig. 3 *Joseph Chamberlain, 1836–1914, was an influential businessman, politician and statesman. He was appointed colonial secretary by Lord Salisbury*

Cross-reference

Joseph Chamberlain appears throughout this book, but his profile can be found on page 67.

Key terms

Joint-stock company: commercial enterprise with varying amounts of capital (stock) supplied by shareholders. The profits were divided in proportion to the amount of capital subscribed.

Salisbury, who had long despised what he called the 'sterile' and 'dangerous' policy of isolation, was stuck with a label for his non-aligned but heavily engaged foreign policy, which was far more complex, subtle and intelligent than crude isolationism. The avoidance of joining entangling alliances or European power blocs, which Salisbury considered an inherent threat to peace, was by no means the same as Little England isolationism of which he often still stands accused.

Roberts, A (1999) **Salisbury, Victorian Titan,** *Weidenfeld & Nicolson*

Rather than being responsible for introducing a policy of isolation, Salisbury was aware of Britain's lack of allies when he first entered office in 1885. Britain had few friends in Europe as a result of Gladstone's policies. Gladstone had alienated France over Egypt, upset Turkey and Austria and tensions were high between Britain and Russian over Afghanistan. Salisbury's approach to Bismarck to help mediate between Russia and Britain was politely, but firmly, turned down.

Salisbury regarded France as a threat to Britain's vital naval supremacy in the Mediterranean and the route through the Suez to India. This suited Bismarck as he aimed to keep France isolated, and not able to threaten Germany. In 1882, Bismarck had formed the Triple Alliance between Germany, Austria and Italy. Salisbury maintained a good relationship with the Alliance but always at a distance. Salisbury preferred Britain not to be constrained by the opposing interests of any country, with whom there were friendly relations.

John Charmley sums up the reasoning behind Salibury's cautious approach to alliances (Source 2).

The fears about isolation were secondary to the greater fear of the catastrophe of a European war, and Salisbury never moved from the position that a Continental commitment would cost Britain more than it would benefit her.

2

Charmley, J. (1999) **Splendid Isolation,** *Hodder & Stoughton*

■ Activity

Talking point

Do you think Salisbury was justified in keeping other European nations at arm's length? What were the possible dangers of pursuing such a policy?

Liberal Imperialism

Imperialism was the focus of popular sentiment during the 1880s and a significant group of leading Liberals were in favour of aligning party policy with this movement. There was unhappiness at the Liberal leadership's lack of engagement with the new popular mood and, to make the point, a group within the party led by Lord Rosebery 'styled' themselves Liberal Imperialists. Lord Rosebery was Gladstone's foreign secretary 1892–94, but he could do little to control Rosebery, as he needed his support for Home Rule. Rosebery believed in Imperial expansion in Africa and used British troops to subdue a revolt in Egypt by the Khedive and reimpose Britain's authority. He became involved in a clash with the French over the annexation of Uganda and over-ruled Gladstone, but the issue deepened divisions between Imperialists and anti-Imperialists within the Liberal Party. Rosebery's premiership (1894–5) was too short to pursue a strong Imperial policy and the Cabinet quarrelled constantly. The anti-Imperialists were set against further colonial commitments, particularly the future level of the British presence in Egypt. The issue soured relationships and created lasting hostilities within the party. When Salisbury and the Conservatives came back into government in 1895, the weak and broken Liberal Party could only lick its wounds.

When Henry Campbell-Bannerman became party leader in 1898, it was hoped that the Liberals could set aside their differences and achieve a degree of unity. The outbreak of the Boer War in October 1899 ended these hopes. The Liberal Party was split over its support for the war – the Liberal Imperialists followed their old leader Lord Rosebery in support of the British position in the Transvaal, while the anti-Imperialist pro-Boers spoke out vigorously against the morality of the British response. Campbell-Bannerman missed the opportunity to impose firm leadership on his party by attempting to strike a balance between the two opposing views. The rift in the Liberal Party encouraged the Conservatives to hold an election in October 1900, nicknamed the 'Khaki Election', as a result of which the Conservatives were returned with a comfortable majority.

The historian Robert Rhodes James believes that by the end of the Boer War attitudes towards Imperialism were changing. The Liberal Imperialists, the dominant group in the party, through debate and self-questioning could claim to 'represent a public opinion that believed in empire but had become disenchanted with foreign adventures while grievous social problems remained unresolved at home'. The long period of Conservative rule soon gave way to a new kind of Liberalism.

The challenges posed to Britain by Russia, Germany and the Boers

Russia and Germany

Britain distrusted Russian Imperialism and disliked Russia's autocratic government. A close relationship was always unlikely. Britain remained anxious about Russian ambitions in the Balkans and a possible naval presence in the Mediterranean. There were continuing issues with Russia over the security of India's North-West Frontier. When Salisbury took office in 1885, Russian troops were gathering near the Zulficar pass in Afghanistan. Salisbury took a firm line with Russia leaving the country in no doubt that Britain would fight to safeguard India. The dispute was settled to Britain's satisfaction but, within a few weeks, a serious international crisis blew up in the Balkans that gave scope for Russian interference.

Eastern Rumelia united with Bulgaria in contravention of the terms of the Congress of Berlin. Salisbury maintained a consistent position in support of Bulgaria, in the face of opposition from the other powers. Salisbury's firm diplomacy avoided war and won Bismarck's respect. When the situation developed further, Salisbury supported Germany and Austria in forcing Russia to back down from ambitions in the Balkans.

When Salisbury took office again in 1895, France and Russia had signed a defensive alliance (1894), which was potentially dangerous for Britain. As Germany, Austria-Hungary and Italy were part of a Triple Alliance,

Cross-reference

The Boer War is covered later in this chapter on pages 27–28.

The split in the Liberal Party between Imperialists and anti-Imperialists is covered in Chapter 6.

For the new Liberal rule of the early 20th century, look ahead to Chapter 8.

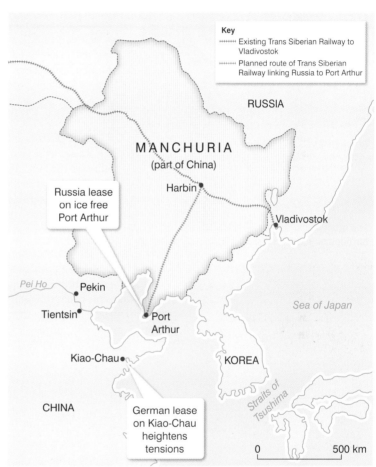

Fig. 4 *Part of China affected by European territorial ambitions, 1897–8*

Exploring the detail

Afghanistan bordered India's North-West Frontier. India was Britain's most prized empire possession. Russia continually attempted to extend its influence into Afghanistan and thus threatened Britain's position in India. This caused great tension between the two countries. For Britain, it was essential that Afghanistan remained as a buffer state between India and Russia.

Fig. 5 *Cartoon showing Britain, Germany, Russia, France and Japan trying to divide up China to suit their interests and ambitions*

Cross-reference

The affair of the Kruger telegram is outlined on page 127.

in European terms, Britain looked rather isolated. Bismarck had made an approach to Salisbury in 1889 about a formal alliance with Britain, but Salisbury would not accept Bismarck's terms and so turned down the offer. Despite this, relations with Germany remained cordial until 1894, when Kaiser Wilhelm took a more prominent role in Germany's foreign and Imperial affairs.

Britain's interests in China were threatened by both Russia and Germany in 1897. Russia turned its attention to China in 1897 and alarmed Britain with the possibility of the weak Chinese Empire being partitioned among the Europeans. Salisbury did not wish to disturb Britain's 'open door' policy with China, which allowed Britain lucrative trading concessions. Russia's bullying behaviour towards China secured the lease of the ice free Port Arthur, to which they planned to link their Trans-Siberian Railway. Germany added to the tension by obtaining a lease of the near-by harbour at Kiao-chau. Britain protested and received ample compensation from the Chinese. Salisbury successfully eased the tension by making an agreement between Russia, Germany and France to recognise clearly defined spheres of influence in China.

The nature of Britain's relationship with Germany changed after 1894. Kaiser Wilhelm seemed to take every opportunity to make trouble for Britain, for example with the Kruger telegram. The Kaiser was irritated that Britain would not formally join the Triple Alliance. But when Chamberlain tried to form an alliance with Germany in 1898 in the aftermath of the Port Arthur affair, it came to nothing. Germany did not want to risk war with Russia over its trading position in China.

The Kaiser's uncompromising attitude to Britain eventually drove Britain towards improving relations with France. The key to Britain's security was its navy. When the Kaiser trumpeted the opening of the Kiel Canal in 1895 and approved a Navy Bill in 1898 to build a powerful fleet, Britain was disturbed. A new German navy would pose a direct threat to Britain's empire and trade routes.

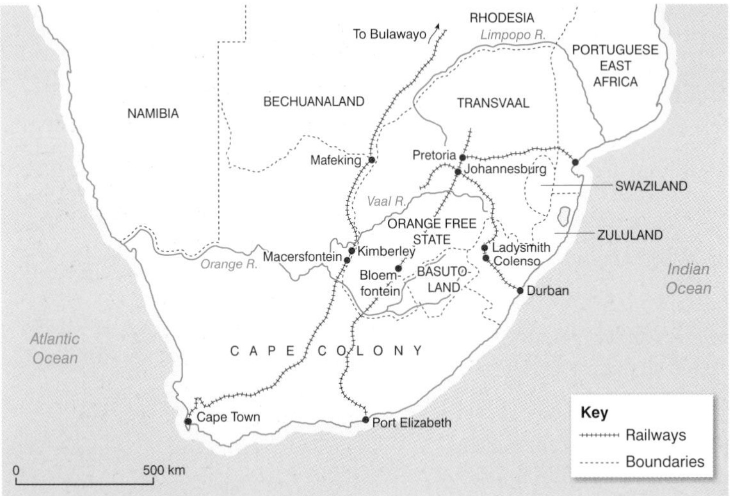

The time was coming for Britain to find reliable allies.

The Boers

There had been rivalry between Dutch Boers and British colonists long before the 'Scramble for Africa'. There were two Boer states in South Africa, the independent Orange Free State and the Transvaal. The Transvaal had won independence in 1881. An uneasy relationship between Britain and the Boers had continued in spite of this. The situation became more complicated with the discovery of gold in the centre of the Transvaal in 1886.

The gold transformed the economy of the Transvaal and gave their president, Paul Kruger, ideas to expand its borders. He came into direct conflict with another large personality, Cecil Rhodes, who was prime minister of Cape Colony (British South Africa) from 1890 to 1896. Rhodes had grandiose plans for British domination of Africa, with a railway running from Cape Town to Cairo entirely through British territory.

Fig. 6 *South Africa during the Boer War*

Cross-reference

The granting of independence to the Transvaal is described on page 83.

With the discovery of gold, prospectors had poured into the Transvaal in the early 1890s. These 'Uitlanders' (outsiders), who almost outnumbered the Boers, were disproportionately taxed and denied political rights by Kruger, to curtail their influence. Rhodes decided to stir up the Uitlanders, who included many British from Cape Colony, with the ultimate objective of overthrowing Kruger. He engineered the Jameson Raid, which ended in international censure of Britain.

Kaiser Wilhelm of Germany congratulated Kruger in a telegram for defending his country against British aggression. Kruger continued to stock-pile German armaments. A meeting between Kruger and Sir Alfred Milner, South African high commissioner, failed to address the Uitlander's grievances and British troops moved to the Transvaal borders. When an ultimatum from the Boers for the British troops to stand down was rejected, the Boers attacked Cape Colony and Natal.

The Boer War that followed lasted from 1899 to 1902, was bitterly fought and ended in defeat for the Boers when the British, with great difficulty, won control of the Transvaal gold mines and absorbed the Boer republics by the Treaty of Vereeniging in 1902. Both the Transvaal and the Orange Free State were incorporated into the union of South Africa in 1910.

The Boer War carried several important implications for Britain socially, economically and politically. As the war continued, it began to lose public support in Britain. The cost in money was estimated at a massive £200m, but in lives it was a soul-destroying 20,000 men. To the ordinary British subject, this seemed too high a price to pay. Many turned away from what they had seen as stability in Conservatism and pride in Imperialism. The Boer War highlighted Britain's isolation. Most

Le Petit Journal
SUPPLEMENT ILLUSTRE

AU TRANSVAAL
Le docteur Jameson prisonnier des Boers

Fig. 7 *Leander Starr Jameson and his troop of 500 men overwhelmed by the Boers and forced to surrender on 2 January 1896*

Fig. 8 *Londoners celebrating the relief of Mafeking. During the Boer War, the British were beseiged at Mafeking from October 1899 to May 1990*

Exploring the detail

Rhodes planned the Jameson Raid, in December 1895, with the help of Dr Leander Starr Jameson, who rode into the Transvaal from neighbouring Bechuanaland. He was expecting support from the discontented Uitlanders, but their lack of organisation threw the raid into chaos and Jameson was easily overcome by the Boers. The incident destroyed Rhodes' reputation and he resigned. Britain's foreign policy was discredited as the raid was seen as an unprovoked invasion of a foreign State. Joseph Chamberlain, the Colonial Secretary, denied any knowledge and rode the storm.

Did you know?
The relief of Mafeking

British people followed the progress of the Boer War with great interest in the press. One of the nail-biting events was the siege of Mafeking by the Boers, which started at the outbreak of hostilities in October 1899 and lasted until 17 May 1900. The resistance to the Boers was organised by Colonel Baden-Powell, later founder of the Scout movement. The town was finally relieved by a contingent of British troops. Back at home, people regarded Baden-Powell as a hero. A cabinet maker from North Berwick, in Scotland, William Auld named his house 'Mafeking' to commemorate the event.

Activity

Research task

The events in the Boer War contain many stories of heroic and dreadful deeds. Carry out some research on these events, either by the using the internet or using books in your school/local library. Try to form your own conclusion on which, if either, side held the moral high ground. Your findings could form part of a class discussion or a display.

Cross-reference

Read this section in conjunction with the section on the Great Depression on page 98.

Cross-reference

The challenges posed by Germany and America are discussed on page 130.

The discovery of gold in South Africa in the 1880s is outlined on page 99.

Table 1 *Estimated levels of unemployment from 1886 to 1900*

Year	Unemployed (%)
1886	10.2
1887	7.6
1888	4.9
1889	2.1
1890	2.1
1891	3.5
1892	6.3
1893	7.5
1894	6.9
1895	5.8
1896	3.3
1897	3.3
1898	2.8
1899	2.0
1900	2.5

*Cook, C. (1999) **The Longman Companion to Britain in the Nineteenth Century 1815–1914**, Longman*

European countries, Germany, France, Austria-Hungary and Russia, supported the Boer cause. Salisbury, elderly and in poor health, resigned his premiership in 1902. It became imperative for Britain to seek and be prepared to be committed to new alliances and bring to a close the long period of 'splendid isolation'.

Changes in the British economy, 1886–1901

Changes occurred in the British economy during the last years of the 19th century. The contemporary view was that Britain was suffering from a long-term depression, which had started in 1873 and lasted until 1896. There were periods of marked cyclical downturns in the economy during the periods 1873–79, 1882–86 and 1890–96. For years Britain had dominated the export markets, but this situation was changing as Britain began to face competition from foreign markets and there was a fall in demand for British goods in the traditional European and American markets. Prices and profits tumbled in both industry and agriculture, and continued to do so for the next 20 years. These events eroded confidence in Britain's economic supremacy.

Prices fell steadily and then picked up in the 1890s as the gold-mining boom in South Africa gave a boost to the economy and the late-1890s saw a return to economic prosperity and a period of affluence.

In June 1885, Salisbury's government was sufficiently anxious about the economy to set up a Royal Commission to inquire into the Depression of Industry and Trade. Its remit was to report on 'the extent, nature and probable cause of the depression prevailing in various branches of trade and industry'. The majority report concluded that agricultural prices had been falling since 1873 and continued the downward trend. It noted an increase in production of most other commodities, but in many instances supply outstripped demand. This led to a reduction in profits, a fall in prices and lower rates of interest on invested capital. There were issues relating to foreign competition. The report, however, commented that there were encouraging signs for the future. The tone of complacency was not shared by everyone.

The thing that concerned businessmen more than production levels was profits. They were in business to make money. When profit levels are low, there is less money available for capital investment. To offset the profit loss, employers have little alternative but to pay off their workforce. In 1886, unemployment had reached a peak of approximately 10 per cent. This created much hardship and a sense of depression. However, for most of this period, unemployment levels remained around 5 per cent.

During this period, falling profits and overseas competition led to increasing unemployemt. In the absence of official statistics, the figures in Table 1 are drawn from various numbers of unemployed in certain unions.

Between 1873 and 1896 there was a 30–40 per cent drop in price levels of most commodities but the price of imports fell more than the price of exports. This meant a beneficial shift in the terms of trade for Britain. By 1900, Britain imported 50 per cent of its foodstuffs and much of its raw materials for industry, and so benefited from the low import prices. Wages did not fall, therefore, so long as a man could stay in a job, he benefited from lower-priced goods and food. The result of this was a significant rise in the standard of living in Britain.

Britain's industrial output continued to grow throughout the period, although the rate of growth certainly slowed. This was not unreasonable after such a lengthy and sustained period of economic expansion, which had lasted most of the 19th century. Britain still relied heavily on its staple industries – coal, iron and steel, shipbuilding and textiles. Output and exports increased in all of these industries, for example coal output in 1870 was 110.4 million tonnes and in 1900 was 225.2 million tonnes. At the same time, there was a marked rise in the level of British imports, as a better standard of living led to an increase in the import of foodstuffs from overseas. This had a detrimental effect on Britain's **visible trade** balance.

A sign of Britain's increasing manufacturing output was the appearance of many new, smaller industries such as boot and shoe manufacture, chocolate, soap, tobacco and beer, which all developed successfully at this time. William Lever started up his soap manufacturing business in 1886 in Liverpool, when unemployment was at its height. It was one of the first companies to manufacture soap from vegetable oils and, with Lever's innovative approach and marketing practices, he successfully opened a sales office in New York in 1895. These examples seem to be at variance with the idea of a depression carrying on into the 1880s and 1890s.

Fig. 9 *Advert for Sunlight household soap c.1890, recommending it to the housewife by claiming it would make life easier. Produced by Lever Brothers at Port Sunlight works in Liverpool*

In order for these new businesses to grow, capital was required. Men like William Lever raised capital by offering limited liability shares in their companies. This led to a rise in the number of large joint-stock companies, whose main loyalty was to their shareholders rather than their workforce. Companies operating in the same line of business amalgamated to form giant corporations like the Imperial Tobacco Company and Vickers-Armstrong, the biggest producers of armaments in Britain.

Key terms

Visible trade: refers to actual goods that are exported and imported and can literally be seen and transported to their destination by road, rail, sea or air. Opposite of invisible trade.

Cross-reference

The figures for the balance of trade between 1866 and 1900 are provided in Table 3 on page 131.

Table 2 *Average prices of agricultural and industrial products in Britain over five-year periods*

Years	Rousseaux price index Take 100 as the norm, so that 120 indicates high prices and 76 low prices
1865–9	115
1870–4	120
1875–9	108
1880–4	100
1885–9	84
1890–4	82
1895–9	76
1900–4	86

*Adapted from Mitchell, B. R. and Deane, P. (1962) **Abstract of British Historical Statistics**, Cambridge University Press*

Activity

Research task

1 Conduct your own research into the manufacture of one of the following:
  - Clark's shoes and boots.
  - Cadbury's chocolate.
  - Lever's soap.

2 To what extent does your research tie in with the concept of Britain being in the middle of a continuing depression in 1886?

Cross-reference

Read this section in conjunction with the section on the Great Depression on pages 98–105.

These developments led to a change in the market for consumer goods. The growing population, continuing urbanisation and the increase in the value of real wages gave rise to a mass market in consumer goods.

The challenges posed by overseas competition

The most crucial change in the economy as far as Britain was concerned was economic global expansion. By the 1880s, the world economy involved a growing number of countries, both in terms of industrialising nations and those trading in primary products. The 1886 Royal Commission of Industry and Trade report noted that Britain's manufacturing supremacy was being challenged by 'foreigners'. The fact that Britain was no longer the only industrial economy could not be ignored. For the first time, Britain was facing stiff competition from other industrialising nations, particularly in Europe and America. Britain's two most formidable opponents were America and Germany.

- **Population growth and immigration**. Population expansion in Germany and America gave both countries a large labour force and a ready home market for manufactured goods. Germany had a larger population than Britain and it was growing at a faster rate. Germany's population rose from 45.2 million in 1880 to 56.4 million in 1900. European immigrants flooded into the America during this period and, as a result, the American population rose from 50.2 million in 1880 to 77.5 million in 1901, a 30 per cent increase in 20 years. The largely immigrant American population were almost, by definition, hard working. Many had arrived in America with few possessions and seeking a better life. They had a vested interest in building a great new nation and threw all of their energy and resources into achieving success.

- **Vast untapped natural resources**. America and Germany both possessed vast quantities of coal and iron ore. This enabled them to forge ahead of Britain in steel manufacture. By 1890, American steel production had exceeded that of Britain and, by 1896, Germany had achieved the same. By 1899, America had overtaken Britain in coal output. America and Germany also competed successfully with Britain in engineering and the production of machinery and armaments. In America, railroads carried raw materials to factories and finished products to towns for home consumption, and to seaports for export, thus diminishing Britain's share of the world export markets.

- **Political stability**. Germany had become one nation in 1871, instead of many small, economically isolated states ruled by reactionary monarchs and princes. Germany unified under the strong leadership of Otto von Bismarck and, by 1886, was pursuing expansionist policies in industry and empire. America had recovered from the worst effects of the Civil War of 1861–5.

Britain's response to this fierce new competition has been criticised for being too complacent. Britain was perhaps slow to respond and too set in its ways to make the necessary changes to be more competitive, allowing America and Germany to forge quickly ahead. A number of factors contributed to this:

- **Britain's outdated equipment and processes**. By the 1880s much of Britain's machinery and production methods were out of date and there was a reluctance to invest capital in the new modern machinery, which was by then being both manufactured and used in America and Germany.

- **British government's lack of investment in technical education**. The Germans had invested money in education, especially technical colleges. The result was a better educated workforce with a range of new skill sets. They undertook vital research in new fields of electrical engineering, motor manufacturing and chemicals during the 1880s. The British government failed to make adequate investment in education and scientific and technological research, and Britain fell behind Germany.

- **Introduction of protective tariffs by overseas competitors**. The introduction of tariff reform across Europe and America was damaging to Britain's export trade and industrial production. In 1870, British goods made up almost one-third of the world's manufacturing output, but the tariffs imposed by other emerging industrial nations made British products more expensive and, therefore, less competitive – Britain's share of the market fell. Germany imposed duties of 13 per cent on manufactured goods in 1879. America followed in 1890 but, by 1900, had raised the tariff to a crippling 57 per cent.

- **Britain's free trade policy**. While other industrialising nations imposed tariffs on imports from abroad, Britain stuck with its free trade principles. A pressure group, the Fair Trade League formed in 1881, put forward moderate demands for a restructuring of Britain's trade policy along more protectionist lines. It argued that, 'Our manufacturers are more and more excluded from the markets of the civilised world, not by fair competition but by oppressive tariffs'. The League was influential in the late-1880s, but neither Gladstone nor Salisbury would be moved on the issue of protectionist tariffs.

Cross-reference

To recap on the issues of protective tariffs versus free trade, look back to pages 57–59.

Britain's balance of payments remained in surplus during the years of the Great Depression, in spite of the fall in exports. The balance of visible trade is the value of imports subtracted from the value of exports. Invisible earnings come from services such as shipping, insurance and overseas investments. The balance of payments is arrived at by adding together the balance of visible trade and the balance of invisible earnings. The balance of payments is the amount left at the end. A surplus is a sign of a thriving economy.

Table 3 *The UK balance of payments, 1866–1900 (annual averages in £m)*

Year	Exports – Imports = Balance of visible trade	Balance of invisible earnings	Balance of payments
1866–70	−65	+106	+41
1871–5	−64	+139	+75
1876–80	−124	+149	+25
1881–5	−99	+161	+61
1886–90	−89	+177	+88
1891–5	−134	+186	+52
1896–1900	−159	+199	+40

Cook, C. (1999) The Longman Companion to Britain in the Nineteenth Century 1815–1914, Longman

Between 1886 and 1901 Britain survived the challenge of foreign competition to its industry and export trade.

- In the 1880s, Britain was still the biggest exporter of industrial products and so did not believe it needed to worry.

Key terms

Invisible trade: refers to services such as banking, insurance, transport and overseas assets, rather than actual goods. Today, invisibles include tourism, consultancy, and the music, television and film industries.

Primary product: refers to food crops, such as tea or wheat and raw materials like cotton, rather than manufactured goods.

Activity

Challenge your thinking

Individually or in pairs, read over the sections on 'Changes in the British economy, 1886–1901' on pages 128–129 and 'The challenges posed by overseas competition' on pages 130–132.

1. What positive aspects were there to Britain's economy between 1886 and 1901?

2. What negative aspects were there to Britain's economy between 1886 and 1901?

3. From the information you have gathered, draw up a conclusions as to the overall state of Britain's economy during this period. Does it seem to you that Britain was suffering from a depression, or do you think on balance the economy was thriving?

Cross-reference

The development of the trade unions, especially the craft unions, and their part in the growth of the Labour Party are discussed on pages 112–113.

Cross-reference

For more information on the SDF, look back to page 114.

The influence of Karl Marx on Socialism and the Labour movement is referred to on page 114.

As the world economy grew, the City of London (the centre of finance and commerce) became more important than ever to the world economy. Britain was the largest exporter of capital and of **invisible trade**, and so still maintained a surplus trade balance.

In spite of overseas competition in shipbuilding, the British shipping industry was still the largest in the world. The British merchant fleet represented about one-third of the total and British ships still dominated the world's shipping lanes.

Britain was the largest outlet for **primary products** such as tea, cane sugar and wheat. It bought 50 per cent of the world's meat exports. By 1900, half of Britain's food was imported. The bonus for Britain was that the overseas producers like Argentina and Uruguay were happy to take British manufactured goods in exchange for their primary produce.

Britain's trade balance remained healthy during this period and the country was able to maintain a dominant position in the world's economy, although it could no longer claim to be the supreme power. Britain had been pushed out of the American market by protective tariffs and, by 1900, Germany and to some extent France were taking over Britain's European markets. Britain was forced to seek new outlets for its industrial goods and, as a result, turned increasingly towards its empire.

The growth of new unionism

The 1880s saw a change in direction in the union movement. It was the beginning of the organisation of unskilled workers, many of whom had endured appalling working conditions for decades, and had lacked any real bargaining power with their employers. Their militant approach, with striking as their first line of attack, was in direct contrast to the craft unions. Subscriptions were low to allow for the workers' poor and often fluctuating wage levels, but the large membership gave the unions funds to support some strike action, albeit not for long. Unlike the craft unions, their funds did not make provision for welfare payments. They became known as mass unions.

There were a number of reasons for the growth of 'new unionism':

The uncertain economic climate of the late-1870s and 1880s contributed to the growth of new unionism. As manufacturing industries began to experience a downturn in demand for their goods and profits, unskilled workers were the first to be laid off. The high levels of unemployment made wage bargaining difficult and strikes ineffective, as there was always plenty of labour to take over from strikers. Those workers lucky enough to be in a job had little choice but to accept the poor rates of pay.

The spread of education among the labouring classes after 1870 and the right to vote for many unskilled labourers in 1884 boosted their confidence. Trade unions had achieved legal status in 1876, and it was inevitable that the unskilled workers would seek the advantages gained by the craft unions by forming their own unions.

Leading socialists from the SDF, some of whom were influenced by the writings of Karl Marx, held meetings outside factory gates to encourage the workers to assert their rights.

A few high-profile strikes by unskilled labour gave impetus to the new union movement.

High-profile strikes

Bryant & May match girls strike – July 1888

In 1888, the audacity of a group of female employees at the Bryant & May match factory to strike for better conditions captured public sympathy and ended in triumph at the end of two weeks. The factory was in the London's east end. The workforce was pulled from the slum areas and was largely young and female. This enabled Bryant & May to keep down their wage bill. Dipping sticks into yellow phosphorous to make matches was highly dangerous and often resulted in a painful, disfiguring and fatal affliction called Phosphorus Necrosis or 'phossy jaw'. A leading socialist, Annie Besant, helped to organise the match girls' strike and give it publicity by writing an article entitled 'White Slavery' in her weekly paper *The Link*.

Fig. 10 *Matchmakers in the east end of London were among the poorest paid workers. Their strike in May 1888 ended in success and led to an improvement in their rate of pay*

A closer look

The Bryant & May match girls

The case of the match girls – who took on their employers and forced them to re-employ all the strikers and stop their underhand practice of imposing unreasonable fines – made national headlines. Annie Besant referred to the plight of the match girls before their action as 'White Slavery' (Source 3).

3

The hour for commencing work is 6.30 in summer and 8 in winter; work concludes at 6 p.m. This long day of work is performed by young girls, who have to stand the whole of the time. A typical case is that of a girl of 16, a piece-worker; she earns 4 shillings a week and lives with a sister, who earns 8 or 9 shillings per week. The salary of 4 shillings is subject to deductions in the shape of fines; if the feet are dirty, or the ground under the bench is left untidy, a fine of 3d. is inflicted; for putting 'burnts' – matches that have caught fire during the work – on the bench, 1 shilling has been forfeited and a fine of 3d. is inflicted for talking. If a girl is late she is shut out for 'half the day'. Such is a bald account of one form of white slavery as it exists in London. But who cares for the fate of these white wage slaves? Born in slums, driven to work while still children, undersized because underfed, oppressed because helpless; who cares if they die or go on the streets, provided only that the Bryant & May shareholders get their 23 per cent?

Besant, A. (1888) 'White Slavery', an article in the newspaper The Link

Activity

Challenge your thinking

The conditions of employment at Bryant & May were unacceptable and the employers were forced to back down. It is, however, important to look at both sides of the argument.

In small groups, consider the strike from the point of view of one of the following:

- The employer.
- The workers.
- Annie Besant.
- The Socialists.

Construct a press release for or against the strike from the point of view of any one of these groups. What were the objectives of each group? How valid were they? What were the future implications for the outcome on both sides?

Activity

Talking point

Read Source 4 – a newspaper article that appeared several years after the match girls' strike. What does this tell you about the attitude of the Bryant & May Company Directors?

Key terms

Collective bargaining: a formula for negotiating pay and conditions between a trade union on one side and employers on the other.

Phosphorus poisoning is one of the most terrible diseases to which the workers are subject. It arises from the inhalation of the fumes of yellow phosphorus used in the manufacture of matches. The Home Office has laid down special rules for factories where this is used, (and) every case (must) be reported to the district inspector. Last month a man, who had been working at Bryant & May's, died. An inquest found that death was due to phosphorus poisoning. It was discovered that no less than seventeen cases had occurred, none of which had been reported. This led to Home Office proceedings.

4   *Article from the **Daily Chronicle**, 2 June 1898*

Gas Workers' Union strike – July 1889

Will Thorne, a member of the SDF, established a Gasworkers' and General Labourers Union in March 1889, which soon had 20,000 members. He organised a strike to reduce the working day by demanding three 8-hour shifts instead of two 12-hour shifts. The Southern Metropolitan Gas Company immediately agreed and the success provided an incentive for other workers to organise unions. This strike resulted in better pay and conditions for all workers in gas, water and electricity companies, where unbroken supplies to the customer were of vital importance and the workforce was regarded as specialised. They won union recognition and an ability to pursue **collective bargaining**.

Dockers' strike – August 1889

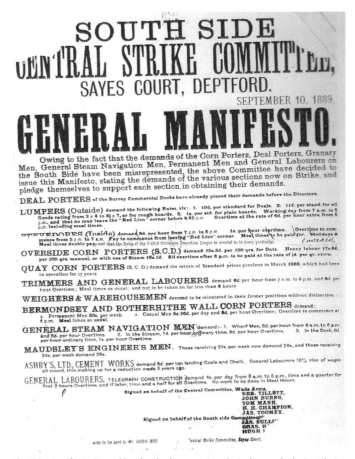

Fig. 11 *Manifesto issued by the dockers stating their demands during their strike of August 1889*

The work of the dockers was irregular and poorly paid. The pay was 5d an hour. Too many dockers were available for the 'call-on'. It was one of the main complaints of the dockers that they hung around half a day for work that either did not materialise or was only for a couple of hours at a time.

> We are driven into a shed, iron-barred from end to end, outside of which a foreman or contractor walks up and down with the air of a dealer in a cattle market, picking and choosing from a crowd of men, who, in their eagerness to obtain employment, trample each other under foot, and where like beasts they fight for the chances of a day's work.

5 *From a pamphlet by Tillett, B. (1910)* **A Brief History of the Dockers' Union**

The depression in trade had created fierce competition between the London dock companies. The dock strike began when dock companies cut bonus rates (the 'plus' system) in order to offer a lower rate to ship owners for using their docks and warehouses. The West India Dock workers, led by Ben Tillett, Tom Mann and John Burns, came out on strike. They had no funds for strike pay but were supported by other dock trades. The port was virtually brought to a standstill.

The main strike demand was a wage of 6d an hour – the dockers' tanner. They wanted the 'plus' systems to be abolished, union recognition and to be taken on for a minimum of four hours a day. A strike committee organised mass meetings and established pickets outside the dock gates.

Contemporary opinion was divided as to the conduct of the dockers during the strike.

> Sir, – During this week I have witnessed the most open intimidation practised by the men on strike – howling crowds going from dock to dock and warehouse to warehouse, stopping business and threatening vengeance on all who did not comply with their demands, until now there are thousands who are out who had no desire to strike, but were compelled to do so. Those who dare to work for their wages are being brutally maltreated and threatened with worse if they dare attempt to work in defiance of the strikers' wishes.

6 *The Times, 24 August 1889*

> It was impossible not to admire the self control of those who could in ten minutes have sacked every shop within a mile and satisfied the craving of nature. Contrast this crowd with the French mob which cried hoarse with passion 'Give us bread'. Not so the English docker, independent still in his direst straits. 'Give me work' he says and in this case a rider is added and 'pay me fairly'. That is the grit of the whole matter, a fair wage.

7 *The East London Advertiser, 24 August 1889*

The strike went on for five weeks and the employers were convinced that hunger would drive the dockers back to work. Unexpectedly, about £30,000 was sent by union supporters in Australia. It saved the day for the London dockers. They were able to negotiate the ending of the strike with the help of the Lord Mayor of London and Cardinal Manning,

Key terms

Call-on: an expression used by the dockers to describe being employed to carry out the loading or unloading of a ship's cargo.

Did you know?

The dockers' demand for a wage of 6d an hour became known as 'the dockers' tanner'. Tanner was common slang for a sixpenny piece. It would be equivalent to 2.5 pence today.

the Roman Catholic Archbishop, and their demands were met. A new General Labourers' Union was formed with a 30,000-strong membership. The immediate result of these high-profile strikes was a rapid increase in union membership and an increase in strike action.

The importance of the strikes

John Burns explains the importance of the strike in Source 8.

> Still more important perhaps, is the fact that labour of the humbler kind has shown its capacity to organize itself; its solidarity; its ability. The labourer has learned that combination can lead him to anything and everything.

8

*Burns, J. 'The Great Strike', **New Review**, Vol. 1 No. 5, October 1889*

The actions of this low-paid, poorly educated workforce, whose basic needs and rights were scarcely considered by their employers, had demonstrated that they could no longer be ignored or exploited without a struggle. The intervention in the strikes of establishment figures, especially the highly regarded Cardinal Manning, was an indication of public sympathy for the strikers and a regard for the way in which they had conducted their cause. The success of the strikes gave confidence to other unskilled workers to form unions, and was a huge boost to the concept of new unionism with its militant leadership, low subscriptions and striking as its main weapon to improve conditions at work. It strengthened the position of the trade union movement as a whole. There was a strong message to the establishment and society regarding the right of all workers to fair and decent wages for a job done. However, there was a long struggle ahead to gain full acceptance of this concept.

The 1890s – a difficult decade for new unionism

The respect and sympathy won from the establishment the previous year quickly evaporated. Flushed with the successes of 1889, the militant union leaders led a number of unsuccessful strikes, mostly among dock workers and seamen, to establish the '**closed shop**'. Employers would not be brow beaten into accepting the closed shop and organised police protection for non-union labour whom they preferred to employ. The most dramatic example was a strike at Hull docks in 1893, which ended in failure for the unions.

Employers' federations were formed, which drew up registers of non-union workers and coordinated **lock-outs** to defeat strikes, although many employers did begin to settle disputes through arbitration under the 1896 Conciliation Act. In 1897, the Federation of Engineering Employers instigated a lock-out and used **blackleg** labour over a demand for an eight-hour day. The Amalgamated Engineering Union was forced to give in and this defeat of such a well-respected union gave impetus to the unions to 'strengthen their political arm as quickly and as decisively as possible' (H. Pelling, *A History of British Trade Unionism*, 1967).

The new mass unions had yet to grasp their potential political importance. By 1900, trade union membership stood at over 2 million out of a population in Britain of 38 million. This represented only about 11 per cent of the total workforce, and a very small proportion of these belonged to the new mass unions. Ben Tillett summed up the ultimate importance of new unionism: 'it marked the beginning of that close alliance in thought and purpose between the Trade Union Movement and the Socialist Movement which produced, in time, the Labour party.'

Learning outcomes

Through your study of this section you have learnt about the deep divisions in the Liberal Party that kept the party out of power, and, by contrast, the political dominance of the Conservative Party under Lord Salisbury.

You should have developed an understanding of the difficult challenges faced by the government over the issue of Home Rule for Ireland, the fierce opposition and passions it aroused and the pivotal role played by Charles Parnell and should be able to appreciate Gladstone's political legacy at the end of his long political career.

You should also be aware of the importance of the development of the Labour movement, which led to the formation of the Labour Party in 1900 and changed Britain's political landscape.

Furthermore, you have gained an understanding of Britain's complex relationships with the other European powers and the importance of, and issues surrounding, Britain's Imperial position. Underpinning Britain's power was its economy and you should be able to appreciate Britain's economic position and the challenges the country faced by the beginning of the 20th century.

Practice question

To what extent was the development of the Labour movement the most significant threat to Gladstone's Liberal Party during the years 1865 to 1900?

(45 marks)

Study tip This question is asking for an assessment of the threats to Gladstone's Liberal Party in 1865–1900 and, as such, is wide ranging. It is, of course, directing you to pay particular attention to the development of the Labour movement. There are two main elements to consider within the Labour movement – the industrial element, i.e. trade unions, and the political element, i.e. the Labour Representation Committee (Labour Party). However, you will need to discuss a wide range of other factors and should make it clear which posed the greatest threat. You will probably wish to include: Gladstone's (sometimes narrow) high-minded principles, which determined his actions and alienated natural Liberal supporters; Gladstone's obsession with Ireland; and the electoral (and pyschological) damage of Chamberlain's split from the party.

8 Liberals in power

Booth's division of population according to level of income (London)

A	the lowest class – occasional labourers, loafers and semi-criminals	0.9% of population
B	the very poor – casual labourer, hand-to-mouth existence	7.5%
C&D	the poor – earnings at irregular intervals (seasonal employment) or small, regular earnings for unskilled work (earnings 18s – 21s [80p – £1.05]	22.3% poverty line
E&F	comfortable skilled working class, with regular employment, plus best paid artisans	51.5%
G	lower middle class – shopkeepers and clerks}	
H	upper middle class – keep domestic servants}	17.8%
	Conclusion – approx. % of population living in poverty	30%

Source: C. Booth, *Life and Labour of the people in London, 1892*, Vol II pages 20–21

Fig. 1 *Booth's classification of the population*

In this chapter you will learn about:

- the Liberal Party in opposition, 1902–6
- the failures of Balfour's government
- the general election of 1906
- the Conservative Party in the years between 1906 and 1915
- Liberal constitutional and social reforms, looking in detail at pensions and National Insurance
- the general elections of 1910 and the reform of the House of Lords.

Source 1 is based on Seebohn Rowntree's survey of living conditions in York. It was published in 1901.

> Wages paid for unskilled labour in York are insufficient to provide food, shelter and clothing adequate to maintain a family in a state of bare physical efficiency. And let us be clear what mere physical efficiency means. A family must never spend a penny on railway fare or omnibus, they cannot save, nor can they join a sick club or a Trade Union. The children must have no pocket money. Should a child fall ill it must be attended by the parish doctor. The wage earner must never be absent from his work for a single day.

1   Rowntree, B. S. (1901) *Poverty: A Study of Town Life*, Nelson

Key profile

Seebohm Rowntree

Rowntree (1871–1954) was a member of the York chocolate-making family and his curiosity about Booth's classification led him to question whether London was a unique case. He completed a more careful investigation on York published in 1901, which drew similar conclusions to Booth. Both reports showed that the main causes of poverty came about through low wages, lack of regular work, supporting large families, ill-health and old age, and with that poverty came appalling living conditions and disease. These reports widely publicised that it was almost impossible to escape from the cycle of poverty without State help.

The real causes of poverty were not properly understood at the beginning of the 20th century. This extract in Source 1, from one of the most influential studies made of poverty at the time, attempts to explain why so many decent hard-working people found it impossible to escape poverty and changes the general perception that poverty was caused by idleness and fecklessness. Its findings were taken up and acted on by the Liberal governments between 1906 and 1914.

Activity

Thinking point

1. What were the real causes of poverty?
2. How did poverty became a vicious circle from which it was almost impossible to escape?

The opening years of the 20th century witnessed a period of political change and unprecedented social reform. In July 1902, A. J. Balfour took over as Conservative prime minister from his elderly uncle, Lord Salisbury, at a time when support for the long era of Conservative government was being challenged by the ideas of new Liberalism and Socialism, which brought increasing pressure for social reform. The Conservative reluctance to act over issues affecting the legal position of the unions led many working-class Conservative voters to switch their allegiance to the Liberals. Aware of the unpopularity of his government, Balfour resigned in December 1905. The Liberal Party swept to power with a resounding victory. They were responsible for introducing a remarkable series of reforms that tackled the wide range of current social and constitutional problems, such as the introduction of old-age pensions, National Insurance and, most controversially, the reform of the House of Lords.

Table 1 *General election results, 1900–10*

	1900	1906	1910 (Jan)	1910 (Dec)
Conservatives	334	133	241	237
Liberal Unionists	68	24	32	35
Liberals	184	400	275	272
Irish Nationalists	82	83	82	84
Labour	2	30	40	42

Liberals and Conservatives

The Liberal Party, 1902–6

In 1902, the Liberal Party under the leadership of Sir Henry Campbell-Bannerman presented an ineffective opposition to Balfour's Conservative government. The real contender for the Liberal leadership should have been H. H. Asquith, a barrister with an astonishing intellect. However, Asquith still depended on his earnings at the Bar and had not put himself forward for the job. The Liberal Party had been in a weakened state since the disastrous split over Gladstone's Home Rule Bill in 1886. The Liberals' previous term in office (1892–5) had merely underlined these divisions and created new ones. However, Liberal fortunes began to change as opposition in parliament and the country mounted against Balfour's government.

Cross-reference

A. J. Balfour is profiled on page 119.

Key chronology

Events of 1902–15

1902 July	A. J. Balfour becomes prime minister; end of Boer War.
	Balfour's Education Act.
1903	Chamberlain resigns from Cabinet post to campaign for tariff reform.
	Lib-Lab Pact.
1906	General election in January sweeps the Liberal Party to victory; Campbell-Bannerman becomes prime minister. Trade Disputes Act. Provision of Meals Act.
1907	Medical Inspection Act.
1908	Children's Charter. Campbell-Bannerman dies; H. H. Asquith becomes prime minister. Old-age pensions introduced.
1909	The 'People's Budget'.
1910	Death of Edward VII; George V becomes king. Opening of first Labour Exchange.
1911	Parliament Act; National Insurance Act for health and unemployment; payment of MPs.
1914	Outbreak of the Great War.

Cross-reference

To recap on the fortunes of the Liberal Party between 1886 and 1901, look back to Chapters 6 and 7.

Fig. 2 *Henry Campbell-Bannermann*

Campbell-Bannerman – the right man for the job?

Sir Henry Campbell-Bannerman

Campbell-Bannerman (1836–1908) was the youngest of six children of Glasgow's Lord Provost. He attended Glasgow High School and Cambridge and was Liberal MP for Stirling for 40 years. When Balfour resigned, Campbell-Bannerman became prime minister, winning the following election. He was mild mannered, but lacked any charisma or obvious leadership qualities. He led a strong, effective government, known as the 'ministry for all talents', and battled with Lords over social reforms. His achievement was self-government for Transvaal (1906) and Orange River Colony (1907). He resigned through ill-health in April 1908, dying two weeks later.

Sir Henry Campbell-Bannerman was, in some respects, a compromise candidate as leader of the Liberal Party. He had a reputation as a safe pair of hands and had plenty of previous government experience. Queen Victoria had once referred to him as a 'good honest Scotchman'. He described himself as having 'an easy-going disposition'. It was this quality that initially made it difficult for him to pull the party together over the issue of the Boer War, but ultimately made him popular across the Party. By the time he took office after the Liberal election victory in January 1906, his reputation was rising, according to historian Robert Ensor (Source 2).

> His name became the watchword of the radicals and the young. It was his nature to move persistently to the left. His countless trials as leader in opposition had brought to light some qualities which none of his rivals possessed in equal degree – shrewdness, steadfast will, directness of purpose and unselfish devotion to his party's cause.

2   *Adapted from Ensor, R. C. K. (1936)* **England 1870–1914**, *Clarendon Press*

The reality was probably less clear cut than this tribute. There was political intriguing among other Liberals immediately before Campbell-Bannerman accepted office. Sir Edward Grey, who was to become foreign secretary reportedly, told Asquith, '**You** must be leader. Under no circumstances would I take office with CB as Prime Minister'. Roy Hattersley in his book *Campbell-Bannerman* (2006) comments: 'Campbell-Bannerman led the Liberal Party into the election of 1906, because he simply ignored the intrigue of his colleagues and got on with the business of preparing for government.'

By the time of Balfour's resignation in December 1905, the divided Liberal Party had been able to overcome most of its differences and make sufficient appeal to the electorate in January 1906 to achieve a landslide victory. But it was the problems faced by Balfour's government and the mistakes it made which had as much to do with the victory as any positive action by the Liberals. From the time Balfour took office in July 1902, his policy decisions on education and tariff reform and lack of any real social reform programme turned the electorate away from voting Conservative. By early 1905, it was quite clear that Balfour's government was doomed.

The failures of Balfour's government

Arthur James Balfour was prime minister for three and a half years and his time in office is often regarded as a failure. Although he was politically astute, his wealthy aristocratic upbringing, outlook and cool detached manner meant he had little in common with ordinary people. Many of Balfour's fellow parliamentarians had similar backgrounds, but Balfour's intellect and philosophical interests increased his aloofness. It was said he believed in parliamentary democracy as long as the masses voted for the upper classes.

During this period the Conservatives lost a series of by-elections, there were resignations from Cabinet on policy issues and an apparent lack of decisive leadership from Balfour. It was mainly the issues of the Education Act and tariff reform that caused this weakening in the Conservative ranks, causing the loss of their popularity in the country and the uniting of the Liberals in a common cause. Other issues relating to adverse publicity after the Boer War, and reluctance to act over the Taff Vale Case, also caused upset among the electorate. It was not, however, all bad news. Balfour's government can be credited with several notable successes, which had positive repercussions in the long term for Britain, for example, the Entente Cordiale with France in 1904 and the setting up of the Imperial Defence Committee that led to important army and navy reforms. Nevertheless, the Conservatives seemed unable to trumpet their successes, and their failures were played out in the full glare of public attention.

Balfour's Education Act, 1902

Balfour's Education Act of 1902 can be regarded as a considerable achievement, but the hostility expressed towards it by the Nonconformists, most of whom were Liberals, was harmful to the Balfour government. The Education Act established State responsibility for secondary education. The old school boards (which had been set up as part of Forster's Education Act, 1870) were abolished and responsibility for the financing and running of secondary schools transferred to the 140 newly created Local Education Authorities (LEAs), run by county and county borough councils.

The LEAs were authorised to build new secondary schools, but there was a religious issue. Under the new scheme, the provision of money from the local rates was also to be used for the Church schools that were included in the reform, but still retained a measure of independence. This brought a storm of protest from Nonconformists, who believed Church schools were being advantaged by the bill. The fact that children from working- and lower-middle-class families could now benefit from an education beyond primary level, for a small weekly fee, did not appear to impress those who opposed the measure. In spite of its success in ultimately establishing a national system of secondary education, it caused considerable controversy and played a part in the Conservative defeat in the general election of 1906. It helped to reunite the Liberals and strengthen their opposition to the government.

'Chinese slavery'

In the aftermath of the Boer War, the Conservatives were met with a public outcry over the issue of 'Chinese slavery'. To assist with reconstruction at the end of the Boer War, the government allowed the Rand mine owners in the Transvaal to bring in thousands of indentured Chinese coolies to overcome a labour shortage. They were contracted to work for a particular mine owner and obliged to live in single-sex

Did you know?

Winston Churchill, son of Lord Randolph Churchill, was so disenchanted with the Balfour government and, in particular, Chamberlain's campaign for tariff reform, that he crossed floor of the House. In other words, he left the Conservative Party and became a Liberal. Churchill was a convinced free trader, but he was also ambitious for promotion that had not come his way in Balfour's government.

Cross-reference

Full details of the Entente Cordiale and Imperial Defence Committee can be found on pages 158–163.

Cross-reference

For the 1870 Education Act, see pages 24–5.

compounds, isolated from the local population. Although they were paid for their work and were far better off than they would have been in China, the whole scheme raised clear comparisons with the slave trade, abolished in Britain a century earlier. There was indignation from the middle-class voters on humanitarian grounds, over the general working and living conditions of the Chinese, although the accusation of slavery was generally accepted to have been exaggerated. It appeared to set a precedent that would undermine the unions in the case of industrial action, if the government could then sanction the import of foreign labour to break a strike and lead to British workers losing their jobs. The strengthening Liberal opposition was not slow to heap criticism on the heads of Balfour's government over their decision to sanction the enterprise.

Balfour and the trade unions

Many groups of workers depended on the support of their trade unions in order to help them improve conditions and wages. The unions had won important legal rights under both Gladstone and Disraeli. The trade unions had been very unhappy with the Taff Vale judgement in 1901, as it attacked union power and implied financial ruin for any union that called a strike. Balfour rejected constant union appeals for amending legislation, which angered the workers and brought a huge increase in support for the LRC. For the Liberals, the spin-off was that the small group of Labour representatives in the Commons looked to an alliance with the Liberals to achieve some of their political aims. By December 1905, the Liberals had not only been brought together in opposing Balfour's policies, they had the prospect of support for the time being of the new Labour Party.

Fig. 3 *The original Oldham Trade Union council banner, which dates from 1867. It has been recently restored and exhibited*

Cross-reference

To review the Taff Vale judgement, look back to page 116.

To recap on the LRC, look back to page 116.

Cross-reference

Britain's free trade policy is discussed in detail on pages 4, 46 and 128.

Chapter 7 also addresses the challenge arising from overseas competition.

Key terms

Imperial preference: if a system of trade tariffs was introduced, it was planned to give favourable terms or exemption to countries in the British Empire, and therefore only tax imports from outside the empire.

Conservative division over tariff reform

The raising of the issue of tariff reform in 1903, by Joseph Chamberlain, Secretary for the Colonies, became a major cause of Balfour's resignation and defeat. The policy of free trade rather than protection had been pursued for the latter half of the 19th century by Liberals and Conservatives, which meant there were no tariffs levied against trade with other nations. The Budget of 1902 had introduced a duty of 1 shilling (5 pence) on imported wheat, to help cover the cost of the Boer war. Chamberlain suggested there could be a reciprocal arrangement between Britain and its empire, **Imperial preference**, which would lift this duty on wheat from the colonies. This would mean a return to a system of protected trade, except for the Colonies, for the first time in 50 years and the proposal divided the Conservative Cabinet.

Chamberlain's proposal for tariff reform came against a background of Britain's contracting global economic and industrial power. He believed that if Britain consolidated its political, economic and military ties with its empire, the country would be able to face any threat from the increasing influences of other countries, particularly Germany and America. As part of his strategy, Chamberlain did envisage some of the revenues being used for education, naval defence and also as an alternative to raising direct taxes. What he failed to do was to take on board that this would be a divisive and damaging policy. When Balfour appeared uncertain as to whether to adopt tariff reform, Chamberlain pushed on without regard for the Conservative Party. Chamberlain can be criticised for his blinkered and inflexible approach, but he did put forward some strong arguments for tariff reform.

In a powerful speech in Birmingham, in May 1903, Chamberlain spoke against those in Balfour's government who stuck to a free trade position. The speech caused uproar and pressed home the split in the Conservatives between the free traders and the tariff reformers. On the same day, Balfour spoke in London in favour of scrapping the shilling tariff on wheat. The lack of consensus in the Cabinet was revealed. In spite of Balfour's efforts to reach a compromise and introduce a limited degree of trade protection, the damage was done. Balfour's Cabinet team was fractured by resignations and dismissals, all to the delight of the Liberals, who, sensing a change in the political climate, began to pull together on what had become a major political issue. Balfour's tactics of not coming down on either side caused confusion and looked weak.

In September 1903, Joseph Chamberlain resigned from office, free to pursue his scheme of tariff reform. He set up a Tariff Reform League to finance his campaign. He moved away from his original argument for Imperial preference to out-and-out protectionism and continued to imply criticism of Balfour for evading any debates on free trade. The tariff reform issue split the Conservative Party in two and reunited the Liberals.

Exploring the detail

Tariff reform

The divisions over tariff reform within the Conservative ranks were so publicly aired that the reaction from the electorate was considerable. It caused anxiety among many ordinary people who feared a general rise in food prices. Cheap food was particularly important to the low-paid agricultural labourers who had been enfranchised in the reform of 1884 and had, so far, largely voted Conservative.

A FREE TRADE FORECAST.

Fig. 4 *There was intense debate about continuing the policy of free trade or introducing tariff reform, to deal with increasing competition to British industry, especially from America and Germany. On which side of the argument are those who issued this cartoon? Explain how you have come to this conclusion*

Assessment of Balfour's options

Balfour was in a tight corner, but it is harsh to blame him entirely for the divisions in his party. If Balfour had chosen to ignore the issues of education and tariff reform, he could perhaps have held on for longer. He might then have been accused of inaction as addressing both of these areas was overdue.

■ Activity

Thinking point

'Gladstone as leader of the Liberals, had broken his party over Home Rule; it was the Conservatives whose own change of front now brought the Liberals together again. And in each crisis it was the voice of Joseph Chamberlain that was decisive' (A. Wood, *Nineteenth Century Britain*, 1969).

Was Joseph Chamberlain a political liability or an asset? (You may wish to undertake some further research into the life and career of Joseph Chamberlain before attempting this question.)

■ Cross-reference

For the formation of the LRC in 1900, see page 116.

■ Questions

1 To what extent did the Conservative policies help to reunite the Liberal Party, which was in disarray in 1902?

2 How did the Conservative policies enable the Liberal Party to strengthen its opposition to the Conservative government?

The Liberals certainly seized the opportunity to whip up Nonconformist opposition to the Education Bill, which took the Conservatives by surprise. The argument about the funding of the Church schools from the local rates lacked logic as, previously, the Church schools had been funded from a central government grant. It was tax payers' money whichever way you looked at it. On balance it was a sensible reform, but the Liberals were able to take political advantage of it.

The issue of trade protection had to be addressed to take account of world economic expansion, but it could be argued that, once Balfour saw how unpopular it was, he would have been wise to drop it.

In addition, the allegiance of a large sector of the working classes could no longer be taken for granted. The formation of the LRC in 1900 should have acted as a clear warning to the Conservative government that if it ignored the concerns of the working classes, it could no longer depend on their vote. In spite of this, Balfour had shown little inclination to introduce a programme of reform to address the problems of the working-class poor. The working class now had political status, better education and unions to represent their interests. Underlying these issues was the fact that the Conservatives had been in power almost unchallenged for two decades, and many voters simply wanted a change.

The general election of 1906

By October 1905 Balfour was in little doubt as to the unpopularity of his government. Both the Liberal opposition and the extreme Protectionists in Balfour's own party were out to bring him down. His authority in his own party was greatly damaged by his inability to resolve the issue of tariff reform. In December, in a last ditch effort to regain political control, Balfour resigned. He hoped that Campbell-Bannerman would have difficulty in forming a united Cabinet and that the old divisive issues of Irish Home Rule and Imperialism would prevent any agreement among the Liberals. An election might then put Balfour back in office. In the event, Campbell-Bannerman succeeded in pulling together what is still today regarded as a government of exceptional quality and outstanding ability. Among the best known were H. H. Asquith, Lloyd George, Lord Haldane, Winston Chuchill and Sir Edward Grey. The new Cabinet also had balance in that it represented the key opinions and beliefs within the party. It included traditional Gladstonians, moderates such as Asquith and Haldane, new left (New Liberals) as represented by Lloyd George and Labour by John Burns. For the first time, the landed classes did not dominate the Cabinet.

With this impressive Cabinet line-up, Campbell-Bannerman called an election for January and the campaign began in earnest after Christmas. It focused on free trade and cheap bread and was a vote winner. It was still the custom for elections to be held over a number of days and, in this case, the election was spread over three weeks. The early results would be known before some people had cast their vote. (There was clearly a need for electoral reform in this respect.) When all the results were in, there was an astonishing landslide for the Liberal Party. They had won 377 seats, which gave them a clear majority over any alliance of any other parties, while the Conservatives had been reduced to 157. Even Balfour had lost his seat. For the first time, there was a good showing of Labour candidates and the Labour Party won 29 seats outright.

Key profiles

Herbert Henry Asquith

Asquith (1852–1928) was Liberal prime minister from 1908 to 1916. His government was renowned for introducing far-reaching social reforms, challenging the power of the House of Lords, conducting an arms race with Germany and taking Britain into the Great War in 1914. Born into an ordinary middle-class Yorkshire family, Asquith's outstanding intellect enabled him to win a scholarship to Oxford, and become a successful barrister. He became an MP for East Fife in 1886, home secretary from 1892 to 1894 and chancellor of the exchequer from 1905 to 1908. Widowed in 1888, he married the flamboyant, aristocratic Margot Tennant in 1894. Their expensive lifestyle meant he could not afford to become leader of the Liberal Party when approached in 1898. He was Campbell-Bannerman's obvious successor in 1908. Payment of MPs was introduced in 1911. Asquith spoke out against female emancipation. He felt compelled to tackle Irish Home Rule, which was shelved when war came. He headed a coalition government in 1915, but was criticised for his handling of the war and was replaced by Lloyd George in 1916.

Fig. 5 *Herbert Henry Asquith*

David Lloyd George

Lloyd George (1863–1945), nicknamed the 'Welsh wizard', is considered to be one of the great reforming politicians of the 20th century. He was appointed president of the Board of Trade by C-B, chancellor of the exchequer in Asquith's government 1908–15, and prime minister of the wartime coalition government 1916–22. Born in Manchester, Lloyd George grew up in Wales and was an ardent Welsh Nationalist. Elected Liberal MP for Caernarvon in 1890, he continued to practise as a solicitor as MPs were not paid until 1911. He came to national prominence for his outspoken attacks on the Conservatives over the Boer War. He could rouse a crowd with his fiery speeches. He was the driving force behind many of the Liberal social reforms, and to pay for these he presented the controversial 1909 'People's Budget'; its rejection by the Lords led to the Parliament Act in 1911. He ran the Ministry of Munitions during the war. He replaced Asquith as prime minister in 1916 with the connivance of the Conservatives. He represented Caernarvon until his death in 1945.

Fig. 6 *David Lloyd George*

Cross-reference

The Liberal social reforms are detailed on pages 150–153.

The People's Budget of 1909 and the Parliament Act of 1911 are covered on pages 155–6.

Fig. 7 *Members of the Labour Party about to take their seats in parliament for the first time after the 1906 general election. Keir Hardie is in the centre and Ramsay MacDonald is second from left*

■ **Did you know?**

During the opening of parliament in October, there was a protest from a group of women who called themselves suffragettes. They wanted the vote for women and thought the Liberals would support their cause – they were to be disappointed. See page 170.

■ **Cross-reference**

The Lords' rejection of the 1909 budget and the ensuing crisis and election are detailed on pages 155–156.

■ **Cross-reference**

For Irish Nationalism between 1903 and 1915, look ahead to pages 168–170.

Before the election, the LRC had enough clout to enter into a secret electoral pact with the Liberal Party, known as the Lib-Lab Pact. The LRC agreed not to put up candidates against Liberals in constituencies where the anti-Conservative vote might be split, in exchange for a free run in 35 constituencies where the LRC had a strong chance of winning a seat. The result in the new parliament was that the Labour group agreed to give support to the Liberals, but it also looked to the Liberal government to address its key concerns over the unemployed and, most immediately, the reversal of the Taff Vale decision. The LRC changed its name to the Labour Party.

It seemed that the general election of January 1906 was about to bring in a new era in politics.

The Conservative Party, 1906–15

In the election of January 1906, the Conservative Party had been reduced to 157 MPs. Of these, 109 were in full support of tariff reform and only 16 were in favour of free trade, the rest supporting trade protection. This meant that the protectionists defined the Conservative Party in opposition during these years.

Balfour was soon returned to parliament in a by-election and resumed leadership of the party. Lord Lansdowne became leader in the House of Lords. The vast majority of the members of the Lords were traditionalist in outlook by virtue of their background. Most of them actively supported the Conservative Party. Balfour took advantage of this and, working closely with Lansdowne, encouraged the Lords to vote against Liberal legislation at every opportunity. Salisbury had used this tactic to defeat Gladstone's Home Rule Bill in 1894 and continued it to bring down Gladstone's successor Lord Rosebery in 1895.

Salisbury had got away with it, but political power was moving away from the landowning elite and its use by Balfour against the Liberal Party, which had formed a government with an overwhelming mandate from the electorate, was unjustifiable and clearly undemocratic. Balfour's policy of using the Lords to attempt to undermine a government that was introducing ground-breaking social reform turned out to be the preliminary round in the greatest constitutional crisis in Britain since the 1832 Parliamentary Reform Act. When the Lords rejected the Liberals 1909 budget with Balfour's encouragement, the ensuing crisis led to the Liberals calling an election, which the Liberals won.

Balfour resigned shortly afterwards, apparently on health grounds, but in reality was pushed out. His successor was Andrew Bonar Law, a tariff reformer and a good debater. Under the new Conservative leader, the emphasis changed towards dealing with the re-emergence of the Irish Home Rule question. The idea of Home Rule was very unpopular in most parts of Britain and especially the Irish Nationalist plan to coerce Ulster into being part of a united Ireland. However, the outbreak of war in 1914 put the Irish question on hold and gave the Conservative Party a new national cause to support.

Key profile

Andrew Bonar Law

Although born in Canada, Law (1868–1923) moved to Scotland at 16 and worked in his family's iron business. He became an MP in 1900 and rose rapidly. He lost his seat in the 1906 general election, but got back into parliament through a by-election. Law became leader in 1911 and continued to serve through wartime even though it was revealed in 1914 that his family's firm had been supplying iron to Germany for armaments. He became chancellor of the exchequer in 1916 and, despite retiring in 1921, came back as prime minister after Lloyd George's disgrace in 1922. However, he suffered ill-health and retired in 1923 and died the same year.

The historian Robert Blake questions why Balfour made such a fundamental error in his misuse of the power of the House of Lords. He finds a clue in a speech by Balfour in 1906:

> *It is the duty of everyone to ensure that the great Unionist (Conservative) party should still control, whether in power or in opposition, the destinies of this great Empire.*

*Blake, R. (1997) **The Conservative Party from Peel to Major**, Arrow Books*

Activity

Challenge your thinking

Read over the above section, 'The Conservative Party, 1906–15'.

1. Explain the ways in which Balfour's tactics in opposition were contrary to parliamentary democracy.

2. Why do you think Balfour thought his tactics were acceptable?

3. Why do you think he made 'such a fundamental error' and misjudged the political climate so badly?

Study tip

To gain a fuller understanding of the issues surrounding this topic, read over the section below on the Reform of the House of Lords. In addition, reading the section page 8 will help you to focus on general issues of parliamentary democracy and be a useful revision exercise.

Liberal social and constitutional reforms, 1906–14

The Liberal government, which swept to power in January 1906, introduced a set of social reforms that were more far-reaching than any measures passed by previous governments. It attempted to deal with the problems of children, the old, the sick and the unemployed. Liberal measures included medical inspection in schools, the introduction of old-age pensions, setting up Labour Exchanges and the introduction of health insurance and unemployment benefit.

Some historians argue that these social reforms laid the foundations of the modern welfare state. Yet, in 1906, many Liberals were still committed to the principle of *laissez-faire*, which meant minimum government intervention in people's lives. There was no clear programme of social reform laid out and, indeed, social welfare had not been a key election issue. There was, however, a group of radical 'New Liberals', that was interested in moving away from the *laissez-faire* ideology of the Gladstonian Liberals to a new view – that increased State intervention was necessary to achieve a minimum acceptable standard of living.

This group proved to be extremely influential in directing Liberal policy. Other important influences, such as the rise of Labour, were brought to bear on the party leaders and caused a re-think of policy. The budget, which was introduced to pay for the reforms, brought the issue of the Lords' inappropriate use of their power to block legislation to boiling point. The Liberal government was then faced with one of the great constitutional crises in British parliamentary history.

Social reform

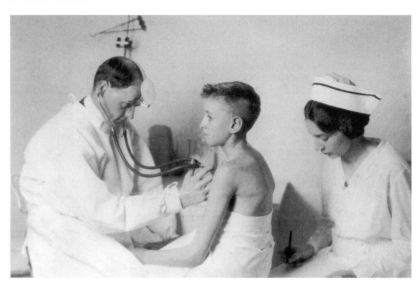

Fig. 8 *A doctor holds a stethoscope to a boy's chest during a medical examination, c.1910*

Under Campbell-Bannerman's leadership the Liberals introduced reforms to improve the health and wellbeing of disadvantaged children. It was not until Asquith took over as prime minister in 1908 that the old Gladstonian Liberalism gave way to the New Liberalism and that the pace of reform quickened.

The motives behind the reforms

The Liberals passed an extraordinary number of far-reaching social reforms, and yet their election campaign was not fought on this issue. This has prompted historians to consider a number of possible motives that led the Liberals to adopt such a policy.

New Liberalism

New Liberalism was a belief in the necessity of tackling poverty through State social welfare and a more humanitarian approach to social problems. The Liberal Party was moving away from the Gladstonian *laissez-faire* Liberalism and Asquith's Cabinet included a number of these New Liberals. The influence of the fresh intake of Liberal MPs began to be felt as they canvassed their leaders to employ the power of the State in response to social problems. Lloyd George, who visited Germany to witness welfare legislation in action, and Winston Churchill were the two most prominent members, but there were others whose ideas had huge influence and who exerted pressure from a more junior position. The journalist H. W. Massingham and philosopher L. T. Hobhouse wrote of the necessity of State intervention; civil servants with strong convictions like Robert Morant and William Beveridge made their views felt in government circles. There were others such as Charles Masterman and Charles Trevelyan. They argued against individualism and for greater **collectivism**. They convinced the moderate members of the party to accept the change in direction.

Political self-interest

The Liberal government was certainly aware of the growing concern over the problems caused by poverty, but it was equally conscious of the potential threat from Labour. Tackling poverty would, therefore, be politically expedient for the Liberals. There was an anxiety among the Liberal leadership that if it did not attempt to meet the needs of the working class, these voters would increasingly turn to the Labour Party. The social reform programme could be viewed almost as an antidote to the spread of Socialism.

Pressure from the Labour Party and the trade unions

The Labour Party and the trade unions were sufficiently confident to pressurise the Liberals into taking action to improve conditions for the working classes. Labour's first demand met with great success, when the Liberal government accepted the Labour proposals for the Trades Disputes Act, which overturned the Taff Vale judgement and gave the unions immunity from prosecution for taking strike action.

Cross-reference

For the Taff Vale judgement, look back to page 116.

Impact of social research

Non-government organisations such as the Salvation Army and other charities were no longer able to deal on any meaningful scale with the problems that beset the impoverished urban dweller. As the industrial cities had grown, the problems of the poor had increased. A number of key reports in the previous decade had put forward clear evidence of the extent of poverty in Britain. The Liberal government could not afford to ignore these findings.

The Report of the Royal Commission on Labour (1895) suggested that ordinary working people could not earn enough to buy basic necessities. The Royal Commission on the Aged Poor (1895) called for some form of old-age pensions and an end to the workhouse as the main system of poor relief. The two surveys that made the most impact on the Liberal Party were Charles Booth's *Life and Labour of the People of London* (1891) and Seebohm Rowntree's *Poverty: A Study of Town Life* (1901), which both concluded that about one-third of Britain's urban population lived in grinding poverty. There was greater public awareness of such information as a result of better education and wider access to newspapers.

Key profile

Charles Booth

Booth (1840–1916), a wealthy, philanthropic Liverpool ship owner, carried out a detailed investigation of the living standards of Londoners over 17 years, meticulously recording his findings. He concluded that 30 per cent of Londoners lived in poverty even though many of these had regular jobs – their wages were too low to buy even the basic necessities. When they were laid off work or sick, there was no support and they had no savings to fall back on. Booth identified only a very small percentage of idle, feckless poor (0.9 per cent). He called for government action such as the introduction of pensions.

Cross-reference

Seebohm Rowntree is profiled on page 138.

Reform in the interests of national efficiency

The poor state of health of the working-class army recruits who came forward for the Boer War had generated widespread shame and concern, which the Liberals could ill afford to ignore. The minimum height requirement for signing up had to be dropped to 5'2" from 5'6" in order to get enough recruits. At a time of growing international tension, it was believed that if Britain was to maintain a strong military reputation, measures had to be taken to improve the state of health of the nation's

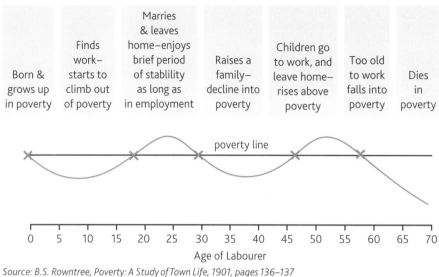

Cycle of Poverty of a Labouring Man

Source: B.S. Rowntree, Poverty: A Study of Town Life, 1901, pages 136–137

Fig. 9 *Cycle of poverty of a labouring man*

children. Social reform could therefore be justified on the grounds of preserving national pride and efficiency.

It would appear that much of the impetus for the Liberals' social reform programme was based on political expediency, rather than a genuine desire to improve the lot of the working classes. However, most Liberals came to believe that some State action was necessary to achieve minimum acceptable living standards for all. It became a challenge to set 'a line below which we shall not allow people to live and labour' – in other words, the poverty line.

Activity

Constructing a spider diagram

Draw a spider diagram to show the reasons for the Liberal governments' social reforms.

The social reforms

Reforms for children

The first social reforms to be undertaken by the Liberal government targeted children and dealt with the provision of school meals and medical inspections. Since education had become compulsory, it became clear that many children were arriving at school hungry, sick and dirty. The initial proposal for school meals provision came from William Wilson, Labour MP, as a private members' bill that the government adopted. The Provision of Meals Act was passed in December 1906. The local authorities could levy a rate to pay for school meals for needy children. Many authorities failed to act until the provision was made compulsory in 1914.

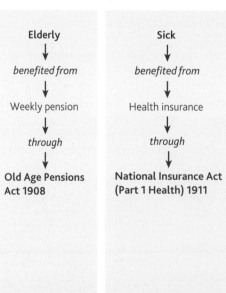

Children
↓
benefited from
↓
Free school meals
Medical inspections
Special protective measures against criminalisation
↓
through
↓
Schools Meals Act 1906
Medical Inspections Act 1907
Children's Charter 1908

Elderly
↓
benefited from
↓
Weekly pension
↓
through
↓
Old Age Pensions Act 1908

Sick
↓
benefited from
↓
Health insurance
↓
through
↓
National Insurance Act (Part 1 Health) 1911

Workers (employed/unemployed)
↓
benefited from
↓
Compensation for injuries at work
Eight-hour day for miners
Assistance to find work
Minimum wages for 'sweated' industries
Half-day off for shop assistants
Unemployment insurance
↓
through
↓
Workmen's Compensation Act 1906
Coal Mines Act 1908
Labour Exchanges 1909
Trade Boards Act 1909
Shops Act 1911
National Insurance (Part II umemployment) 1911

Fig. 10 *Liberal social reform*

The introduction of medical inspections in schools in 1907 was introduced as a result of the efforts of Robert Morant, who was adamant that unhealthy children could not benefit from attending school. Most education authorities chose to ignore the clause to provide free medical treatment, until the act was tightened up in 1912, and additional government grants were given to set up school clinics.

The Children's Act (or Charter) brought together a collection of measures to protect and decriminalise children. Juvenile courts and borstals were set up so that children who faced court proceedings and detention were not mixed up with hardened adult criminals, who might have a further corrupting influence on them. The emphasis was not on punishment but on rehabilitation of children back into normal society. There were new penalties for the ill-treatment of children. It became illegal for children to beg on the street. The sale of cigarettes, tobacco and unsealed alcohol (i.e. beer in a jug) to children under 16 was banned.

The Children's Charter was important in establishing new attitudes towards the welfare of children. It set the precedent that the State must take responsibility for its children's welfare. The principle became accepted that it was a child's right to receive these services and protection. It also underlined the fact that children were not the only vulnerable group in society who deserved State support.

Reforms for the elderly

The Old-Age Pensions Act was passed in 1908. It provided a non-contributory pension of 5 shillings per week for people aged 70 and over, with an annual income under £21. The pension could be collected from the local post office.

The main criticism was that it was insufficient to raise an elderly person above the poverty line. Its importance lay in the fact that the pension was given as a right and not as a charitable handout and removed the stigma of applying for help under the poor law system. It was non-contributory, so that there was no financial burden attached to receiving it. It established a collectivist principle of State intervention in the lives of the elderly poor, using government funds for their relief. It also assumed that you had saved for your old age.

Reforms to safeguard the workers

The Liberal government passed a number of measures to safeguard workers from exploitation, to secure better working conditions and to help the unemployed back into work. Many thousands of workers, mainly women and children, were involved in 'sweated industries', such as tailoring and lace making, which were not covered by the Factory Acts. They worked long hours in ill-lit back-room factories, or at home for piece money. They had no union to represent them. Churchill's Trade Boards Act fixed minimum wages for the various trades involved. It was another unprecedented intervention by the government, but continued to excluded many trades. The Shops Act gave assistants a half-day holiday a week, but did not control the maximum hours that could be worked. The Mines Act limited the number of hours a miner could work

Activity
Thinking point
What evidence is there that the Liberal reforms reflected a new attitude to the care of children? In pairs, draw up a list of child reforms and consider what problem each addressed to help to come to a conclusion.

Activity
Talking point
What differences are there in attitudes to the care of children today?

Question
Why do you think it was important that pensions were paid at post offices?

Fig. 11 *Men lining up at one of the new Labour Exchanges opened in 1910, hoping to find work*

underground in a day, but did not include the considerable time spent getting to and from the coal face.

The setting up of Labour Exchange Offices across the country was a practical innovation influenced by William Beveridge. The Exchanges advertised local job vacancies and, after 1911, paid out unemployment benefits. Beveridge pointed out in his book *Unemployment – a Problem of Industry* that the practice of men standing outside a factory gate waiting to be taken on for casual work was inefficient. A Labour Exchange would bring together worker and employer at one location. The scheme was criticised as there was no requirement for the unemployed to register and employers were not encouraged to use the Exchange. When they did, it was usually to find skilled rather than unskilled workers.

The National Insurance Act, 1911

The National Insurance Act was a compulsory scheme organised in two parts, the first relating to health insurance and the second to unemployment insurance. It should be regarded as Lloyd George's outstanding peace-time achievement. This was the most far-reaching example of State intervention to support workers who were temporarily unemployed or sick through no fault of their own.

Health insurance

In the interests of national efficiency and alarm at the high incidence of tuberculosis among the working class, Lloyd George drew up a scheme whereby a worker paid a regular contribution and received a measure of sickness benefit. It was a compulsory scheme that provided health insurance for workers earning less than £160 per year. The deal was that the worker would contribute 4d (d = old pence), the employer 3d and the State 2d to the scheme, which in turn would provide sickness benefit of 10 shillings a week for 13 weeks, with free medical attention and medicine.

Fig. 12 *Leaflet entitled 'Dawn of Hope' published to promote Liberal social reforms*

The final legislation was a watered-down version of Lloyd George's original scheme. He had wanted to include widows and orphans, but objections came from insurance companies that already catered for those groups on a private basis and wished to protect their business. Their inclusion in administering the final scheme, in which they handled the contributions, meant that they could expand their business as long as they accepted State supervision. Objections came from the British Medical Council that the scheme interfered with doctors' independence. The *laissez-faire* politicians argued that it was wrong to force workers to part with some of their wages. It was sold as a bargain for workers with the slogan '9d for 4d', to which the socialist quip was 'why not five pence for nothing?' The Liberal publicity machine travelled around the country persuading workers that the scheme was advantageous to them.

It was innovative, but limited in that it only catered for the worker and not his family (apart from a generous maternity benefit of 30 shillings). It excluded the majority of the workforce. The entitlement lasted only 26 weeks. There was no free hospital service. It did not create a national health service, but it did point future governments in that direction.

Unemployment insurance

This was a compulsory scheme of unemployment insurance for workers in trades that were most affected by seasonal variations: shipbuilding, mechanical engineering, construction, iron founding and saw milling. It was run on the same principle as the health insurance, with weekly contributions from the employer (2.5d), employee (2.5d) and the State (3d). The benefit was 7 shillings (35 pence) a week for 15 weeks in a 12-month period. The scheme covered over 2 million workers, but was not comprehensive enough. There was no safety net when the 15-week period was over. Many felt that the State contribution was too small.

Other significant reforms

The early social legislation of the Liberal government came about through pressure from the Labour Party as much as through Liberal conscience, although in the case of reversing the Taff Vale decision the Liberals were fulfilling a pre-election pledge. Measures had to be taken to safeguard the unions from ruinous financial penalties in future disputes. In the end, the act was far more extensive than many Liberals felt necessary, but they gave in to pressure from Labour to avoid open conflict. The Trades Disputes Act, 1906, established that no case could be brought against a union for damages caused by strike action and it finally made peaceful picketing legal. It gave the trade union movement a strong legal position as a basis for the future and secured their industrial power for decades to come.

Assessment of the Liberal social reforms

The success of the Liberal reforms is a matter of debate among historians. The main objective of the Liberal reforms was to alleviate poverty, but some argue that the measures had limited success. Between 1901 and 1914 the value of real wages rose very little. The Poor Law with its workhouse system still remained, although its importance was diminishing. The pension provision was regarded as inadequate. The National Insurance Act was not comprehensive enough. There was no inclusion of benefits for the very low-paid agricultural workers. The major issues of education and housing were ignored. Some low-paid workers could access free medical treatment, but the scheme excluded the majority of working men. There was no policy of full employment, and inadequate relief through the Poor Law system remained the option for the long-term unemployed and their families.

However, it can be argued that the Liberal reforms were a significant departure from traditional minimal State interference. Setting up Labour Exchanges went against the principles of market economy and laissez-faire Liberalism. It was the first time any government had provided welfare benefits as a right, although this fell well short of creating a **welfare state**, established years later in 1945. The concept that the wealthier members of society should contribute to the welfare of the poorer was applied in Lloyd George's 'People's Budget', through raising taxes on high salaries, land and luxury items. This established an important model for future governments to follow.

To some extent, the Liberal reforms signalled a departure from individualism and the end of the patronising Victorian attitudes of self-help and *laissez-faire*. The old idea that poverty was caused by individual fecklessness or laziness was disappearing, and with it reliance on the unpopular and humiliating methods of Poor Law relief. The move towards government responsibility for those who could not help their poor circumstances, in other words collectivism, began to gain acceptance.

Key terms

Welfare state: the government accepts that it has the primary responsibility to make comprehensive provision for the wellbeing of its citizens in education, health, employment, old age and housing. A welfare state was established in Britain in the years immediately after the Second World War. It was largely the work of Atlee's Labour government (1945–51).

Cross-reference

For more on the 'People's Budget, look ahead to page 155.

Activity

Challenge your thinking

How successful were the Liberal reforms in tackling the problems of poverty?

When trying to answer this question, Historians have reached different conclusions. Draw up a list of positive points and negative points. Try to draw a conclusion that reflects a balanced view based on the evidence you have collected. Don't forget to include financing the reforms in your assessment.

Constitutional reform – the reform of the House of Lords

The role and conduct of the House of Lords

Fig. 13 *Poster produced by the Labour Party for the general election of 1910, which was called by the Liberal government to gain support for the constitutional crisis. Use the poster to explain how the Labour Party intends to capitalise on the situation*

With each step in the progress of parliamentary reform, during the 19th century, the power of the House of Commons increased and conversely the power of the House of Lords diminished. By 1901, they were on an even footing. A parliamentary bill could be introduced into either the Lords or the Commons and, as long as it passed each of three readings in both Houses and amendments were considered, it would become law once it received the monarch's approval. However, the last word really lay with the Lords. They had the power to veto a bill after it had passed the Commons. It had become the custom for money bills (i.e. budgets) to be raised only in the Commons and not be vetoed by the Lords, as parliamentary business would be brought to a standstill.

As the Commons became more democratic, with the extension of the franchise to the working classes, and more representative, with the redistribution of seats to densely populated areas, the power of the Lords, as the unelected representatives of the landed classes, to veto any government bills, became increasingly questionable.

There were 591 members of the House of Lords. Of those, 561 were hereditary peers, 24 were Anglican bishops, 2 were Archbishops and 4 were law lords. Over two-thirds of the Lords were Conservatives and the remainder Liberals. The size of the House of Lords could be increased by the monarch's creation of new peers. As things stood, the Conservatives had an almost invincible majority in the Lords.

The constitutional crisis of 1910, which came about as a direct result of Lloyd George's controversial 1909 budget and led to the reform of the House of Lords, could be said to have stemmed from the political game played first by Salisbury and later Balfour, in opposition, to outwit the Liberal government, by encouraging the Lords to veto their measures. The Campbell-Bannerman and Asquith governments became increasingly frustrated at the House of Lords' tactics in blocking worthwhile legislation. The progressive element in the Liberal Party had become uncomfortable with the undemocratic nature of the House of Lords, while many in the Labour Party were opposed to its existence. Lloyd George often expressed contempt for the House of Lords in his speeches, for example to the National Liberal Federation in 1906 (Source 3).

■ Cross-reference

The 1909 budget and the resulting constitutional crisis are detailed on page 155.

The use by Salisbury and Balfour of the House of Lords to block legislation which they opposed is described in on page 146.

The House of Commons represents the industry of the country. What does the House of Lords represent? It represents the idleness of the country. What about the House of Lords? There is not a workman there. They are not men who are there because of any special gifts, but purely from the accident of their birth.

3   *Lloyd George, D. (1906) **The Government and its Work**, Liberal Publication Department*

The People's Budget, 1909

Lloyd George, as chancellor of the exchequer, had two objectives in his first budget. The first was to raise enough money to finance the building of Dreadnoughts in response to public clamour in the face of a growing naval threat from Germany. The second objective, closer to his heart, was to fund old-age pensions and set a precedent for future social reform. Many historians think that his hidden agenda was to get the better of the Lords and raise money by taxing the rich and 'wage implacable warfare against poverty and squalidness'.

The focus of the budget was to raise government revenue by direct taxation, rather than by tariff reform and this displeased many Conservatives. Lloyd George raised income tax from 1 shilling (5 pence) to 1 shilling 2d (6 pence) in the pound on those earning over £3,000 p.a. and introduced a super tax on annual incomes over £5,000. He introduced, for the first time, a road fund licence and petrol duties. Few but the wealthiest owned cars. Lloyd George increased death duties, taxed alcohol and tobacco and, most controversially, introduced a 20 per cent tax on profits made on the sale of land. The House of Lords reacted strongly at what they perceived as an attack on their landed wealth and privilege by breaking the convention of never vetoing a money bill. In November 1909, they threw out Lloyd George's budget and set in motion a major constitutional crisis.

Lloyd George's speech at Newcastle in October 1909 contains more than a hint of confidence that he would succeed in bringing the House of Lords to its knees (Source 4).

> Let them realise what they are doing. They are forcing a revolution, and they will get it. The Lords may decree a revolution, but the people will direct it.

4   *Lloyd George's speech at Newcastle, October 1909*

The general elections of 1910 and the 1911 Parliament Act

Fig. 14 *The passing of the 1911 Parliament Act in the House of Lords, from a drawing by S. Begg*

Asquith declared the Lords' action as unconstitutional and called an election for January 1910. The Liberal victory was narrow, with 274 seats over the Conservatives 272. It meant the balance rested with the Irish Nationalists, who held 82 seats, and the Labour Party, who held 40.

Key chronology

Constitutional crisis

1909 November Lloyd George's budget rejected by Lords.

1909 December Asquith calls election to seek popular approval to curb power of Lords.

1910 January Election results give Liberals tiny majority, and Irish Nationalists balance of power.

1910 March Parliament Act introduced, to abolish Lords' power of veto.

1910 April Threat of Parliament Act encouraged Lords to pass budget.

1910 May Death of Edward VII. George V becomes king.

1910 November George V secretly agrees to create Liberal peers to swamp Lords if Parliament Act is rejected.

1910 December Parliament dissolved and election gives 272 seats each to Liberals and Conservatives.

1911 May Parliament Act passed by Commons.

1911 July Lords try to amend bill – George V threatens new peers.

1911 August Lords pass bill 131 votes to 114.

The Parliament Act, presented to the Commons in March 1910 by Asquith, sought to end the power of veto of the Lords. It proposed to deny the Lords power to amend or veto a money bill (i.e. a budget); impose a maximum delay of two years on any other act; and to hold elections every five years instead of the current seven years. The Irish leader, John Redmond, agreed Irish Nationalist support to get the act through on condition that Home Rule for Ireland was reintroduced. The Lords finally passed the 1909 budget, but held out against the attack on their power.

A genuine attempt to negotiate a settlement of the crisis was attempted when Liberal and Conservative politicians held a series of meetings, known as the Constitutional Conference, without success. Asquith risked another election in December, which again resulted in the Irish and Labour holding the balance.

In May 1911, the Parliament Act was passed in the Commons. When the Lords employed delaying tactics, Asquith revealed an agreement he had made with George V to create enough Liberal peers to swamp the Conservative peers in the Lords if they rejected the act. The threat was enough to convince the Lords to accept the act. After an impassioned debate in the Lords, the 1911 Parliament Act became law by a majority of 17 votes.

The Parliament Act was a triumph for democracy and reduced the power of the unelected second chamber. It brought an end to the long period of political dominance of the aristocracy and marked the ascendancy of the House of Commons. It prevented the undemocratic Conservative exploitation of their majority in the Lords. It confirmed the principle that a democratically elected government should be allowed to carry out their work, as long as they had the confidence of the House of Commons, which reflected the will of the people. There were other consequences too: the 1910 elections had given the balance of power to the Irish Nationalists again, and the price for their support was a Home Rule Bill. For Labour, it removed the barrier to their eventually achieving their own legislative programme through the democratically elected House of Commons.

Exploring the detail

The 1911 Parliament Act

- The House of Lords had no right to either amend or veto a money bill.
- The Speaker of the Commons was to define what is a money bill.
- Any other bills could be amended or rejected, but only for a period of two years, when they automatically would become law.
- General elections were to be held every five years instead of every seven.

Did you know?

Payment for MPs was introduced in 1911 at a salary of £400 p.a. It opened the House of Commons to men who lacked independent means. They could stand for parliament and establish their right to be a representative of the people, as well have the right to vote. It was another step forward in the road to democracy.

Summary question

What was the political importance of the reform of the House of Lords?

9 Changing relationships at home and abroad

Britian needs you to run the war.

Britian needs my military experience.

Fig. 1 *Asquith appoints Kitchener as Secretary of State for War*

In this chapter you will learn about:

- foreign affairs and the search for allies

- the end of splendid isolation and relationships with European powers to 1914

- the challenge to Liberalism from the Labour Party

- the development of Irish Nationalism

- the suffragettes and their campaign for votes for women

- the Liberal reaction to the start of the Great War to 1915.

Historians L. C. B. Seaman and Trevor Royle have expressed differing views of Kitchener's appointment as Secretary of State for War.

> On August 5th 1914, Asquith appointed Lord Kitchener as Secretary of State for War. This was not only because it was good for morale and for the government's shaky reputation. It represented accurately the view that Asquith and most politicians of the day might be expected to take on the outbreak of war. War was a specialized under taking, the soldier was the expert whose advice and competence no politician was qualified to question. However, throughout his career, Kitchener had worked in aloof isolation, attended by a small group of favourite subordinates; with the result that the techniques of delegation and coordination essential to the running of the war department were beyond him. It was a mistake on Asquith's part to rely so heavily on a colonial soldier whose capacities were largely a matter of myth and whose chief effectiveness was as a model for a recruiting poster.

1

Adapted from Seaman, L. C. B. (1991)
***Post Victorian Britain**, Routledge*

Key chronology

Key events, 1906–15

1902	Salisbury retires from office.
	Coronation of Edward VII: Anglo–Japanese Alliance.
1903	Emmeline Pankhurst founds the Women's Social and Political Union.
	Liberal and Labour parties make secret electoral pact.
1904 February	Russo–Japanese War.
	April Entente Cordiale with France.
1905	Foundation of Ulster Unionist Council and Sinn Fein.
	First Moroccan crisis.
1906	Liberal landslide in general election.
1907	British Entente with Russia.
1908	Bosnian Crisis.
1910	Union of South Africa established.
1911	Agadir Incident, 1911.
1912	Third Irish Home Rule Bill introduced.
1912–3	Balkan Wars.
1913	Home Rule Bill is rejected twice and rejected by the Lords.
1914 4 August	Britain declares war on Germany.
1914 23 August	BEF in action at Mons and Le Cateau.

Did you know?

Lord Salisbury handed over the job of foreign secretary to Lord Lansdowne in 1900. He had managed that role as well as that of prime minister for most of his years in office. It was Lord Lansdowne who started to seek out allies for Britain.

Cross-reference

To recap on foreign policy in the years 1887–1901, see pages 121–128.

To the man in the street all was well now that Britain had secured the services of its greatest soldier in its hour of need, and much of the anxiety that had gripped the nation on 4 August evaporated when the headlines proclaimed Britain's new warlord. In their eyes Kitchener could do no wrong. His imperial process had seen him defeat all who had dared to stand before him, victory was his friend, and his very presence – his huge frame, the luxuriant moustache, the fixity of his gaze – had become a symbol of British pluck and resolve. In short, he was nothing less than a national institution whose existence would strike terror into the hearts of Britain's enemies. In that respect Asquith had shown great discernment in engineering Kitchener's services at such a critical time.

2   *Royle, T. (1983) **The Kitchener Enigma**, Michael Joseph*

Lord Kitchener (1850–1916), a career soldier, spent most of his adult life in postings to various parts of the empire, in the Sudan, Egypt and South Africa. He was Commander-in-Chief in India (1902–9), where he reorganised the Indian army and was promoted to Field Marshall in 1910.

Foreign affairs and the search for allies; the end of splendid isolation

The main thrust of Salisbury's foreign policy during the 1880s and 1890s had been not to get too involved in alliances with other European nations which might lead Britain into an unnecessary war. One result of this policy meant that by 1902, when Salisbury retired from office, Britain had no close allies. All the other great European powers belonged to defensive alliances. Britain's isolation had been highlighted by international disquiet at the Jameson Raid and the country's subsequent handling of the Boer War. It made Britain aware of its vulnerability if war was declared on Britain by any one of the other powers.

In reality, Britain's island security could only be broken by naval attack. The building of the Kiel Canal (1895) and the passing of the Navy Laws (1899–1900) in Germany alerted Britain to the potential threat to its naval supremacy and the need for allies especially in Europe. A final attempt was made to form an agreement with Germany, over what Britain believed to be mutual concerns in their trading position in the Far East. It failed.

Throughout the Salisbury era, Britain had remained closer to the Triple Alliance of Germany, Austria and Italy than to the Dual Alliance of France and Russia. There had been years of tension between Britain and Russia, over Russian designs on Constantinople and an outlet into the Mediterranean via the Black Sea; anxiety over the security of India from Russian expansion into Afghanistan and, more recently, suspicion over Russian ambitions in the Far East. Russia's activities potentially disturbed Britain's lucrative trading arrangements in China. An increase in Russian military presence in northern Manchuria in January 1901 indicated Russia's continuing pursuit of colonial expansion and prompted Britain to consider its first alliance for many years.

The Anglo–Japanese Alliance, 1902

Britain's signing of an alliance with Japan in 1902 signalled the end of its period of 'splendid isolation'. Japan was an emerging industrial nation and naval power, and was also anxious about the Russian military build-up in its sphere of influence. If either Britain or Japan were attacked by more than one power, the other would help. Japan recognised British interests in China and the Pacific and Britain recognised Japan's rights in Korea. Agreement was reached over the size of the naval presence in the Pacific. A naval force 'superior in strength to that of any third power' would be maintained. This allowed Britain to concentrate on its fleet nearer home. It was also a warning to Germany who had colonies in the Pacific.

When a newly confident Japan went to war against Russia in February 1904, Britain was able to abide by the terms of the agreement as well as steer clear of the dispute. France, which was allied to Russia, did not want any involvement and looked more keenly towards Britain for a conclusion to recent friendship talks.

Relationships with European powers to 1914

Entente Cordiale, 1904

The hostility engendered between France and Britain over Britain's occupation of Egypt had come to a head at Fashoda in 1899 and brought the two countries to the brink of war. By 1902, most of these colonial issues had been settled, but it was not until this point that Britain felt ready to engage in new friendships with its European neighbours. France was prepared to lay aside resentment of Britain over Egypt and was more anxious about the potential threat from Germany. Britain's alliance with Japan concerned them, because of tensions between Japan and France's ally Russia. War between Japan and Russia could cause problems between France and Britain.

In the face of the build-up of German naval power, a stronger relationship with France would make sense for Britain.

The signing of the Entente Cordiale between France and Britain in April 1904 was a clear reversal of British policy. Britain's rapprochement with France signified a closer involvement with Europe. France recognised British occupation of Egypt and the Sudan. Britain recognised French interests in Morocco. France conceded defeat in a dispute over fishing rights along the Newfoundland coast and received territory in Gambia. The Entente was not a defensive alliance, or an anti-German alliance. It was simply a friendly agreement. It brought an end to Britain's fear of any Franco–Russian naval cooperation, which would pose a serious threat to Britain's Mediterranean fleet.

The Entente Cordiale moved Britain closer to the possibility of cordial relations with France's main ally, Russia, although British suspicions of Russia remained. It minimised any potential damage caused by the Russo–Japanese War (1904–5). It upset the Kaiser and created tension between Germany on the one hand, and Britain and France on the other. There was a slight shift in the balance of power in Europe, but to the frustration of the Kaiser and to a lesser extent France, Britain avoided clarifying the extent of its allegiance to France. It was a situation of growing unease between old neighbours, who had always been suspicious of each other's motives. There were no further references to Britain's 'splendid isolation'.

Cross-reference

Details of Britain's Imperial tensions are provided on pages 121–127.

The build-up of German naval power is discussed on page 160.

Exploring the detail

Entente Cordiale, 1904

Several leading British politicians were involved in the cross Channel talks that took place before the Entente was signed, and a great deal of publicity was given to the State visit of Edward VII to Paris at the time, but Balfour should be seen as being the driving force behind the Entente. It was a major achievement and one for which he is rarely given credit. Robert Rhodes James comments: 'King Edward passed into legend as the Peacemaker. Arthur Balfour went down to political eclipse' (R. R. James, *The British Revolution*, 1976).

Question

Why did Britain seek to end its period of 'splendid isolation' after 1900?

Key profile

Sir Edward Grey

Foreign secretary, 1905–16, Grey (1862–1933) made the defence of France against German aggression the main object of his policy, but sought opportunities to mend fences with Germany. He was critical of the Kaiser's short-sighted blunders, which heightened tension. He was criticised for secret diplomacy with France. Had he been more open about commitments to France, it might have deterred German aggression. Grey fulfilled Britain's 'obligations to honour' Belgian independence when Germany invaded France through Belgium. Grey was shocked by the rapid descent into large-scale conflict and prophesied, 'The lamps are going out all over Europe; we shall not see them lit again in our lifetime.'

Sir Edward Grey as foreign secretary carried much of the responsibility for conducting Britain's relationships with the other European powers from 1905 until the outbreak of war in August 1914. Increasing international tension and mutual suspicion made relationships very difficult and Europe was brought to the brink of war on several occasions before 1914. Grey aimed to strengthen Britain's new friendships with France and Japan and, at the same time, lessen the mistrust between Britain and Germany. This was difficult with the continuing build-up of German naval strength. It was imperative for Britain to maintain a naval presence in several places worldwide, yet keep a big enough North Sea fleet to keep German naval expansion in check.

German rivalry

The Kaiser regarded Britain as a commercial and Imperial rival. His ambitions to create for Germany an overseas empire – 'a place in the sun' – justified the expansion of his navy. Germany had always been considered to be a land power, and had a huge conscripted army to protect its extensive borders with its European neighbours. Germany had a short coastline and relatively few colonies, compared with Britain. The passing of the Navy Laws in Germany in 1899 and 1900 alarmed the British government as it made provision for the build-up of the German High Seas Fleet. It was seen as a direct threat to Britain's security as an island. As part of its defence strategy, Britain operated the two-power standard. Britain maintained the same strength in fighting ships as the sum of the next two naval powers.

Fig. 2 *The* Kaiser Wilhelm der Grosse *dreadnought, commissioned in 1909 and launched in 1912*

Britain's naval supremacy was as yet unquestioned, but the difficulty the country now faced was preserving its strong naval presence across the world to protect its trade routes and colonies, and also concentrate enough ships in the North Sea to compete with the growing German fleet.

Naval build-up

After 1905, neither Britain nor Germany could deny the naval rivalry that existed. For the next 10 years they tried to outdo each other in the construction of battleships. Plans to improve naval defence were started under Balfour's government. Sir John Fisher, First Sea Lord, was responsible for organising the building of the first dreadnought. It was a revolutionary design in terms of armour, guns, size and speed.

The deadnought quickly made all other battleships obsolete. Its launch resulted in an arms race between Britain and Germany.

Dreadnoughts	1906	1907	1908	1909	1910	1911	1912	1913	1914	Total
Great Britain	1	3	2	2	3	5	3	7	3	**29**
Germany			4	3	1	3	2	3	1	**17**

Attempts by Britain to persuade Germany to halt the race failed. Campbell-Bannerman had reduced the number of dreadnoughts being built in 1906, but Germany responded by speeding up its production. Reports in the British press caused public alarm. Pressures from public and naval chiefs persuaded the government to increase dreadnought production. The cost to finance rapid construction of the dreadnoughts was immense and was partly responsible for Lloyd George's controversial budget in 1909. By 1914, Britain had a clear lead. The British navy had 29 dreadnoughts, compared with Germany's 17 (including those under construction). An Atlantic fleet based at Gibraltar was created to take pressure off the Mediterranean fleet.

Fig. 3 *The naval base*

Cross-reference

For details of Lloyd George's 1909 budget, refer back to page 155.

British army reforms

Anxiety over mounting German hostility persuaded the Liberal government to review the state of the British army. R. B. Haldane, Secretary for War, was responsible for making Britain's small professional army as well trained and efficient as possible. It could never compete in size with the conscripted armies of the other European powers, especially Germany. Haldane introduced a General Staff to achieve better planning of operations and coordination and a volunteer territorial army to supplement the professional army. An Officers' Training Corps was established in public schools under the direction of the War Office.

Did you know?

The revolutionary battleship *HMS Dreadnought*, launched in 1906, was so successful it gave its name to all battleships built to that specification. The size of the dreadnoughts led the Germans to widen the Kiel Canal in 1911. This caused further alarm to the British government and Admiralty.

The Moroccan Crises and the Entente with Russia

The Kaiser, upset by the Entente Cordiale, tried to cause a rift between Britain and France and at the same time test the strength of their relationship. Morocco was one of few semi-independent territories remaining in Africa and France was keen to increase its sphere of influence there. It was adjacent to French Algeria; it had extensive iron ore deposits; it had a strategically important position at the entrance to the Mediterranean; and it had a weak ruler. The Kaiser visited Morocco, declaring his support for its independence and criticising French ambitions. The Kaiser called for an international conference at Algeciras, in Spain, to settle Morocco's position. Grey came out in support of France's claims over Morocco, followed by Russia, Spain and Italy. Germany was defeated and isolated, except for its close ally Austria-Hungary.

The Algeciras conference had brought France and Britain closer together and led to the start of informal Anglo–French military talks, in which plans for possible future military action were discussed. The Kaiser's action had created a real anxiety that Germany was trying to establish its domination of Europe, but it was a short-sighted policy and made Grey determined to continue his support of France and look towards an understanding with France's ally Russia.

In 1907, Britain signed an Entente with Russia, putting aside its distaste for the reactionary tsarist regime. Most areas of conflict between them were settled. Britain had given up support of Turkey over the Armenian massacres in the 1890s and Russia's defeat by Japan in 1905 had ended the Russian threat in China. It was now possible to plan to concentrate Britain's Expeditionary Force (BEF) in Europe and not the north-west Indian frontier.

In 1911, French troops occupied the Moroccan capital Fez, to protect the Sultan from an internal revolt. The Kaiser claimed compensation for German citizens living in Morocco and sent a warship to the Moroccan port of Agadir. Britain responded at once to the Kaiser's bullying tactics and he was left in no doubt that Britain would come to France's aid if necessary. The Entente between Britain and France was looking more like an alliance than an understanding. Britain and France started naval talks. Anti-German feeling was developing in Britain, encouraged by Winston Churchill and Lloyd George, whose anger against Germany was backed up by the British press. The tension between Germany and Britain was dangerously close to an outbreak of hostility, but neither side wanted war.

Bosnia and the Balkans

Annexation of Bosnia

In 1908, Austria took advantage of a revolt in Turkey and annexed Bosnia and Herzegovina. This action roused nationalist feelings in Serbia and increased its hostility towards Austria. It stirred up Russian protests. The Balkans was not an area of immediate concern for Britain or France. Germany, Austria's main ally, perhaps unwisely, took the opportunity to undermine Russia by putting pressure on Russia to recognise Austria's annexation. Britain and French concerns about German ambitions were raised.

Russia, angered by its humiliation, embarked on a rearmament programme to strengthen its position. Cautious references were made to a Triple Entente between Britain, France and Russia. It remained a diplomatic alliance, but emphasised the alignment of the European powers into two blocs. Germany's clumsy diplomacy was putting Germany in danger of the encirclement it most feared, that of Britain, France and Russia. The Triple Alliance was primarily defensive, and it should be remembered that neither system was made as a preparation for war, but rather as an attempt to preserve peace.

The Balkan Wars, 1912–13

Britain did involve itself indirectly in the Balkan Wars in 1912 and 1913, in an attempt to prevent hostility escalating between Austria and Serbia. The Balkan League of Serbia, Greece and Bulgaria defeated the Ottoman Turks and finally chased them out of Europe. It was a victory for Balkan Nationalism. Germany, Russia and Austria each had cause for concern at the potential power of the victorious independent Balkan nations. Austria, however, was particularly concerned at the growing influence of Serbia on its doorstep. Sir Edward Grey took the initiative and called the Conference of London to settle the territorial outcome of the war. It was carried out with agreement between Britain, Germany and Austria and to the general satisfaction of the European powers.

Serbia and Bulgaria immediately fell out over their gains and there was a brief second Balkan War. Bulgaria was defeated and a large and powerful Serbia was created, causing Austria renewed anxiety. This time, Germany advised restraint. There had been agreement in London, involving both Germany and

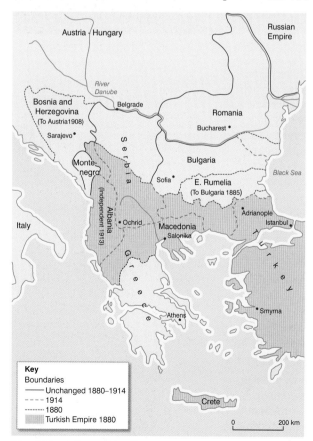

Fig. 4 *The Balkans, 1880–1914*

Britain and, as a result, tensions eased between them. The head of the Foreign Office, Arthur Nicholson, wrote in May 1914, 'Since I have been at the Foreign Office, I have not seen such calm waters'. It was a case of the calm before the storm.

Europe at war, June to August 1914

On 28 June 1914, Archduke Franz Ferdinand, the heir to the Austro-Hungarian Empire was assassinated, while on an official visit to the Bosnian capital Sarajevo. This action lit the fuse that sparked off the Great War that lasted from August 1914 until November 1918, and brought untold death and misery to many parts of Europe. Austria accused Serbia of complicity in the assassination and declared war on Serbia on 28 July. On 1 August, Russia came to the aid of Serbia and Germany declared war on Russia. When Germany declared war on France on 3 August, it looked as though Britain would be drawn in.

On 3 August 1914, German troops marched into Belgium as part of their wider plan of attacking Paris, knocking France out of the war and then concentrating their efforts on France's ally, Russia. The immediate reaction of Asquith's Cabinet was to make Germany's breach of the Treaty of London of 1839 (guaranteeing Belgium's neutrality) Britain's *casus belli* (an incident that justifies war). Britain declared war on Germany on 4 August 1914.

Fig. 5 *A crowd in Trafalgar Square in London surrounding recruitment poster with a message from the King, 1914*

Reasons for Britain's entry into the war

Britain had been concerned at the unfolding events in Europe, but had hoped they would be contained within the Balkan region, which did not directly affect Britain's interests. There was disbelief in Germany that Britain would go to war over a 'scrap of paper' and Germany suggested Britain had other motives. Britain was not obliged to assist France, but there was a moral duty to take action. The attack on France potentially threatened Britain's security. Any hostile German naval activity in the Channel would cause anxiety, although by 1914 Britain had clearly overtaken Germany in the naval arms race. Britain had twice as many naval vessels of every category as the Germans and was in no obvious danger at sea and Britain's trade routes were secure. Relations between Germany and Britain had worsened considerably over the previous decade, but there was no outstanding dispute between them, which would have made war a likely outcome. The Kaiser's posturing had irked the British government, but his aggressive attitudes were not a cause for war. Britain's fear was that Germany would defeat France and Russia and be in a position to dominate Europe. Britain could not run that risk.

The Germans did not think Britain would feel strong enough to mount a challenge on land with its small British Expeditionary Force, which was far outnumbered by Germany's army. Haldane's reforms in the army in 1907 had produced an effective well-organised force, which contributed in delaying the German advance into Paris in the early weeks of the war.

Exploring the detail

Belgian neutrality

The Treaty of London was signed in 1839 by the European powers including Prussia (later part of Germany), France and Britain recognising Belgian independence. Belgium agreed to remain neutral and the signatories agreed to uphold its neutrality. Seventy-five years later, when Germany marched its armies into Belgium, it was breaking the agreement. However, the terms of the treaty placed no clear obligation on those who signed it to defend Belgium if it was attacked. Yet Britain stated it was the reason for declaring war against Germany.

Did you know?

The Kaiser referred to the British Expeditionary Force as a 'contemptible little army'.

Activity

Talking point

Why did Britain go to war in 1914?

Activity

Revision exercise

Read over the chapter so far. Using a copy of the table below, summarise the key points of Britain's relationship with Germany, France, Russia and Austria-Hungary in 1902, and again in 1914 before the outbreak of war. Make an assessment of how the relationships have changed over the period.

	Key factors affecting Britain's relationship in 1902	Key factors affecting Britain's relationship in 1914
France		
Germany		
Russia		
Austria-Hungary		

The challenge to Liberalism

The Labour Party

Decline of the Liberals?

Liberalism had traditionally gone hand-in-hand with Radicalism. In 1906, the Liberal Party enjoyed one of its greatest electoral successes. It followed this up by establishing a government of extraordinary energy and talent, which carried out far-reaching reforms in an attempt to address the problems of poverty that existed in Britain at the turn of the 20th century and bring benefits for the working class. These reforms, both social and constitutional, took Britain along a road towards greater social responsibility, and with a more democratic parliament. The Liberals were then faced with the challenge of taking Britain through the first total war with its European neighbours, where there was no immunity for any class or either gender. A few years after the end of the war, the power of the Liberals had vanished and in its place was a Labour Party ready to take the reins of government for the very first time. It was an astonishing political turnabout. However, there were many indicators along the way.

By the time the Liberals formed a government in 1906, they had left behind the bitter divisions over Home Rule and Imperialism of the 1880s and 1890s, on the face of it. The ideological split that still existed between the moderate *laissez-faire*, self-help Liberals and the new collectivist Liberals, who pushed for greater State intervention, did not interfere with the party's programme of reform between 1906 and 1914. It is difficult to tell whether or not the earlier divisions had weakened the party sufficiently to contribute to the growth of the Labour Party.

In considering Liberal election successes in 1906 and January and December 1910, the figures suggest that the victories were due as much to divisions in the Conservative ranks as to Liberal's own strengths. It could be argued that after 1910 the Liberal Party was only able to remain in power with the votes of the Irish Nationalists who were hoping to achieve Home Rule. The Labour share of the vote increased, but it was not a dramatic increase.

Cross-reference

For the election results of 1906 and 1910, pages 144 and 155 and for the failures of Balfour's government see page 144.

Although there was a huge wave of patriotism in Britain at the outbreak of war and trade unionists and suffragettes laid aside their disputes with the government, managing the war effort created new dilemmas for the Liberals. The necessity of bringing resources and manpower under government control in wartime (for example the introduction of conscription) was an anathema to many Liberals. By 1915, Britain was facing a major crisis in terms of shortage of men and munitions at the Western Front. A split developed between those like Lloyd George, who believed extraordinary government measures were required to survive the war, and those like Asquith, who wished to continue the same policy. Lloyd George became prime minister of a Liberal-led coalition government. The Liberal Party was irrevocably weakened.

The Labour Party in 1906

Woven into that Liberal Party pattern of difficulty and decline was the effect of the growing public perception of the Labour Party as a viable alternative to the other political parties. The Taff Vale judgement and the refusal of Balfour's Conservative government (1902–5) to introduce legislation to protect the unions had brought about a huge increase in union support for the LRC. With increased funds, the LRC were able to put up more candidates for elections. The Lib-Lab Pact agreed in 1903 had been crucial for the advance of the Labour Party. The election of 29 Labour MPs in 1906 was an undeniable success and Labour was keen to maintain the agreement for the immediate future and work on strengthening its central organisation.

They cooperated with the Liberal government to pass the Trade Disputes Act in 1906. Other Liberal reforms such as provision of school meals and legislation in the workplace were welcomed by Labour, but were strongly criticised for not going far enough. To assume, however, that the Liberals were pressurised into carrying out reforms to appease Labour, is to ignore the Liberals' overwhelming election victory in 1906. The Liberals were able to pursue their policies (e.g. contributory nature of National Insurance provisions) and the Labour Party was not yet wealthy enough or had a strong enough electoral base to bring them down.

Labour's failure to make an impact, 1910–15

The Osborne Case, 1909, and payment of MPs

Walter Osborne, a Liberal, objected to his trade union, the Amalgamated Society of Railway Servants (ASRS), using part of his union subscription to support Labour and the case went to the House of Lords. The decision was made in favour of Osborne, which meant it was illegal for trade unions to use their funds for political purposes. It was a huge blow for the Labour Party, whose MPs could not afford to take their seats without financial backing from their union. The party's continuing pact with the Liberals became vital. The situation was eased by the Liberals' introduction of payment to MPs in 1911 and rectified by the partial reversal of the Osborne Judgement in 1913 with the Trade Union Act. This allowed the unions to set up a separate political fund. The threat to the Labour Party had been largely removed by the actions of the Liberal government, but the government had done it in its own time and not at Labour's behest.

Criticism of Labour

There was criticism from Sidney and Beatrice Webb of the influential Fabian Society that the Labour Party had failed to put its socialist

Cross-reference

Details of the Taff Vale judgement are provided on page 116, and of the LRC on page 116.

Details of Lib-Lab Pact are covered on page 145.

Details of Balfour and the unions can be found on page 142.

Cross-reference

Liberal social reform is the subject of page 150.

Cross-reference

The Fabian Society is outlined on pages 113–114.

Did you know?

In 1911, the *Daily Herald* was the first national daily to back Labour.

■ **Key terms**

Syndicalism: belief in the principle of industry owned and run directly by workers. It encouraged sympathy strikes by other unions to increase pressure on government and employers. Its ultimate objective was the overthrow of Capitalism. 'Syndicat' is French for trade union. Dockers' leader Tom Mann was a syndicalist.

principles into practice to attract the working-class voter, lacked leadership and appeared to be merely a wing of the Liberal Party. The weak, quarrelsome leadership was lambasted by Ben Tillett (Source 3).

> I do not hesitate to describe the conduct of these blind leaders as nothing short of betrayal. The winter will have passed and these unctuous weaklings will go on prattling their nonsense while thousands are dying of starvation.

3   *Leaflet by Tillett, B. (1908) **Is the Parliamentary Labour Party a Failure?***

Labour came bottom of the poll in every by-election it contested from 1910 to 1914 and lost four seats.

Trade union unrest, 1911–14

This was a period of significant industrial unrest, with many strikes and lock-outs. Trade union membership doubled to about 4 million. A triple alliance of the miners, the railwaymen and the transport workers was formed for mutual support during strike action. The rise of **Syndicalism** among some unions, where they demanded change through direct action (rather than action through parliament), could have had a detrimental effect on the Labour Party, but it had a limited following in Britain compared with other European countries, especially France. The tensions within the union movement encouraged the leaders of the traditional trade unions to move away from middle-class Liberalism and lend much-needed support to Labour.

Fig. 6 *Rail strike, 1911: Soldiers escorting Pickford vans used in the strike across Waterloo Bridge in London*

■ **Question**

Why would the Labour Party be reluctant to end its pact with the Liberal government?

■ **Exploring the detail**

In 1911, there were 8 million registered voters in Britain, 30 per cent of the total adult population and 63 per cent of the total adult male population. There were half a million plural voters, i.e. about six per cent of the electorate.

In 1906, there were 1 million trade union voters affiliated to the Labour Party, increasing to 1.5 million by 1914.

Adults who had no vote in Britain were as follows:

■ All women.

■ Live-in servants.

■ Adult sons living at home.

■ Paupers (12 per cent of adult male population).

■ 2.5 million qualified to vote but unable to register, largely through ignorance of the system.

Historians' viewpoint

Historians are divided as to whether the main challenge to Liberalism from Labour came before 1914. Paul Thomson and Henry Pelling both think that the middle-class character of the Liberal Party made it impossible for the party to hold on to working-class support once the working class had gained enough political freedom to form its own party. Ross McKibbin in *The Evolution of the Labour Party 1910–24,* (1984) maintains that the growth of trade unionism enabled Labour to present a threat to the Liberals by 1914. Labour was only held back by legal obstructions, such as the Osborne Judgement, and an electoral system that militated against working-class voters.

George Dangerfield in *The Strange Death of Liberal England* (1935) argued that the crises over the House of Lords, labour unrest, near civil war in Ireland and the violence of the suffragette campaign, were too complicated for a divided party to deal with, and that Britain was on the verge of anarchy in 1914. This view is seen by others as extreme.

Trevor Wilson in *The Downfall of the Liberal Party, 1914–35* (1968) believes that, in spite of the uncomfortable effects of these crises, the Liberal Party was in a strong position in 1914 and, although challenged by Labour, its decline was not inevitable. Wilson maintains it was the events of the war that split the party and caused its decline. K. O. Morgan in *The Age of Lloyd George* (1971) maintains that Liberal reformers of the calibre of Lloyd George had put the party in a strong position and 'to view these years as a kind of Indian summer for a party on the verge of imminent collapse is a basic distortion of political history'.

Impact of war on the Labour Party

The outbreak of war in 1914 divided the Labour Party, but had no long-term effects on its unity. Some members were vehemently opposed to the conflict, but the majority put country before politics and offered full support. There was close cooperation between trade unions and government to achieve the smooth running of industries essential to the war effort. In this climate of pulling together, trade union membership almost doubled and increased Labour Party funds. The war enabled the Labour Party to forge strong connections to the working classes and created a desire for a more equal society in Britain, which ultimately benefited the Labour Party.

Historian Martin Pugh outlines what a typical new Labour politician could offer the electorate (Source 4).

> [He] offered a battery of proposals including the eight-hour day, reversal of the Taff Vale decision, employers' liability, old age pensions, poor law reform, the feeding of necessitous school children, taxation of land values, free trade, Home Rule, nationalisation of mine royalties, payment of MPs, curtailment of the House of Lords and universal suffrage. There was virtually nothing in this that was not acceptable to the new Liberals, or to the Gladstonians for that matter.

4　　　*Pugh, M. (2002)* **The Making of Modern British Politics**, *Blackwell*

Activity

Challenge your thinking

Re-read the section 'Liberal social and constitutional reforms, 1906–14' on page 147, the section 'Challenge to Liberalism' on page 164 and Source 4 above.

1 In Source 4, which 'proposals' offered by the 'new Labour politician' had not been introduced by the Liberal government by 1914?

2 Of the proposals not introduced, which one, if made law, would have had the most impact on increasing Labour votes? Explain your answer fully.

3 Pugh seems to suggest that the Labour politician has little different to offer the voter. Do you think this represents a challenge to the Liberal Party or is it more of a problem for the Labour Party?

4 Using all the information, why do you think the working class would vote for Labour in the future rather than the Liberal Party?

Irish Nationalism

The Irish Nationalist push for self-government had faded after the failure of Gladstone's second Home Rule Bill in 1894, and bitter internal feuding kept the parliamentary Home Rule Party weak and divided. The party split after the death of Parnell in 1891. The underlying support remained, but there was little open rebellion. Salisbury's policy of tough measures to deal with disorder followed

Cross-reference

To revise the issue of Home Rule and to follow the fortunes of the Irish Nationalist Party up to 1906, re-read Chapters 2, 5 and 6.

by sturdy reform had quietened the calls for Home Rule. In 1903, Wyndham's Land Purchase Act finally brought in terms that were favourable to the majority of tenants to buy the land they worked, and the landlord was content with the amount he was paid. To achieve this, the government poured a massive £86m into the scheme. By 1915, almost two-thirds of Irish farmers owned their land.

Re-emergence of Home Rule

John Redmond led the minority Parnellite Nationalists during Salisbury's government and had maintained a low profile. In 1900, he was able to reunite the party. Its influence during the first Liberal

Fig. 7 *Sir Edward Carson, leader of the Protestant Ulster Unionists, set up the Ulster Volunteer Force to resist implementation of Home Rule in Ulster*

government was non-existent, because of the huge Liberal majority. After the 1910 elections, with over 80 seats, they once more held the balance of power between the Liberals and Conservatives. Asquith needed the promise of the Irish Nationalist vote in the Commons to deal with the constitutional crisis over the House of Lords. It was given by Redmond. The reward was the 1911 Parliament Act, which meant that the Lords would no longer be able to block the passing of a Home Rule Bill.

Feelings were running high between all parties as they contemplated the outcome of the Home Rule issue. Asquith dutifully introduced another Home Rule Bill in 1912. It was passed by the Commons, with the Irish Nationalist vote, but rejected by the Lords. The Parliament Act would only allow a two-year delay and it was expected that this Home Rule Bill would become law in 1914.

Ulster, 1912–14

This, however, was not the happy ending to a campaign of sustained electoral support for Home Rule, which had run from 1880 to 1914. The whole question of Ireland's future was again thrown into the melting pot as the Protestant Ulster Unionists threatened to revolt if they were pushed unwillingly into a Catholic-dominated Ireland and forced to sever ties with Britain. The Ulster Unionists began to resist the introduction of Home Rule by mobilising their forces. They were led by a brilliant and unscrupulous Dublin lawyer, Sir Edward Carson, who whipped up support for separate treatment for Ulster. He recruited an 'army' of 100,000 Ulster volunteers – the Ulster Volunteer Force (UVF). It was an illegal organisation prepared to use force. Carson bought guns from Germany. He organised the signing of the Ulster Solemn League and Covenant, which was a Protestant pledge to defend their right to remain part of the union.

The new Conservative leader, Canadian born Andrew Bonar Law, with strong Protestant Scottish-Ulster connections, resented the Parliament Act and the power it gave the Irish Nationalist MPs. Relations between the politicians at Westminster became extremely tense as the Conservatives sought means to preserve the union. Bonar Law dropped a bombshell by promising Conservative help for the Ulster rebels in their defiance of the will of parliament. Asquith was faced with a dangerous and seemingly intractable situation.

■ **Cross-reference**

The constitutional crisis and the Parliament Act of 1911 are discussed on pages 155–156.

■ **Did you know?**

Estimates vary of the number of signatures on the Ulster Covenant from 250,000 to 500,000!

The Curragh mutiny

The Liberal government accepted that it was necessary to offer a special concession to Ulster, to appease its Protestant majority. Asquith, with Redmond's agreement, inserted an exclusion clause in the Home Rule Bill. It would allow the people of any Irish county to vote to opt out of a united Ireland, as a temporary measure to be reversed after six years. The compromise was dismissed by Carson with contempt. The danger of civil war became very real and, in March 1914, alarm was increased at rumours that British army officers stationed at the Curragh, south of Dublin, would 'prefer to accept dismissal' than fight against fellow Protestants. Bonar Law was implicated in this act of near treason, but so also, unwittingly, was Asquith's war minister, Sir John Seely, who was forced to resign after he agreed not to use the army in Ulster. Asquith can be criticised for weak handling of this situation in which army officers appeared to be dictating government policy, and for underestimating the seriousness of the threat from Ulster.

Re-emergence of Irish Nationalism

Various movements for Irish Nationalism were emerging at the turn of the 20th century. The formation of the Gaelic League in 1893 encouraged an Irish Literary revival. The Irish Republican Brotherhood, the remnants of the Fenians, resurfaced in Ireland at this time. Sinn Fein was founded by a journalist Arthur Griffith in 1905, and argued for a separate independent Ireland, but made little political impact before 1914. Another group led by James Connolly, leader of the Irish Labour movement, campaigned for a socialist society. He set up the Irish Citizen Army. Nothing much was heard of any of these groups until the Home Rule crisis. Although there was dissension between them, they shared a dislike of English domination of Ireland and they preferred independence rather than Home Rule.

In November 1913, the Irish Volunteers were formed as a response to the Ulster Volunteers. They were nominally under Redmond's control, but they were soon infiltrated by the Irish Republican Brotherhood, who were were ready to challenge the government if Ireland was denied its freedom. Sinn Fein increased its influence as Redmond's control slipped and moved towards a demand for outright independence.

Home Rule for Ireland

The Home Rule Bill passed through the Commons for the third time in May 1914. There was still no solution for Ulster and an all-party conference in July failed to find an acceptable compromise. Arms smuggling and gun running by both the UVF and the Irish Volunteers brought Ireland to the edge of civil war. Home Rule was due to become law in September 1914 but, when hostilities between the major European powers broke out at the end of July, it was agreed to suspend the operation of Home Rule until the end of the war.

Carson's UVF immediately signed up to join the war effort. Redmond persuaded the Irish Volunteers to do the same. Both sides hoped that their loyal action would bring the government around to their point of view. Asquith appears to have been relieved to shelve the problem and he has been criticised for his 'wait and see' attitude. In the end, Home Rule failed to offer the solution Ireland required. While the majority of Irish Volunteers followed Redmond, a small extreme group split and prepared

Exploring the detail

Events at the Curragh – mutiny or not?

R. F. Foster debunks the theory that the incident at Curragh was mutiny (*Modern Ireland 1660–1972*, 1988):

'Officers stationed at the Curragh camp were, after a series of misunderstandings, given the option by their hysterical commanding officer of resigning rather than "coercing Ulster". In fact there was no government plan to suppress the UVF. The idea of exempting Ulster officers from service in the province would have applied to only 5 out of 57 officers. But the political assumptions and prejudices of a few high-ranking officers had enforced on an inept war secretary a potentially disastrous admission: the army would not in any event, be used to "coerce" Ulster into Home Rule.'

Cross-reference

The Irish Republican Brotherhood and the Fenians are outlined on pages 31–35.

for insurrection against the British government. They carried this out at Easter 1916. After the war, there were many troubled years ahead for both the Irish people and the British government.

The suffragettes and their campaign for votes for women

In 1903, Emmeline Pankhurst and her daughters, Sylvia and Christabel, formed the Women's Social and Political Union (WSPU) to win 'immediate enfranchisement' for women by 'political action' and also to put right other social injustices suffered by women.

Fig. 8 *Suffragettes being carried triumphantly through the streets after their release from Holloway Prison, where they had served a sentence for violent disorder in 1908*

The rights of women and the pattern of their lives were very different from those of men, even at the start of the 20th century, although the social and political restrictions on women that had existed throughout most of the 19th century were beginning to be lifted.

In family life, a married woman was largely dependent on her husband, and unmarried daughters on their fathers. It was not until the 1882 Married Women's Property Act that husbands lost the automatic right to claim their wives' property. Divorce was more difficult for women than men and it usually meant the woman losing custody of her children. In 1912, a Royal Commission on divorce recommended equal rights for men and women seeking divorce, but these were not achieved until 1924.

Girls received the same basic level of education as boys, but few had the opportunity to go on to university and even fewer to enter the professions. Office work and school teaching were common female occupations, although, once married, women were obliged to give up their careers. The first women had started practising medicine in 1870s amid great opposition. Nursing was felt to be more appropriate for women. There was a strong class element in attitudes to women working. It was the norm for working-class women to have full-time employment and they often endured unequal pay and unsuitable conditions in factories and shops. Their male employers were happy to make use of a cheap workforce.

In political terms, women had few rights. They could not vote in a general election, nor become MPs. Women householders had the right to vote in local council elections, after 1888, but most men perpetuated the idea that it was unbecoming and inappropriate for women to be involved in the affairs of State, irrespective of their level of education, or the illiteracy of male voters. They argued that women were too emotional, too fragile for the rough and tumble of politics and they could not fight for their country in time of war. Women's political judgement would be unsound. If women entered the political world, there was an implied threat to the stability of family life. As long as a husband or father had political power and privilege, he could speak for his wife or daughters – a sort of virtual representation! Men in parliament certainly did not wish to share their political power with women.

The National Union of Women's Suffrage Societies (NUWSS), whose members were known as the suffragists, formed in 1897 by Millicent Fawcett, had carried on a quiet campaign for years for female emancipation, but had met with intransigent opposition from both sexes. They had campaigned for equal rights with men instead of pursuing universal suffrage. Some women became impatient with the suffragists'

Did you know?

Elizabeth Garrett Anderson (1836–1917) was the first Englishwoman to qualify as a doctor and she was active in the suffragette movement. She died in 1917, a year before women were given the vote.

lack of progress and this led to the formation, by Emmeline Pankhurst, of the WSPU in 1903.

The slogan of the new WSPU was 'deeds not words', emphasising Mrs Pankhurst's intended strategy of direct action rather than the gentle and ineffective persuasion of the suffragists. The *Daily Mail* first referred to the new group as suffragettes. It was a mainly middle-class organisation, although there was support from female labour groups in the industrial areas of northern England and central Scotland. Annie Kenny, a Lancashire textile worker, was foremost in this group. A petition for female suffrage was presented to parliament in 1904 and rejected. When the new Liberal government dodged the issue of women's suffrage in 1906, the suffragettes mounted a tough campaign in which they were prepared to break the law.

Campbell-Bannerman was not against female suffrage in principle, but apart from support from open-minded politicians like Lloyd George, there were too many Liberals like Asquith who were vehemently opposed to the idea. There was also a fear among Liberals that if the vote was given only to middle and upper-class women, they would support the Conservative Party and damage future prospects for the Liberals to remain in power. Another argument against giving women the vote was that they were in the majority, and the fear was that they would swamp the male vote. The Conservatives were equally divided on the issue and, although great encouragement came from the Labour Party, they were not willing to take on the suffragette cause at this early stage of their history, when there were more pressing issues on their agenda.

The Qualification of Women Act (1907) gave women the right to be elected on to local councils and to take the position of mayor. The Liberal government appeared to be moving in the right direction, but a private member's bill introduced shortly after was overwhelmingly defeated. The suffragettes responded to this by organising marches and demonstrations, and heckling in the House of Commons. The authorities were obliged to arrest the most disruptive trouble makers. The women continued to break up political meetings, smash windows, chain themselves to railings, refuse to pay fines and, when arrested, some went on hunger strike. Their intemperate actions alienated much moderate support from both men and women. The suffragists were dismayed at what they considered to be damaging to the cause and verbally attacked the suffragettes' methods, arguing for a constitutional approach.

During the 1910 general election, Asquith finally agreed to a free vote on a franchise bill for women. It was one of a handful introduced in the following parliamentary sessions, but none ever got passed the second reading. When one of these franchise bills was thrown out on a technicality in 1912, Mrs Pankhurst sanctioned a new phase of violence often referred to as the 'wild period' of suffragette actions. They resorted to physical attacks on government ministers – setting fire to post boxes, and worse, they attacked houses with fire bombs and burnt down churches. The suffragists and even some suffragettes were appalled by the level of violence and the irresponsibility of Emmeline Pankhurst in involving the women in activities that could have caused members of the public serious injury or death. Even Lloyd George's home was bombed in retaliation for his speaking out against one franchise bill, not because of the principle, but because it was a bad bill.

The government toughened up on the suffragettes and ordered force feeding of the women who had gone on hunger strike. When this raised public sympathy for the women, the government passed the Cat and Mouse Act in 1913, which released the suffragettes when they were weak with hunger, gave them time to recover and rearrested them.

Did you know?

The most shocking suffragette action was that of Emily Davison, from Morpeth in Northumberland. She was a suffragette activist and had been imprisoned on several occasions for minor acts of vandalism. On Derby Day in June 1913, she ran across the racecourse at Epsom in front of the King's horse Anmer. She died four days later from severe head injuries. Some of the newspaper reports at the time focused on the inconvenience to the King, the loss of the horse, which had to be shot, the slight injury to the jockey and, lastly, outrage at Miss Davison's reckless behaviour!

Activity

Talking point

Discuss the attitudes to women that prevailed in the early 20th century. Were any of them reasonable? How would they have hindered reform? Was the suffragette campaign the best way of changing those attitudes?

Question

How effectively did the activities of the suffragettes promote their cause?

Fig. 9 *Central London recruiting depot in 1914. Thousands of young men volunteered to join up at the start of the war*

In hindsight, the extreme violence was probably not necessary as the Liberal government had by 1912 accepted the principle of female suffrage, but had not worked out the detail of how far to extend the franchise without disadvantaging their electoral prospects. This too was a futile and short-sighted approach by the Liberals, as they could not control the will of the electorate once the inescapable fact of universal male and female suffrage had been achieved.

When war came in 1914, the suffragettes did not hesitate to call off their campaign and threw themselves wholeheartedly into the war effort. It seemed as though they had nothing to show for their efforts. Over the following four years, the indispensible contribution they made to the successful conduct of the war meant that it became inevitable that when the war ended women would at last be given the vote. The Representation of the People Act (1918) enfranchised all propertied women aged 30 and over and all men over 21.

The impact of the coming of war, 1914–15

British public opinion was completely unprepared for war and many spoke out against British involvement. However, the news of the assassination at Sarajevo caused many to change their minds and support intervention. The extract in Source 5 creates an impression of great enthusiasm for the war.

> In London, the people's enthusiasm culminated outside Buckingham Palace when it became known that war had been declared. The news was received with tremendous cheering, which grew into a deafening roar when King George, Queen Mary and the Prince of Wales appeared. Union Jacks were everywhere to be seen, and the air was filled with the sound of patriotic songs; Trafalgar Square was almost impassable. A hostile crowd assembled outside the German embassy and smashed the windows.

 5   *Daily News, 4 August 1914*

'Business as usual'

In response to the outbreak of hostilities with Germany, Asquith received the confidence of the Commons to continue in government and manage the war, although many had wavered and there were two resignations from the Liberal Cabinet. Asquith appointed Lord Kitchener Secretary of State for War and believed it best to leave the conduct of the war to the military experts, and so virtually relinquished political control. The view of historian L. C. B. Seaman is that this was a mistake and contributed to Asquith's poor reputation as a war leader.

Having taken the decision to send the troops to Belgium, the government and most of the British population thought the war would be 'over by Christmas'. The very British response was that while it lasted they must make the best of it. The very gloomy prophecies by Kitchener about preparing for a long war were largely ignored. The attitude of the government and the people was summed up by Churchill, to continue 'business as usual'.

A wave of patriotism at home encouraged young men eager for adventure and new experiences to respond to Lord Kitchener's appeal for volunteers to swell the army's ranks. The appeal met with great success and by the end of 1914, 1 million volunteers had come forward. They were given basic weapons training in army bases in Ireland before being shipped off to northern France to face the enemy across no man's land between opposing trench lines.

A closer look

The first year of the war on the Western Front

In the early months of the war, the allies held the key position of Ypres in Belgium, which safeguarded the channel ports from the Germans. The Germans attacked there in October 1914, but after weeks of bitter fighting the allies held the centre ground around Ypres, which became known as the Ypres salient.

The importance of the first Battle of Ypres was that the Germans failed to win the war on the Western Front and it marked a new and ultimately destructive phase – the establishment of trench warfare. The line of trenches that extended almost unbroken from the North Sea coast in Belgium, across northern France, to the Swiss border remained virtually unchanged for the remainder of the war. Methods of fighting developed that were previously unknown. Battles went on for weeks or months without a definite victory or defeat and left senior army officers perplexed as to how to break the deadlock. The war of movement had ended and a war of attrition had begun.

The human toll among those fighting on the front line, officers and men, is almost impossible to imagine. New instruments of war, such as machine guns, mortars and shells maimed and killed tens of thousands of men in the first year of the war and left many more emotionally and mentally scarred with the shocking memories of trench warfare.

The Defence of the Realm Act (or DORA as it was known) was passed quickly in August 1914, giving the government wide powers to introduce restrictions on the civilian population at any time while Britain was at war. Measures were introduced slowly, but it was a remarkable piece of legislation for a Liberal government in that it approved of total State intervention in a single move. Control of railways and dockyards were given to the Board of Trade and income tax was doubled in the budget of November 1914. Press censorship meant that newspapers were restricted in the information they were allowed to print, particularly regarding military disasters, mutiny in the ranks and execution of deserters. Heavy casualty figures were manipulated. The destruction caused by German Zeppelin attacks on Britain's east coast towns was played down. The government believed its 'economy with the truth' was in Britain's best interests and would help to keep morale high. An agreement was made with the union leaders in March 1915, to ensure full cooperation from the workforce for the war effort and to reduce the risk of damaging strikes. Striking was later made illegal in essential occupations.

In May 1915, Asquith brought several Conservatives, such as Bonar Law, Balfour and Lord Lansdowne, and Labour's Arthur Henderson into the Cabinet, effectively creating a coalition government. It avoided the necessity of a general election, which was due to be held in 1915. However, the move was mainly to stem growing criticism of Asquith's handling of the war and the scandal of the shortage of shells at the front. Lloyd George was appointed Minister of Munitions and took immediate responsibility for resolving the shell crisis, but to do this effectively, it

Fig. 10 *A munitions factory, where production was stepped up to deal with the shell crisis in 1915*

became essential to extend government control over industry. It also increased pressure on Asquith to introduce conscription, although the idea of interfering with an individual's freedom of choice was an anathema to many Liberals. The volunteer army of 1914 had been decimated and it became increasingly difficult to argue against conscription.

Asquith's performance as a wartime prime minister has come in for much criticism. He was seen as too cautious and lacked the decisiveness and sense of urgency and energy that Lloyd George possessed. The unity of the Liberal Party was severely tested by the war. Conscription became a divisive issue; the shell crisis caused major strains within the party and many Liberals did not accept the necessity of abandoning their firmly held *laissez-faire* principles of individual freedom to accommodate the conduct of the war. By 1916, Lloyd George had replaced Asquith as prime minister with Conservative support. The war seemed to have brought the 'Liberal revival' to a shuddering halt.

Activity

Talking point

What effect did the experience of war have on the Liberal Party?

Learning outcomes

Through your study in this section you have learnt about the reasons for the revival of the Liberal Party after years in the political wilderness and how it established its reputation as a party of reform. You should be aware of the Conservative Party's problems and understand its attempt to resist democratic change over the constitutional crisis of 1910–11, which reduced the power of the Lords.

You have also looked at the development of a third political force, the Labour Party, and have considered the extent to which it posed a long-term threat to the Liberal Party. You have seen how the Liberals faced challenges from Irish Nationalism and the suffragettes, and how their policy of ending isolation eventually led to the greatest challenge of all – the outbreak of war in 1914.

Practice question

'In the years 1906–14 the Liberal government was more concerned with national efficiency than social welfare.' Assess the validity of this view.

(45 marks)

Study tip This question requires you to analyse the reasons for the Liberal social reforms of 1906–14. It might be helpful to begin by making a list of these and recording beside each whether its purpose was primarily national efficiency, i.e. creating an efficient workforce and strengthening the country, or social welfare, i.e. providing for citizens who were unable to provide for themselves. Of course, some reforms may have been passed with both aims in mind, but you will need to decide which factor was, on balance, the more important to the Liberal government that promoted them. This may lead you into some consideration of the major reformers, especially Lloyd George and Winston Churchill. You should set out your argument in your introduction and argue the issues throughout your answer, presenting both sides of the case, but showing why you favour one over the other. Your conclusion should flow naturally from what you have written.

5   Conclusion

Fig. 1 *Lieutentant Patrick Lyon in August 1914, just before he joined his regiment for active service in France. He was killed on 27 August 1914 – an early victim of the war*

By 1915, Britain was one year into a war with its European neighbours, which was already taking on a character very different from any previous war. The technology of war had changed, but the methods by which the older generation of generals conducted the war had not. The result was a horrific toll of casualties on a daily basis. By 1915, the young soldier in the photograph, Patrick Lyon, and two of his brothers had become casualties of what was called at the time the Great War. Had Patrick Lyon joined the army in 1865, and come from a privileged background, his father would have bought him a commission. He would have enjoyed, and probably survived, an army career that usually involved overseas postings to various parts of Britain's vast empire. Although in the 50 years to 1915 there had been battles fought and lives lost in distant parts of the empire, Britain had not been involved in a major conflict during this period, with the exception of the Boer War from 1899 to 1902. Instead, Patrick Lyon enlisted in an army that had undergone significant reform and in which merit, and no longer privilege, was designed to bring reward. For him, and almost a million other young British Empire men, the possibility of contributing to the more liberal, egalitarian and democratic society, which had been developing since 1865, was denied through the folly of war.

In 1865, Britain was at the height of its power. It was the wealthiest, most highly industrialised country in the world. It possessed the largest overseas empire, from which it shipped quantities of raw materials to be manufactured into goods to sell at home or trade abroad. During the next 50 years Britain was able to reap the benefits of early industrialisation. It was confident enough to make free trade the basis of its commercial policy. In spite of the onset of the Great Depression from 1873 to 1894, and stiff competition from newly industrialising countries such as America and Germany, Britain had developed a strong integrated economy that continued to grow, albeit at a slower pace. Britain's trade balance remained healthy and the country maintained a dominant position in the world's economy, although it could no longer claim to be the supreme power.

Britain's empire continued to expand during this period, even though Gladstone was anti-Imperial and Disraeli, although pro-empire, was not expansionist. Most territorial expansion took place under Salisbury in the 1880s and 1890s and Britain succeeded in taking the lion's share of Africa. By then, Britain possessed one-fifth of the world's land surface and controlled one-quarter of the world's population.

Queen Victoria, Empress of India, died in 1901 and with her death came the passing of an age. Victorianism had encouraged self-confidence, self-help and thrift. Deference, religious observance and high moral standards were demanded. It produced an unbending attitude of mind that destroyed the career of Charles Parnell. It suggested moral authority rather than monarchical power, which was limited under the constitution. Queen Victoria often interfered in matters of State and choice of prime minister, but as the party system developed in the House of Commons, her influence declined. When Edward VII succeeded his mother in 1901 and George V followed in 1910, royal influence declined and the monarch became a figurehead.

By 1910, the issue facing parliament was curbing the power of the House of Lords. When the Parliament Act was passed in 1911, it was a triumph for democracy and confirmed that real political power belonged to the people's elected representatives. In 1865, although Britain had been regarded as a liberal democracy in Europe, by today's standards participation was very limited. The franchise was based on property, which meant only the wealthy could vote. The growing industrial towns were under-represented and the views of the non-voting working classes were ignored. The non-elected House of Lords in theory had the same powers as the elected House of Commons. By 1915, the franchise had been extended to include working-class men, although it still excluded many men and all women. The size of constituencies corresponded to population distribution. MPs were paid and the recently formed Labour Party offered voters more choice.

In 1865, there were two main political parties, Liberals and Conservatives. Gladstone and his political legacy (he died in 1898) dominated the Liberal Party until 1906. He clung to individualism, rather than moving forward to the modern idea of collectivism. It was up to his successors in 1906 and the influence of the 'New Liberals' to instigate an extensive programme of social reform. By this time the Labour movement had spread and the working-class electorate that Gladstone had created had formed their own 'Labour' Party.

By 1915, the strains of war caused divisions in the Liberal government, which created serious differences between Asquith and Lloyd George. These were proving to be as damaging as the splits over Gladstone's insistence on Home Rule and Rosebery's Liberal Imperialism in the 1880s and 1890s. There was a serious question mark over the ability of the Liberal Party to survive, but an equally intriguing issue as to whether the Labour Party would be well-enough supported to form an alternative government.

In 1915, the questions of Home Rule for Ireland and votes for women had been shelved because of the outbreak of war. It was Gladstone who had taken a fresh look at the Irish question and placed it firmly on the political agenda. The issue of land tenure had been addressed, but there had been no political solution for Ireland. John Stuart Mill had raised the question of female suffrage in 1867, but in 1914 it seemed to many women that there was no certainty of a vote at the end of the war. However, the war had forced the politicians to accept the suffragettes' offer to take men's jobs in transport, heavy industry and in munitions factories, making it more difficult to argue against female suffrage in the future and, by 1915, married women, in particular, had more freedom, more education, and more choice in controlling the size of their family than in 1865.

In 1865, the population of Britain had stood at around 30 million. On the eve of the outbreak of war in 1914, it was officially estimated at 46 million, suggesting a healthy annual increase over the previous 50 years. In 1865, the annual birth rate was approximately 35 per 1,000 and the death rate 22 per 1,000 of the population. By 1915, both figures had fallen, to 25 births and 15 deaths per 1,000 of the population, confirming the trend towards smaller families and improvements in medical knowledge and care. By 1915, the standard of living for most

British families had risen and, in spite of the intervention of the war, continued to do so. Indicators of rising standards can be seen in increased consumption and an increase in real wages. There was mass production not only of foodstuffs such as jam, margarine and chocolate, but also consumer goods such as gas cookers, bicycles, sewing machines and electric lighting.

Eighty per cent of the population of 1915 lived in urban areas, but increasingly the middle classes had moved to the suburbs while the poor remained in the city centre slums. Disraeli's permissive Artisans Dwelling Act of 1875 had not been followed up by any compulsory measures. According to the surveys of Booth and Rowntree, conducted around 1900, one-third of city dwellers lived in poverty. The Liberal reforms alleviated some of the problems and the sick, the old and the unemployed could expect some State assistance. Furthermore, all children could benefit from a basic education as a result of the 1870 Forster Education Act and the Balfour Education Act of 1902, so most of the population was literate. However, poverty had not yet been eliminated.

Fig. 2 *These British soldiers were victims of a German gas attack. The Germans started using gas as a weapon in 1915. Although it had devastating effects on its victims, it was never a decisive weapon*

The period covered by this book starts on a note of high optimism in 1865, but ends on a note of unimaginable uncertainty in 1915. Britain had reaped the benefits of peace and prosperity and had to come to terms with the upheavals brought about by involvement in 'total war'. By 1915, it was impossible to see the end in sight.

As you read this book, think about the questions that it raises. Why was the Liberal Party with its impressive record of electoral and social reform unable to find a formula to maintain its unity and ensure its survival? Why did the Labour Party look set to replace them? Why was the Irish question so intractable? Why did a peaceful and prosperous Britain become embroiled in such a disastrous war? Your reading of this fascinating period of British history should provide you with some of the answers, and encourage you to draw conclusions about the issues raised.

Glossary

A

Adoptive legislation: a law that allows organisations or individuals at whom it is directed the choice of whether or not to carry out its requirements. It is sometimes refered to as permissive legislation. Adoptive legislation reflects the *laissez-faire* attitudes of the period.

Amnesty: a general pardon usually granted by a government to political prisoners who are then released without further penalty.

Arbitration: when a dispute is settled by each side agreeing on a third party whose decision is binding.

Authoritarian idea: belief that stresses the importance of authority.

Authority: power that comes from holding an influential or official position, e.g. a headteacher in school.

B

Belgian neutrality: an agreement that no country would make alliances with or invade Belgian territory.

Belligerent: person (or country) acknowledged as waging war.

Blacklegs: employees who ignore a union call to strike because they are not union members, or simply do not want to support the strike.

Board schools: the popular name given to the new elementary schools set up by the 1870 Education Act.

Borough/county franchise: until the Third Reform Act in 1884, there existed distinct franchise qualifications for dwellers in boroughs and counties. The value of property that qualified a man to vote in the borough was not the same as the value of property that gave a man the right to vote if he lived in the countryside. This made the system very unfair.

Borough: a town granted special privileges often by royal charter became known as a borough and had the right to send two representatives to parliament. Its origin dates from medieval times.

Boycotting: the term came into use during the land war in Ireland meaning to shun or ostracise anyone taking over land from an evicted tenant. The origin can be traced to the treatment given to Captain Charles Boycott by the Land League. Boycott was agent to a wealthy absentee landlord in Co. Mayo and had evicted tenants. He was mercilessly targeted by Land League supporters and needed almost permanent police protection.

Brinkmanship: going to the very edge of something, e.g. war or disaster, but just holding back at the last possible point.

C

Cabinet: the committee at the centre of the British political system that is responsible for making decisions in government. Its members are chosen by the Prime Minister from among their ministers. Both Disraeli and Gladstone had small Cabinets by today's standards (of approximately 15 members). Cabinet meetings have been held in the same room, the Council Chamber at 10 Downing Street in London, since 1856.

Call-on: an expression used by the dockers to describe being employed to carry out the loading or unloading of a ship's cargo.

Catalyst: an agent that alters the rate of change of a process or event.

Chartist movement: founded in 1838, as a result of popular discontent at limitations of reform for the working class. The main aim of the movement was to achieve universal male suffrage.

Civil Service: the body that is responsible for the public administration of the State.

Closed shop: a workplace that only employs people who are members of a trade union. Union leaders often put pressure on employers to adopt this restriction to keep their members in work when jobs are scarce and to increase their bargaining position with the employer.

Coercion: government by force.

Collective bargaining: a formula for negotiating pay and conditions between a trade union on one side and employers on the other.

Collectivism: the belief that it was the responsibility of government to address the basic needs of its people. From 1870, governments started to move away from the principle of *laissez-faire* and took more action to deal with social problems.

Conscription: compulsory enrolment for armed forces.

Constituency: a district that is represented by a member of parliament. Britain is now divided into constituencies of equal size in terms of population, for the purpose of electing representatives to parliament at each general election. A large city such as Manchester is divided into several parliamentary constituencies. In the 19th century, rapid industrial growth made constituencies very uneven and many districts had no MP to represent their interests.

Constitutional monarchy: a form of government in which a hereditary monarch is head of State, but whose powers are defined and limited by parliament.

Copyholder: possessed a written copy of his lease over his land and qualified for a vote if the land had an annual rateable value of £5 or more.

Craft/model unions: these trade unions of skilled workers repesented a particular trade or craft and emerged around 1850. One of their objectives was to persuade politicians and employers that unions could be beneficial to the community through promoting and practising self-help and settling issues with employers without resorting to strike action.

D

Democracy: a form of government in which the people collectively hold political power. There are several forms of democracy. In Britain it is a representative democracy, in which the people elect representatives to use power on their behalf. During the 19th century, Britain could not claim to be fully democratic as privileges and rights were restricted to certain classes and categories of people.

Demography: study of size, density and distribution of the population.

Denominational schools: schools belonging to a particular religion, e.g. Anglican schools were run by the Church of England.

Disendowment: when a regular provision or means of support or gift is removed, most often with reference to a church. In this context, it can take the form of money or property.

Disestablishment: separation of the Church from the State so that the State no longer takes any official part in supporting the Church or upholding its decisions.

Dominion status: a state that was part of the British Empire, but which also had autonomy in domestic and foreign affairs. Canada received 'dominion status' in 1867. The term went out of use in 1845.

E

Entente: an understanding or friendly agreement between two states, as opposed to an alliance that carries a greater commitment to give support, for example, if one member of an alliance is attacked by another country.

Entrepreneur: a person who undertakes an enterprise, often involving a financial risk.

Excommunication: expulsion from membership of a Church. If a Roman Catholic was excommunicated from the Church, he/she feared eternal damnation and hell when they died.

Expedient: appropriate, meets the need.

F

Fenianism: an Irish republican movement that grew up in the aftermath of the Irish famine in the 1840s. Its members swore a secret oath and vowed to work towards Irish independence.

Filibustering: a tactic adopted by Irish Nationalist MPs to 'talk out' a bill – i.e. prevent its passage through parliament by making long speeches until the time for discussing bill ran out. This disrupted the legislative programme of the government.

Franchise: in historical and political terms, the franchise is a voting qualification – 'the right to vote' or simply 'the vote'. During the 19th century, only 'male persons' had the franchise and that was based on a property qualification.

Free trade: the economic policy that involves a free exchange of commodities (goods) between nations without imposing duties or tariffs. Adam Smith's book *The Wealth of Nations* (1776) inspired the free trade movement, which was taken up by Gladstone and the Liberals.

Freeholder: owned his land and, if it was worth 40 shillings in annual rateable value, he could vote.

Friendly societies: (or mutual societies) were formed among workers to enable them to make savings as an insurance against an event such as accident or sudden death. Every subscriber became a member of the society.

G

Government: the body of people (usually a political party with majority vote) who are authorised to manage and direct the affairs of the State.

H

Habeas Corpus: this term comes from Latin meaning 'you have the body'. It exists to preserve the right of the individual not to be detained illegally. It takes the form of a writ to a jailer to produce the person in court, to establish the legality of the detention. It has a long history, stretching back to before the Magna Carta in 1215, at which time it was common law. Very occasionally it is suspended by the government during social unrest.

Hierarchy: the group of people in a body, organisation or society, who exercise control.

I

Imperial preference: if a system of trade tariffs was introduced, it was planned to give favourable terms or exemption to countries in the British Empire, and therefore only tax imports from outside the empire.

Imperialism: when a State adopts a policy of extending power and dominion over another country or region, usually by territorial acquisition or by taking political or economic control. Because it always involves the use of power, whether military force or some subtler form, Imperialism has often been considered morally reprehensible. The term is frequently used in international propaganda to denounce and discredit an opponent's foreign policy.

Incursion: an invasion or hostile attack.

Indentured: contracted (usually) to carry out some form of employment.

Individualism: the commonly held belief that individuals should take responsibility for their wellbeing and that of their families through thriftiness and hard work. To accept charitable hand outs was seen as degrading. It was based on a *laissez-faire* approach that it was not the business of government to interfere in people's lives. It involved the Victorian self-help ethic, promoted by Samuel Smiles and encapsulated in his phrase: 'God helps those who help themselves'.

Insurgent: a person who opposes, or revolts against the government or established authority.

Invisible trade: refers to services such as banking, insurance, transport and overseas assets, rather than actual goods. Today, invisibles include tourism, consultancy, and the music, television and film industries.

J

Jerry-built: houses built quickly and cheaply out of poor quality materials.

Jingoism: the term came from a music hall song that became popular in Britain at the time of the Russo–Turkish war. It had been particularly associated with Palmerston's foreign policy in the 1850s. To say 'by jingo' was a mildly threatening oath at that time. Jingoism has since come to mean patriotism.

Joint-stock company: commercial enterprise with varying amounts of capital (stock) supplied by shareholders. The profits were divided in proportion to the amount of capital subscribed.

Judicature: system of courts, or body of judges.

K

Khedive: a Turkish word meaning 'Lord', and signifying a high-ranking position as a ruler's representative, or governor in an outlying province of an empire. It became the term used to describe Turkish viceroys who ruled Egypt between 1867 and 1914. The title Khedive was first used in Egypt by Muhammad Ali Pasha, regarded as the founder of modern Egypt, in 1805. The Turks still retained authority (suzerainty) over Egypt and would not accept the use of the title Khedive until 1867.

L

Laissez-faire: doctrine that the State should not interfere in the workings of the market economy. It was a basic principle of 19th century Liberal governments and came from the teachings of the great political economists Adam Smith (1723–90) and David Ricardo (1772–1823). It was closely associated with Gladstone's activities as chancellor of the exchequer (1852–5 and 1859–66) when he followed a policy of free trade by abolishing duties on goods.

Lobby: a group of people who campaign to persuade parliament to pass laws that favour their particular interests.

Lock-out: when employers prevent employees who have been on strike from returning to work on the strikers' terms and, instead, take on non-union members to carry out the work.

M

Marxism: the theories of Karl Marx (1818–83), the German philosopher, were concerned with the conflict between capital and labour. He put forward ideas that encouraged others to believe in the destruction of Capitalism in order to establish a classless society.

Militant nationalists: people who are active in support of a particular cause and are reacting against foreign domination.

Minority government: the government in office has fewer seats in the House of Commons than the opposition. This can occur when a prime minister resigns and a new government is formed from the opposition party without holding a general election. It can reduce the government's ability to carry out its legislative programme.

N

Nationalism/national identity: akin to patriotism, especially in the 19th century, in having a love of one's country. Nationalism includes the belief that one's country is a sovereign State, which means it accepts no other country's authority over it. Nationalism is the attitude that people conscious of a common language, culture and tradition, and sometimes religion, should join together into an independent nation State. National identity addresses a basic need in people to belong to a country they can call their own.

Nepotism: showing favour to one's relatives or close friends.

New model unions: after 1850 skilled workers formed unions for their own craft/skill. Their subscriptions were high and they paid out generous benefits to members for illness or unemployment. These unions were generally against taking strike action.

Nonconformists: Protestants who do not accept the practices of the Anglican Church. They were sometimes known as 'dissenters', but this word has an unpleasant edge to it, and the blander term 'Nonconformist' became more common. Nonconformists include Presbyterians, Quakers and Methodists. Their numbers grew in the 19th century as religious, civil and political restrictions against them had been withdrawn. Their political allegiance lay mainly with the Liberal Party.

O

Old Testament: the first part of the Christian Bible, which tells the history, traditions and law of the Hebrew people.

P

Patrician: usually refers to someone who belongs to aristocracy, to the ruling elite.

Patriotism: devotion to or love for one's country.

Patronage: the right to give privileges or make appointments.

Petit bourgeois: a member of the lower-middle class.

Picketing: the action taken by strikers to persuade non-striking workers to join the strike.

Picketing was only legal if it was conducted peacefully. In practice, it was an intimidating experience for non-strikers to 'cross the picket line' to get into their place of work.

Pressure group: a number of like-minded people who by their actions and words try to influence public opinion or government policy on an issue that is important to them.

Primary product: refers to food crops, such as tea or wheat and raw materials like cotton, rather than manufactured goods.

Protectionists: protection or protected trade is when the government imposes a tax on imported goods to support home production.

Protestant Ascendancy: expression used to describe the position of the Protestant landowning class in Ireland that dominated cultural, economic, political and social life. The land had been forfeited from the Catholics by Cromwell in 1650 and redistributed among his Protestant supporters. Cromwell's action against the majority Catholics left a bitter legacy.

R

Rack-renting: charging an exorbitant amount for rented property.

Radicalism: any set of ideas, usually of the left, that argue for political and social change, which is not part of the political mainstream.

Retrenchment: to economise or cut expenditure.

Ribbonmen: Ribbon Societies were a network of secret societies across Ireland based mainly in the towns, with political aims and a tradition of violence and direct action. The Ribbonmen included clerical workers, school masters and artisans. Its members wanted freedom from British rule and civil and religious liberties for all. The Ribbonmen formed a direct link with the Fenian movement after 1858.

Romantic nationalists: people who take a pride in their nation's past glories and history, and uphold national traditions in music, art and literature.

S

School boards: locally elected committees established by the 1870 Education Act to run the new elementary schools.

Secular: connected with worldly matters, civil or state issues rather than religious or spiritual issues.

Security of tenure: legal right to occupy a leased property (in terms of Irish Land Acts).

Self-help: this could be seen as a by-product of *laissez-faire*. It was made popular by Samuel Smiles in his book *Self Help* (1859), in which he praised the hard-work ethic of inventors and engineers who succeeded through their own efforts. A good standard of living and prosperity was the reward of the middle class for thrift and hard work. Self-help became the virtue of the skilled workers in their campaign to promote themselves as respectable and hard working.

Semaphore: a method of signalling originally developed for use at sea between ships. The message was conveyed by a man moving his arms (or flags) up and down.

Socialism: 'a system under which the wealth of a country and the means of production are owned and managed by the state.' Socialism is the opposite to the Victorian ideal of *laissez-faire*, in which the State leaves the people as free as possible to manage their own affairs. The idea of Socialism is that the State controls the nation's affairs, to make sure that everyone has a share of the good things in life, to try and achieve equality for all.

Splendid isolation: the term used most often by historians to describe Britain's position in relation to other nations in the late-19th century. It refers to Britain's reluctance to become involved in the complex system of European alliances, which other countries formed to safeguard their own interests and security. In a way, the term is a compliment, as Britain was perceived as being strong enough not to need friends. Lord Salisbury is the politician most closely associated with conducting an isolationist policy, between 1885 and 1902, though this view is now challenged.

Status quo: the situation remains as it was; the existing condition.

Suffrage: a very similar meaning to franchise, but is more of a concept of having the power or right to exercise the vote. For example, we talk about the campaigns for female suffrage when referring to attempts to persuade government to give women the vote.

Suzerain: a State having supremacy over another.

Suzerainty: position of a suzerain.

Syndicalism: belief in the principle of industry owned and run directly by workers. It encouraged sympathy strikes by other unions to increase pressure on government and employers. Its ultimate objective was the overthrow of Capitalism. 'Syndicat' is French for trade union. Dockers' leader Tom Mann was a syndicalist.

T

Tariff barriers: taxes on the import of goods and materials from another country, which, if they were cheaper than the home product, could inhibit the growth of the home country's manufacturing industry.

Tenant: rented land on a less secure basis than copyholders, but qualified for a vote if the land had an annual rateable value of £12 or more.

Tenets: the opinions or principles that a person or a group believes in and believes to be true. It comes from the Latin word *tenet* meaning 'he holds'.

Tory democracy: the phrase used to describe the policies advocated by Disraeli when he became prime minister in 1874. The Conservative Party maintained its support of established institutions – constitutional monarchy, the British Empire, the Church of England – but at the same time it would support a degree of social reform. This was an attempt by Disraeli to gain working-class support.

Trade union: an association of workers, often belonging to a single trade, who act together to protect their economic interests and welfare in the workplace. Trade unions began to form with the growth of industry.

Viceroy: (in the context of this book) governor of a part of the British Empire, who rules as a reresentative of the monarch.

Visible trade: refers to actual goods that are exported and imported and can literally be seen and transported to their destination by road, rail, sea or air. Opposite of invisible trade.

Voluntary schools: those schools that had so far been run by two religious societes, one Anglican and one Nonconformist, during the 19th century. They had survived on generous government grants, but needed to upgrade to meet additional demands for school places. Progress had been hampered by long-running and petty disputes between the two societies about religious issues. They were included in Forster's

Education Act, but the religious wrangles continued, taking the focus off education.

Welfare state: the government accepts that it has the primary responsibility to make comprehensive provision for the wellbeing of its citizens in education, health, employment, old age and housing. A welfare state was established in Britain in the years immediately after the Second World War. It was largely the work of Atlee's Labour government (1945–51).

Bibliography

Students

Martin, H. 2000, *Britain in the 19th Century*, Nelson Thornes.

Rubinstein, W. 1998, *Britain's Century: A Political and Social History, 1815–1905*, Hodder Arnold.

Murphy et al 2003, *Britain 1738–1918*, Collins.

Peaple, S. 2002, *European Diplomacy, 1870–1939*, Heinemann.

Aldred, J. 2004, *British Imperial and Foreign Policy 1846–1930*, Heinemann.

Rees, R. 2003, *Britain 1890–1939*, Heinemann.

Paterson, D. 2001, *Liberalism and Conservatism, 1846–1905*, Heinemann.

Lee, S. 2005, *Gladstone and Disraeli*, Routledge.

Goodlad, G. 2004, *Gladstone*, Collins Educational.

Dicken, M. 2004, *Disraeli*, Collins Educational.

Culpin, C. and Tweedie, P. 1998, *Gladstone*, Longman.

Lowe, N. *Mastering Modern British History*, Palgrave.

Mayer, A. 1999, *The Growth of Democracy in Britain*, Hodder & Stoughton.

Chapple, P. 1999, *The Industrialisation of Britain, 1780–1914*, Hodder & Stoughton.

Teachers and Extension

Hoppen, K T. 2000, *The Mid-Victorian Generation, 1846–1886*, OUP.

Searle, G R. 2005, *A New England? Peace and War 1886–1918*, Clarendon Press.

Pugh, M. 1999, *State and Society: A Social and Political History of Britain, 1870–1997*, Hodder Arnold.

Foster, R F. 1988, *Modern Ireland 1600–1972*, Allen Lane, Penguin.

Hinton, J. 1983, *A History of the British Labour Movement*, Wheatsheaf Books.

Magnus, P. 1963, *Gladstone*, John Murray.

Lee, S J. 2005, *Gladstone and Disraeli*, Routledge.

Roberts, A. 1999, *Salisbury: Victorian Titan*, Weidenfeld & Nicolson.

Hattersley, R. 2006, *The Edwardians: Biography of the Edwardian, Age* Abacus.

Grigg, J. 2002, *Lloyd George: The People's Champion, 1902–1911*, Penguin.

Charmley, J. 1999, *Splendid Isolation?* Hodder & Stoughton.

Jenkins, R. 1986, *Asquith*, Collins.

Royle, E. 2003, *A Social History 1750–1997*, Arnold.

Royle, T. 1985, *The Kitchener Enigma*, Michael Joseph.

Blake, R. 1997, *The Conservative party from Peel*, Heinemann.

Laybourn, K. 1988, *The Rise of Labour*, Edward Arnold.

Belchem, J. 1990, *Class, Party and the Political System in Britain 1867–1914*, Blackwell.

Pugh, M. 1990, *The Evolution the British Electoral System*, Historical Association.

Hay, J R. 1978, *The Development of the British Welfare State 1880–1975*, Edward Arnold.

Emy, H V. 1973, *Liberals, Radicals and Social Politics; 1892–1914*, CUP.

DVD

Life in Victorian Britain (DVD by Terry Molloy)

The Boer War (DVD 2003)

Electric Edwardians – The Films of Mitchell and Kenyon (DVD 2005)

Mrs Brown, John Madden (*dir*) (DVD 1997)

Zulu, Cy Endfield (*dir*) (DVD 1964)

The Young Winston, Richard Attenborough (*dir*) (DVD 1972)

Literature 1865–1915

A selection of novels and poems written during the period which reflect some of the thinking and social and political concerns of the time

Charles Dickens, *Our Mutual Friend*, 1865

Elizabeth Gaskell, *North and South*, 1855

George Eliot, *Middlemarch*, 1872

Thomas Hardy, *Jude the Obscure*, 1895

D H Lawrence, *Sons and Lovers*, 1913

W B Yeats (1865–1939). Any collection of his poetry and prose.

Acknowledgements

The author and publisher would also like to thank the following for permission to reproduce material:

p3, *Gladstone 1875–1898*, H.C.G. Matthew, Clarendon Press-Oxford, 1995. p3, *The English Constitution*, Walter Bagehot, Intro by R. H. S. Crossman, The Fontana Library, 1867, 1968. p8, *Life in Victorian England*, W. J. Reader, B. T. Batsford Ltd., 1967. p11, *The Formation of the British Liberal Party*, John Vincent, Hassocks Harvester Press, 1976. p11, *Gladstone, New Perspective*, Vol. 2, E. J. Feuchtwanger, Sept 1996. *The Formation of the British Liberal Party*, John Vincent, Hassocks Harvester Press (etc.), 1976. p15, *Disraeli and Victorian Conservatism*, T. A. Jenkins, Palgrave Macmillan, 1996. p15, *Old and New Birmingham*, R. K. Dent, 1880. Quoted in *The Age of Improvement*, Asa Briggs, Longman, 1967. p18, *Old and New Birmingham*, R. K. Dent, 1880. Quoted in *The Age of Improvement*, Asa Briggs, Longman, 1967. p28, *The Making of Modern British Politics*, Martin Pugh, Blackwell, 2002. p29, *Modern Ireland, 1600–1972*, R. F. Foster, Allen Lane, the Penguin Press, 1988. p33, *The Times* newspaper, March 12th 1867. Quoted in *Ireland Since the Famine*, F. L. S. Lyons, Fontana Press, 1985. p33, *Ireland Since the Famine*, F. L. S. Lyons, Fontana Press, 1985. p34, *The Times* newspaper, 16th March 1867. p36, *Modern Ireland, 1600–1972*, R. F. Foster, Allen Lane, the Penguin Press, 1988, R. F. Foster, Allen Lane, 1988. p38, *The Times* newspaper, 1st May 1869. p38, *Gladstone, Heroic Minister 1865–1898*, Richard Shannon, Allen Lane, 1999. p38, *Gladstone's Irish Policy: Expediency or High Principle?* In *Modern History Review*. p38, *Ireland's Holy Wars; the struggle for the nation's soul*, Marcus Tanner, London; New Haven; Yale University Press, 2001. p38, adapted from *Gladstone Heroic Minister 1865–1898* and from *Gladstone Papers 44419, 243*, Richard Shannon, Allen Lane, 1999. p44, adapted from *Gladstone Heroic Minister 1865–1898* and from *Gladstone Papers 44419, 243*, Richard Shannon, Allen Lane, 1999. p45, *New Illustrated Directory entitled Men and Things of Modern England*, 1858. p46, *The Age of Empire 1875–1914*, E. J. Hobsbawm, Weidenfeld & Nicolson, 1987. p49, *The industries of Scotland*, David Bremner, 1869. p50, *The First Industrial Nation*, Peter Mathias, Routledge, 1990. p51, *The industries of Scotland*, David Bremner, 1869. p55, http://www.victorianlondon.org/publications/mayhew1-8.htm, p58, *Self Help, with illustrations of character and conduct*, Samuel Smiles, 1859. p59, *The First Industrial Nation*, Peter Mathias, Routledge, 1990. p63, *The Conservative Party from Peel to Major*, Robert Blake, Heinemann, 1997. p64, *The Conservative Party from Peel to Major*, Robert Blake, Heinemann, 1997. p64 *British Political History*, Malcolm Pearce and Geoffrey Stuart, Routledge, 2002. p64, *The Conservative Party from Peel to Major*, Robert Blake, Heinemann, 1997. p65, *Disraeli*, Paul Smith, CUP, 1996. p65, *The Conservative Party from Peel to Major*, Robert Blake, Heinemann, 1997. p74, *Britain and the Eastern Question*, G. D. Clayton, Hodder Arnold, 1974. p74, *Disraeli*, Paul Smith, CUP, 1996. p75, *Disraeli and Victorian Conservatism*, T. A. Jenkins, Palgrave Macmillan, 1996. p77, *Splendid Isolation*, John Charmley, Hodder, 1999. p86, *Gladstone 1875–1898*, H. C. G. Matthew, Clarendon, Oxford, 1995. p87, *Gladstone 1875–1898*, H. C. G. Matthew, Clarendon, Oxford, 1995. p87, *Modern Ireland, 1600–1972*, R. F. Foster, Allen Lane, the Penguin Press, 1988. p88, *Land and Popular Politics in Ireland: County Mayo from Plantation to Land War*, Donald E. Jordan Jr, Cambridge University Press, 1994. p88, *Land and Popular Politics in Ireland: County Mayo from Plantation to Land War*, Donald E. Jordan, Cambridge University Press, 1994. p88, *Land and popular Politics in Ireland: County Mayo from Plantation to Land War*, Donald E. Jordan Jr, Cambridge University Press, 1994. p89, *Gladstone 1875–1898*, H. C. G. Matthew, Clarendon, Oxford, 1995. p95, *Disraeli and Victorian Conservatism*, T. A. Jenkins, Palgrave Macmillan, 1996. p95, *Disraeli and Victorian Conservatism*, T. A. Jenkins, Palgrave Macmillan, 1996. p96, *Disraeli and Victorian Conservatism*, T. A. Jenkins, Palgrave Macmillan, 1996. p96, *Gladstone 1875–1898*, H. C. G. Matthew, Clarendon, Oxford, 1995. p97, *Ireland since the Famine*, L. S. Lyons., Fontana, 1985. p97, *Salisbury, Victorian Titan*, Andrew Roberts, Weidenfeld & Nicolson, 1999. p97, *Salisbury, Victorian Titan*, Andrew Roberts, Weidenfeld & Nicolson, 1999. p97, *Salisbury, Victorian Titan*, Andrew Roberts, Weidenfeld & Nicolson, 1999. p100 *The Eclipse of a Great Power, Modern Britain 1870–1992*, Keith Robbins, Longman, 1994. p102, *A Century of the Scottish People, 1830–1950*, T. C. Smout, Fontana, 1967. p103 Chapter 9 'The Liberal Age 1851–1914' in *The Oxford Illustrated History of Britain*, H. C. G. Matthew ed. Kenneth O. Morgan., OUP, 1989. p107, *The British Revolution*, Robert Rhodes James, Hamish Hamilton, 1976. p108, *Nineteenth Century Britain, 1815–1914*, Anthony Wood, Longman, 1969 (8th impression). p108, *The British Revolution*, Robert Rhodes James, Hamish Hamilton, 1976. p110, *Salisbury, Victorian Titan*, Andrew Roberts, Weidenfeld & Nicolson, 1999. p110, *The Conservative Party from Peel to Major*, Robert Blake, Heinemann, 1997. p111 Chapter 9 'The Liberal Age 1851–1914' in *The Oxford Illustrated History of Britain*, H. C. G. Matthew ed. Kenneth O. Morgan., OUP, 1989. p114, *The Rise of Labour: the History of the British Labour party 1890–1979*, K. Laybourn, London, Edward Arnold, 1988. p117, *Nineteenth Century Britain*, Anthony Wood, Longman, 1969 (8th impression). p117, *Nineteenth Century Britain*, Anthony Wood, Longman, 1969 (8th impression). p120, *Salisbury, Victorian Titan*, Andrew Roberts, Weidenfeld & Nicolson, 1999. p124, *Salisbury, Victorian Titan*, Andrew Roberts, Weidenfeld & Nicolson, 1999. p124, *Splendid Isolation? Britain the balance of power and the origin of the First World War*, John Charmley, Hodder & Stoughton, 1999. p125, *The British Revolution British Politics, 1880–1939*, Robert Rhodes James, Hamish Hamilton, 1977. p133, Annie Besant's paper, The *Link*, Annie Besant, 1888. p134, *Daily Chronicle* newspaper. p135, *A Brief History of the Dockers Union*, Ben Tillett, 1910. p135, *The Times* newspaper 24 August 1889. p135, The *East London Advertiser*, 24 August 1889, John Burns. p136, *A History of British Trade Unionism*, Henry Pelling, The Chaucer Press Penguin Books Ltd, 1967. p138, *Poverty: A study of Town Life*, B. S. Rowntree, 1901. p140, *England 1870–1914*, R. C. K. Ensor, Clarendon Press, 1936 (1st edn). p140, *Campbell-Bannerman*, Roy Hattersley, Haus, 2006. p154, *The Government and its Work*, David Lloyd George, Liberal Publication Department, 1906. p157, *Post Victorian Britain*, L. C. B. Seaman, Routledge, 1991. p158, *The Kitchener Enigma*, Trevor Royle, London, Michael Joseph, 1983. p159, *The British Revolution British Politics, 1880–1939*, Robert Rhodes James, Hamish Hamilton, 1977. p163, *The British Revolution British Politics, 1880–1939*, Robert Rhodes James, Hamish Hamilton, 1977. p166, pamphlet 'Is the Parliamentary Labour Party a failure?', Ben Tillett, 1908. p167, *The Age of Lloyd George*, K. O. Morgan, Weidenfeld & Nicolson, 1974. p169, *The Making of Modern British Politics*, Martin Pugh, Blackwell, 2002. p172, *Modern Ireland 1660–1972*, R. F. Foster, Allen Lane, 1988.

Photographs courtesy of:

Ann Ronan Picture Library; 0.1, 1.6, 3.2, 3.3, 3.4, 3.5, 4.2, 4.3, 5.2, 5.5, 5.6, 5.7, 7.6, 9.1, 9.7, **World History Archives**; 0.2, 1.1, 1.2, 1.3, 1.4, 1.8, 2.1, 2.2, 2.3, 2.4, 2.5, 2.6, 4.1, 4.4, 4.5, 4.6, 4.7, 4.8, 5.1, 5.3, 5.4, 6.1, 6.2, 6.3, 6.4, 6.5, 6.6, 7.1, 7.2, 7.3, 7.7, 7.8, 8.1, 8.4, 8.5, 8.6, 9.2, 9.6, **National Galleries of Scotland**; 1.5, **Bridgeman Art Library**; 3.6, **World History Archive**; 8.3, 9.3, 9.4, **www.revolutionaryplayers.org.uk**; 3.1, **Edimedia archive**; 7.4, 7.5, 9.5, **The Literature Archive**; 5.8, 3.7, **Sante Archive**; 10.2, **Topfoto**; 8.9, **Getty**; 8.7, 8.8, **Haileybury School**; 10.1, **Gallery Oldham**; 8.2, **Public Domain**; 8.11.

Index